AN ACTOR'S GUIDE

Making It in New York City

2nd Edition

AN ACTOR'S GUIDE

Making It in New York City

2nd Edition

GLENN ALTERMAN

ALLWORTH PRESS
NEW YORK

15 14 13 12 11   5 4 3 2 1

Published by Allworth Press
An imprint of Skyhorse Publishing
307 West 36th Street, 11th Floor, New York, NY 10018.

Allworth Press® is a registered trademark of Skyhorse Publishing, Inc.®,
a Delaware corporation.

Cover design by Mary Ann Smith and interior design by Mary Belibasakis
Page composition/typography by Integra Software Sevices Pvt., Ltd., Pondicherry, India

Library of Congress Cataloging-in-Publication Data
Alterman, Glenn, 1946–
    An actor's guide—making it in New York City / Glenn Alterman. — 2nd ed.
      p. cm.
    Includes bibliographical references and index.
    ISBN 978-1-58115-763-5 (alk. paper)
    1. Acting—Vocational guidance—New York (State)—New York.   I. Title.
    PN2055.A453 2011
    792.0'28023—dc22
                                                                2010051017

Printed in Canada

CONTENTS

ACKNOWLEDGMENTS

The author wishes to acknowledge the following for their assistance: Francine J. Tory, Sue Henderson, Doug Barron, Robert Kim, John Rubin Gould and Claire Abramowitz, Shea Connelly, and Tad Crawford at Allworth Press.

INTRODUCTION

This book is more than just a revision of the original edition. When I first began working on it, I had no idea how much things had changed in the entertainment business in the last decade. Much of the information in the original edition needed to be totally updated. Many interviews from that edition had to be deleted, with many new ones added. The world, and certainly the entertainment industry, has changed dramatically since 2001. The change in the economy has had a major impact on all businesses, including show business.

The Internet plays a far more significant role in all aspects of entertainment now, especially in how projects are cast. The chapter in this book on the Internet is extensive and completely updated. It includes a listing of many important Web sites of which actors need to be aware. There's even a section on how to set up your own Web site.

My goal in this revised edition was to give actors the most up-to-date, comprehensive information on being a New York actor. I believe my research will be of value to the actor just moving to New York City as well as to the seasoned pro. I wanted this to be the definitive source book, the go-to book for any questions you may have about being a working actor in New York. There are several other books out there that cover some of the same topics I've covered in this book. I didn't want to simply rehash information that's already available. I wanted this book to be as current as possible, with information not available anywhere else.

When I began work on this book, I thought that my target audience would primarily be young actors coming to New York for the first time. But as so often happens when you're researching and interviewing, new areas opened. As I continued with my research, I began learning a tremendous amount about an industry about which I thought I knew almost all there was to know. I've been an actor in New York for more than forty years and have written many theater-related books. I thought that by now, there was little I didn't know about this field. Boy, was I wrong! Truth be told, I probably learned more from the research and interviews that I did for this book than in any of my previous ones. I sought out the opinions, advice, and insights of many of the major players in the New York theater, TV, and film communities. I think you'll find their interviews particularly informative and helpful.

Because this book is for the New York actor, I felt that a chapter specifically on Manhattan and the outlying areas was necessary. Everything from what's where, to where to live (and how much it'll cost you), to shopping, to nightlife is covered.

I think that you'll find the acting teacher interviews interesting and inspiring. I interviewed three of the top acting teachers in New York. Their focus was primarily on the craft of acting, not just the commercial aspects. Does everyone need to study acting? What is the best training? What should you be wary of when seeking out instructors? How long should you study with a teacher? When should you terminate with a teacher? How much training is enough?

The marketing and networking chapters are the flip side of the coin. Here, I wanted to explore the best ways to turn your talent into something marketable in today's economy. To succeed in this business, you need a strong game plan, a well-thought-out strategy. You need to know how to network effectively. I suggest different ways to set up shop and operate as a businessperson. You don't have to sit around waiting for that cell phone to ring anymore.

Learning how to effectively work with agents, casting directors, and personal managers was something I felt every actor needed to know. These are the people with whom you come into contact on a daily basis. They can have a major impact on how successful you are in your career. During the interviews, I asked very specific questions to which I felt all actors want to know the answers. How do you find an agent? Do you need a personal manager? What's the best way to get a casting director to know you? What's expected in the actor-agent or personal manager–actor relationship? What are the main pet peeves of agents, personal managers, and casting directors? I think that you'll be surprised at some of the responses.

There are chapters on commercial print modeling, extra work, and survival strategies. Very few actors come to New York and make it right away. I felt that these peripheral ways to earn a living were well worth investigating.

One of the things you'll discover as you read through this book is that talent is only part of a successful acting career. As you may be aware, there are many very talented actors who are unemployed simply because they haven't yet learned how to market themselves effectively. Effective marketing, self-promotion, and networking strategies, although not always held in the highest esteem by some actors, are a very necessary part of a successful acting career. Unless effective action is taken, a dream to succeed in this business will quite often remain just that—a dream. This book is for those who are ready to take charge, to do something. It is a step-by-step guide for actors who want to realize their dreams. If you have the talent and the desire to succeed, this book can be your best friend. Of course, no one can guarantee a successful acting career to anyone. But the more information you have, the better your odds are. This book is meant to inform, inspire, and point you in the right direction; the rest is up to you. Stay focused on your goals, do something every day to further your career, and more than anything, never give up.

—Glenn Alterman

PART I

They Say the Neon Lights Are Bright . . .

BEFORE YOU LEAVE FOR NEW YORK

For years, you've dreamed of one day becoming an actor. In your imagination, you may have seen yourself on Broadway, in movies, or as a soap opera star. Dreams. Daydreams. Wishes. So you took it a step further, perhaps took some drama classes in school, maybe got the lead in the school play, did some community theater. The dreams grew, the wishes became stronger. For some people, the dream grows so powerful that it becomes an obsession. For these people, the question is never, "Should I become an actor?" but rather, "How, when, and where do I need to go to become an actor?" Much of the information in this book deals with "how" you become a working actor. The answer to the question about "where" is usually New York or Los Angeles. That's not to say that you can't find substantial acting work anywhere else in the country (especially several major cities), but rather that New York and Los Angeles offer the most opportunities to actors.

The journey from "hoping" to "becoming" an actor can be a tough ride. Unless you're willing to give it everything, perhaps you should rethink your dream. But if you're serious, if you're really sincere about being an actor, this book is for you. I've tried to answer every question to dispel many myths.

New York or Los Angeles: Which Is Best for You?

Before moving to New York, you should consider if this is really where you want to go to pursue your acting career. New York and Los Angeles offer the serious actor different work opportunities. The main distinction between the two (aside from the geographical differences) is the kind of work you'll find. New York's strong suits are theater, TV commercials, and print modeling. Los Angeles is better known as the TV and motion picture capital. But that's certainly not to say that there isn't theater (and some very good theater) in the Los Angeles area. Or that there isn't a lot of TV and film casting in New York. These days, many movies, films, and TV commercials cast their projects on both coasts. The primary distinction is the *quantity* of work offered on each coast.

Another important factor to consider is lifestyle. New York is a bustling, energetic, crowded place with people out on the streets twenty-four hours a day—all-night subways, restaurants, clubs, Fifth Avenue, Broadway, four different seasons, distinctly different neighborhoods, uptown, downtown, a melting pot of different types of people. It's an energetic, round-the-clock, "in your face" people everywhere place.

Los Angeles is quite different. It has palm trees, Rodeo Drive, movie studios, the Sunset Strip, beaches, year-round lovely weather, beautiful views, freeways, smog, and everywhere you look, cars, cars, cars. You won't see many folks out walking on the streets of LA.

If you can afford it—and it can be very expensive—some actors live on both coasts at different times of the year. They are known as "bicoastal" actors. Each town has its busy seasons. For instance, Los Angeles casts for new TV pilots at specific times of year. Auditioning, and then perhaps being cast in a TV pilot, can give an actor's career quite a boost.

How Long Will It Take?

Sorry, there are no guarantees. No one can tell you in advance how long it will take you to start (if ever) working as an actor. Many variables go into a successful acting career. You'll need talent, of course; but more than that, you'll need luck, and lots of it. Opportunities come and ago in the blink of an eye, and you'd better be smart enough to see when they're coming your way. You have to learn to live with a lot of uncertainty in this business; for some, that is very difficult.

Deciding on New York

One reason that many actors begin their careers in New York is that New York is known for having some the best acting teachers and schools in the world. Another reason is that most people in the industry have a tremendous respect for actors experienced in theater. New York's Broadway, Off-Broadway, and Off-Off-Broadway offer many opportunities for actors to both hone their craft and perhaps make a splash for themselves. There are countless stories of actors opening in plays in New York, getting rave reviews, being "discovered" overnight by agents and casting directors, and having their careers take off. Stage-experienced actors seem to make the transition to film and TV more easily than actors going the opposite route. Many agents and casting directors I spoke with felt that actors should spend at least a couple of years in New York, learning their craft and getting some serious stage experience, before (if ever) moving to Los Angeles.

New York Scouting Excursions

If you've decided to move to New York, I strongly suggest that you visit the city at least once prior to actually moving here. Come with your family or with a friend to check out the New York scene. It's a large, complicated city. There's a lot that you'll need to know before you actually move here. A New York scouting expedition will help eliminate many fears and anxieties about the city. I suggest staying here for at least a couple of weeks. Don't try to do it in just a few days. On your scouting expeditions to New York, you'll need a temporary, inexpensive place to stay. The following places offer daily, weekly, and monthly apartment rentals:

Radio City Apartments
142 West 49th Street
New York, NY 10019
(212) 730-0728

Markle Residence
(for women 18-50 years old)
123 West 13th Street
New York, NY 10014
(212) 242-2400
All rooms include maid service, phone, and bath, plus two meals per day

Bedford Hotel
118 East 40th Street
New York, NY 10016
(212) 697-4800

YMCA West Side
5 West 63rd Street
New York, NY 10023
212-875-4100

Chelsea International Hostel
251 West 20th Street
(212-647-0010)
New York, NY 10011-3501
(Rates as low as $33 per night!)

Hotel Wolcott
4 West 31st Street
New York, NY 10001
(212) 268-2900

Pickwick Arms Hotel
230 East 51st Street
New York, NY 10022
(212) 355-0300

The Reality Factor: How Much Will It Cost?

New York is one of the most expensive cities to live in in the United States. Finding inexpensive housing has become nearly impossible, especially in the past few years. (See chapter 3 on apartment rentals.) That being said, there are ways to get by and not pay an arm and a leg. Actors, by and large, are incredibly resourceful. If you network with other actors, you can find out where the best bargains exist, from housing to shopping to entertainment. What follows is a preliminary discussion of some basic expenses you'll come across. A more detailed account of expenses will follow in chapter 3.

More than likely, rent will be one of the largest expenses you will have. Housing in New York City is not cheap. There are many stories, though, of actors who luck out with a long-term, inexpensive sublet or miraculously find an apartment where the rent isn't ridiculously high. Depending on where you live, the costs will vary a great deal. In New York, for the most part, heat and water are included with your rent. You'll be paying extra, however, for gas and electricity.

At this time, the basic cost for telephone installation is $75. Depending on which features you add to your service (call waiting, caller ID, etc) and which calling plans you'll use, the rates vary a great deal.

While you are out there pounding the pavement (more about that later), you'll need to have a cell phone with an inexpensive plan. I wouldn't depend much on public pay phones in New York. Many of them are broken or overpriced. There's another reason why a cell phone may be a worthwhile investment. Casting directors and agents will need to contact you for auditions and bookings. The quicker they can reach you, the better. Some combination of cell phones, beepers, and answering services and machines are necessary to actors. Once again, depending on how you go, prices can vary wildly. You can get answering machines for as low as $20 or as much as $200. Answering services can be a cheap as $15 a month or as high as $75 (or more). Beepers and cell phones run the gamut from $50 a month and up. Most of the talent agents and casting directors that I spoke with said they prefer contacting actors on their cell phones.

Depending upon where you shop, you'll spend an average of $50 to $90 a week on groceries. One thing you'll discover is that the range of markup in different groceries in your neighborhood can be quite substantial. You'll need to shop around for the most economical food stores in your area. Food prices in New York supermarkets tend to be slightly higher than outside the city, although that can vary widely, depending on the area. If you take advantage of the wonderful ethnic markets located throughout New York (especially Chinatown) and the diverse neighborhood restaurants that serve up international home cooking, you may actually end up spending less on food than you do outside New York (but don't count on it).

For actors, watching movies and theater is not just entertainment but also a vital part of keeping up with business. It's important to see what's out there. The cost of a Broadway show has just gone up to $135, and movie tickets are now up to $12.50. But there are several ways to cut the high cost of entertainment.

The Theatre Development Fund (TDF) has a half-price theater ticket booth (TKTS) at Broadway and 47th Street and also offers discounted tickets by mail. TDF can be contacted by mail at 520 8th Avenue, Suite 801, New York, NY 10018. In addition, an organization called Audience Extras offers tickets for plays on and Off-Broadway for only $3.50 per ticket. There is an initial membership fee of $115 ($85 for the AE Annual Membership Fee plus an initial deposit of $30 put in a fund to start purchasing tickets). Audience Extras is at 109 West 26th Street, Suite 3B, New York, NY 10001, (212) 686-1966, Web site *www.audienceextras.com*.

Theater Extras, like Audience Extras, offers theater tickets at $4 each. They charge $99 per year. You can reach them at (914) 304-4093 or (212) 802-7277, *www.theaterextras.com.*

And Play By Play also offers theater tickets. They charge $99 (plus an $8 processing fee) for Internet. You can reach them at (212) 868-7052, *www. play-by-play.com.*

If you belong to the Screen Actors Guild (SAG) or Actors' Equity (AEA), you can take advantage of the free and low-cost tickets to performances and screenings (see chapter 14 for contact information for these unions).

Other expenses include

- Internet service ($30 to $50 a month),
- clothing (varies),
- grooming ($15 to $75 per month),
- health clubs ($300 to $1,200 per year),
- classes ($200 to $400 per month),
- union dues (vary, depending on the union—see chapter 14),
- other professional expenses that you'll come across on a day-to-day basis.

BASIC STATS FOR THE *NEW* NEW YORKER

You'll come to New York because you have a dream of becoming an actor, but you will also be making a life for yourself here. You'll have to work, play, and survive here; so the more information you have about the city, the better. Since Manhattan is the borough that most people think of as the Big Apple, I'll start with it.

New York: Basic Facts

Size
New York City: 301 square miles (485 square km)
Manhattan: 22.7 square miles (36.5 square km)
Length: 13.4 miles (21.5 km)
Width: 2.3 miles (3.7 km) at the widest section, 0.8 miles
(1.3 km) at the narrowest section

Population
8.3 million (2008 census)

Religions
Catholic   43.4 percent
Jewish   10.9 percent
Baptist   10.7 percent

Average Temperatures
Spring: 49–80 degrees Fahrenheit
Summer: 63–85 degrees Fahrenheit
Fall: 31–66 degrees Fahrenheit
Winter: 26–49 degrees Fahrenheit

*For basic information, contact The Convention
and Visitors Bureau, 810 7th Avenue, 3rd Floor,
New York, NY 10019. Or go to www.nycgo.com.*

Fifth Avenue divides Manhattan between east side and west side. Street numbers begin at 5th Avenue. For instance, 1 West 44th Street is the first building on the west side of 5th Avenue, and 1 East 44th Street is the first building on the east side of 5th Avenue. You'll discover that most of the streets in Manhattan are one-way. With a few exceptions, traffic on even-numbered streets travels east, and traffic on odd-numbered streets travels west. Traffic on some of the crosstown streets, such as Canal, Houston, 14th, 23rd, 34th, 42nd, 57th, 72nd, 79th, and 86th streets, travels in both directions. Generally, when someone says that a location is "downtown," they mean that it is south of 14th Street; when they refer to "uptown," they mean north of 14th Street.

The Neighborhoods of Manhattan

Each of New York's neighborhoods has a distinct flavor and unique history. As you travel through each different neighborhood, you'll discover its individuality. I'd like to briefly discuss each of the neighborhoods, but the best way to really learn about them is to experience them yourself. In many of the sections that follow, I list some of the theaters and theater companies in that neighborhood. This is just a sampling of the hundreds of theaters in the city. Theaters and theater companies come and go. The ones listed here are not the only ones in an area, only those that are better known.

The Financial District

At the southern tip of the island is the Financial District. Due to the World Trade Center disaster, some of this area has been destroyed. Rebuilding has begun and will continue to restore the area.

The Financial District is the oldest section of Manhattan. It is where the first European settlers arrived. There are still centuries-old buildings, overshadowed by new skyscrapers.

Battery Park got its name from the forts that the American army built to fend off the British. Here, you can catch the ferries to Ellis Island and the Statue of Liberty. At the eastern edge of Battery Park, you can catch the free Staten Island Ferry, a great way to see many of the popular sights of the city in only twenty-five minutes. There are fantastic views of New York Harbor, Lower Manhattan, Ellis Island, and the Statue of Liberty.

The Battery Park Esplanade, a lovely place to visit, is a ninety-two-acre commercial and residential complex, running a mile and a half long, up to Chambers Street. It's amazing to think that this area was built entirely on landfill at a cost of $4 billion. There are many beautiful sculptures by some well-known artists, as well as some serene and lovely views.

Bowling Green is just north of Battery Park. This small square, located at the corner of Broadway and Battery Place, is the oldest park in the city.

Not far away, on Broadway and Wall Street, is historic Trinity Church. The present structure was completed in 1846 and was the tallest building in Manhattan for most of the nineteenth century. In the cemetery next to the church, you'll find the tombs of such notables as Alexander Hamilton. The burial ground goes back to 1681.

Nearby on Wall Street is the New York Stock Exchange. If you go inside, up to the balcony, you can catch the daily action. Once again, this is a freebie (but tough to get into sometimes). Be prepared for high security and individual inspections.

Across the street and east a bit is the Federal Hall National Memorial, the site of George Washington's 1789 inauguration. It's also the location of the country's first capitol building. In 1702, the first city hall was built here.

Going uptown, you'll come to city hall, the office of the mayor of New York. The building is a Federal-style landmark (1803–1812). The Alliance for Downtown New York has a salmon-colored jitney that stops at all major places of interest in the Financial District. Like the Staten Island Ferry, it's free. One last place I suggest stopping while in the area is the South Street Seaport. There are cobblestone streets and a wooden pier that has some lovely views. Mainly, the area is filled with tourist shops and singles bars that really come to life after work hours.

While at the South Street Seaport, you might want to visit the Shooting Star Theater (in the Seaport) at 40 Peck Slip, New York, NY 10038. The telephone number is (646) 825-1864.

Tribeca

Tribeca (TriBeCa) was actually named by real estate developers in the 1970s. The name refers to the *Tri*angle *Be*low *Ca*nal Street. Back in the seventies, there were barely 250 people living in this area north of the Financial District. Back then, the area consisted of run-down warehouses. The real estate developers aggressively changed the look of the area (and all within a decade). At first, the rents were quite inexpensive, attracting artists and people in show business to the area. Performance spaces, art galleries, cafés, bistros, and charming little shops sprouted up seemingly overnight. But as often happens, the area became very popular, rents started to skyrocket, and many members of the art community were forced out. Now, the area is filled with upscale housing, chic restaurants, and shops all tucked into the little streets. Many film companies have their offices and screening rooms down there, and popular restaurants such as the Tribeca Grill and Nobu are located there.

The FleaTheater, 41 White Street, New York, NY 10013, (212) 226-0051

Soho

The area south of Houston Street (and north of Canal Street, between 6th Avenue and Lafayette Street) is called Soho. Here, you'll discover many wonderful old cast-iron buildings, some of which have been turned into artist's studios, lofts, trendy restaurants, and chic shops. In Soho, you'll find many "downtown" artists and designers, boutiques and galleries. What was once a bohemian section of the city has become a very trendy, very expensive location. Soho is also well known for its great art galleries.

Some theaters to contact in this area are

- Soho Rep, 46 Walker Street, New York, NY 10013, (212) 941-8632;
- Synchronicity Space, 55 Mercer Street, New York, NY 10003, (212) 925-8645;
- Performing Garage, 33 Wooster Street, New York, NY 10013, (212) 966-3651;
- HERE Arts Center, 145 6th Avenue, Ground Floor, New York, NY 10013, (212) 647-0202.

Chinatown

Gravitating out from Canal Street, Chinatown contains over a third of New York's Asian population. Many of the people who live here are from Thailand, Vietnam, Cambodia, and Malaysia. Supposedly, the first Chinese residents relocated here (at 8 Mott Street) in 1858. You can find exotic produce markets on the neighborhood's many narrow streets, as well as vendors selling ginseng, stir-fried noodles, and other Asian delicacies. The corner of Mott and Pell Street is the unofficial center of Chinatown. You should take a walk down Mott Street to visit the many shops.

Little Italy

Little Italy is a charming section of lower Manhattan located between Canal, Houston, Elizabeth, and Lafayette streets. Since the 1960s, the area's borders seem to be shrinking due to the expansion of Chinatown. What are left are some lovely streets, shops, and restaurants. There are some great authentic Italian restaurants located on Mulberry Street. For you, lovers of sweets, there's the Ferrara pastry shop at 195 Grand Street. This is supposedly America's oldest pastry shop.

Every autumn, Little Italy holds the San Gennaro Festival. This eleven-day celebration is famous for the authentic Italian food and music, the carnival games and the partylike atmosphere.

The Lower East Side

At one time, this area was the first stop in the city for Irish and German immigrants. Then it became home to Eastern European Jews, who lived there from the mid-nineteenth to the mid-twentieth century. There were more than four hundred thousand people living in the cramped Lower East Side in 1920. Yiddish theater flourished on Second Avenue. These were the theaters where you could catch the beginnings of Irving Berlin, George Gershwin, and the Marx Brothers. Check out Katz's Deli at 205 East Houston Street to get a taste of some of the foods from those times.

If you walk down Orchard and Delancey streets, you can find some real bargains on vintage clothing, shoes, junk jewelry, even designer clothes.

Some theaters on the Lower East Side include

- Theater for the New City, 155 1st Avenue, New York, NY 10003, (212) 254-1109;
- New Federal Theatre, 292 Henry Street, New York, NY 10002-4804 (212) 353-1176, info@newfederaltheatre.org;
- Teatro LA TEA, 107 Suffolk Street, New York, NY 10012, Performance Space 122, 150 1st Avenue, New York, (212) 477-5829, *www.ps122.org.*

The Village

The Village is located from river to river between Houston Street and 14th Street. The West Village, or Greenwich Village, is located between Broadway and the Hudson River. To many, this is "the Village." This area was originally built in the mid-1800s. It was the home of Edgar Allan Poe, Walt Whitman, and Mark Twain. There were lovely upper-class homes and lots of churches in the area. Eventually, theaters, galleries, and clubs followed. By the end of the nineteenth century, many working-class Italian immigrant families moved into the area south of Washington Square Park. It was at that same time that a gay subculture started to grow in the area. The Village was home to many social causes and political movements, from the antiwar protests of the sixties to gay rights in more recent years.

The geographical center and heart of the Village is Washington Square Park. At one time, there were public gallows there. Today, it is a popular place for street performers and chess players. It is the place to hang out and the unofficial New York University campus.

The East Village is considered a hip place to live and still has some reasonable rents, inexpensive restaurants, and very cool bars. At one time, it was the home of the Beat generation's Allen Ginsberg and William S. Burroughs. Check out Tompkins Square Park, which is located between 7th and 10th streets, between avenues A and B. As Washington Square Park is to the West Village, so Tompkins Square Park is the heart of the East Village, and a nice place to hang out on a warm summer day. Don't miss St. Mark's Place on East 8th Street, east of 3rd Avenue. It's the main drag in the East Village, filled with nifty shops and lots of street vendors.

Some theaters to take note of in the Village are

- the Cherry Lane Theater, 38 Commerce Street, New York, NY 10014, (212) 989-2020;
- the 13th Street Repertory Theater, 50 West 13th Street, New York, NY 10011, (212) 675-1011;
- Pan Asian Repertory Theater, 47 Great Jones Street, New York, NY 10012, (212) 505-5655;
- LaMaMa Experimental Theater, 74A East 4th Street, New York, NY 10003, (212) 254-6468;

- the Public Theater, 425 Lafayette Street, New York, NY 10003, (212) 260-2400;
- the Minetta Lane Theater, 18 Minetta Lane, New York, NY 10012, (212) 420-8000;
- MCC Theater at The Lucille Lortel Theatre,121 Christopher St, New York, NY 10014, (212) 727-7722;
- Classic Stage Company, 136 East 13th Street, New York, NY 10003, (212) 677-4210.

Chelsea

Chelsea stretches from 5th Avenue to the Hudson River, between 14th and 26th streets. At one time, this area was a shipping district. For a while, it was an industrial area. Eventually, it became a run-down, low-income area. Today, it is a very trendy section of the city with a large gay population. You can also find some of the best art galleries in this area.

Some theaters in this area include

- Theaterworks/USA, 151 West 26th Street, New York, NY 10001, (212) 647-1100;
- the Atlantic Theater, 336 West 20th Street, New York, NY 10011, (212) 645-8015.

The Flatiron District and Gramercy

Located between 5th Avenue and the East River, from 14th to 26th Street, this area was once the home of the Astors and the Roosevelts. Edith Wharton, O'Henry, and the playwright Eugene O'Neill all lived in this vicinity. Gramercy Park, at 20th and Irving Place, is a private green. Only those living in the immediate area are given keys. Not far from Gramercy Park is Theodore Roosevelt's birthplace (28 East 20th Street), a lovely Victorian brownstone.

The Flatiron District is named after the triangular, terra-cotta office building located at 23rd Street and Fifth Avenue. The building is home to several model agencies, photographers, and many others involved in the fashion world.

Some theaters in this area include

- the Blue Heron Art Center Theater, 123 East 24th Street, New York, NY 10010, (212) 979-5000;
- Abington Theater Company, 312 West 36th Street, New York, NY 10018, (212) 868-2055;
- Workshop Theater Company, 312 West 36th Street, New York, NY 10018, (212) 695-4173;
- the Barrow Group Theater Company, 312 West 36th Street, New York, NY 10018, (212) 760-2615;
- the National Asian American Theatre Co, 520 8th Avenue, Suite 308, New York, NY 10018, (212) 244-0447.

Midtown

The area between the rivers from the thirties to the fifties in called "midtown." It is a densely commercialized area. Times Square, theaters, concert halls, the Empire State Building, and Rockefeller Center are all located here. Times Square itself is located at West 42nd Street and 7th Avenue. Known as the "Crossroads of the World," this thirty-square-block neighborhood is midtown Manhattan's central intersection. It's filled with restaurants, hotels, theaters, shops, and razzle-dazzle signs. This is an important area for actors as the major Broadway theaters are located in this area. Most transportation goes to Times Square, and taxis are plentiful, so save yourself a lot of trouble and do not drive to this area. More than 1.5 million people walk through Times Square every day. The flagpole on the roof of One Times Square is where you'll see the ball drop every New Year's Eve.

You'll also find many department stores in the midtown area, as well as St. Patrick's Cathedral on 5th Avenue, which runs right through the middle of midtown. The eastern and western edges of midtown are primarily residential areas.

Take a stroll over to Bryant Park on 42nd Street and 6th Avenue, right behind the world-famous New York Public Library (42nd and 5th). Bryant Park was the home of the 1853 World's Fair, and it's a nice place to relax in midtown on a nice spring day. A couple of blocks east of Bryant Park is Grand Central Terminal (42nd Street and Park Avenue). Built in 1913, this neo-Renaissance-style landmark is one of the city's most impressive architectural accomplishments. Not far from Grand Central is the Chrysler Building (Lexington Avenue and 42nd Street). This was the city's first skyscraper (seventy-seven stories). It was built in 1930 and is an art deco masterpiece.

As an actor, it's important that you know where all the Broadway theaters are. Quite often, producers hold auditions there.

Broadway Theaters

The Ambassador Theater, 219 West 49th Street
The American Airlines Theater, 229 West 42nd Street
The Brooks Atkinson Theater, 256 West 47th Street
The Ethel Barrymore Theater, 243 West 47th Street
The Vivian Beaumont Theater, 150 West 65th Street (Lincoln Center)

♦ ♦ ♦ ♦ ♦ ♦ ♦ ♦ ♦

The Belasco Theater, 111 West 44th Street
The Booth Theater, 222 West 45th Street
The Broadhurst Theater, 235 West 44th Street
The Broadway Theater, 1601 Broadway (at 53rd Street)
Circle in the Square Theater, 235 West 50th Street
The Cort Theater, 138 West 48th Street

♦ ♦ ♦ ♦ ♦ ♦ ♦ ♦ ♦

Foxwoods Theatre, 213 West 42nd Street
The Gershwin Theater, 222 West 51st Street
The John Golden Theater, 252 West 45th Street
The Helen Hayes Theater, 240 West 44th Street

The Al Hirschfeld Theater, 302 West 45th Street
The Imperial Theater, 249 West 45th Street
Bernard B. Jacons Theater, 242 West 45th Street
The Walter Kerr Theater, 219 West 48th Street
The Longacre Theater, 220 West 48th Street
The Lunt-Fontanne Theater, 205 West 46th Street
The Lyceum Theater, 149 West 45th Street
The Majestic Theater, 247 West 44th Street
The Marquis Theater, 1535 Broadway (at 46th Street)
Henry Miller Theater, 124 West 43rd Street
The Minskoff Theater, 200 West 45th Street
The Music Box Theater, 239 West 45th Street
The Nederlander Theater, 208 West 41st Street
The New Amsterdam Theater, 212 West 42nd Street
The New Victory Theater, 209 West 42nd Street
The Eugene O'Neil Theater, 230 West 49th Street
The Palace Theater, 1564 Broadway (at 47th Street)
The Plymouth Theater, 236 West 45th Street
The Richard Rodgers Theater, 226 West 46th Street
Gerald Schoenfeld Theater, 236 West 45th Street
The Shubert Theater, 225 West 44th Street
The Neil Simon Theater, 250 West 52nd Street
St James Theater, 246 West 44th Street
Studio 54, 254 West 54th Street
The Stephen Sondheim Theater, 124 West 43rd Street
August Wilson Theater, 245 West 52nd Street
The Winter Garden Theater, 1634 Broadway (at 51st Street)

Central Park

Central Park runs from 59th Street to 110th Street, between 5th Avenue and Central Park West. This world-famous park is an oasis in the middle of all the concrete. It was designed in 1858 by Fredrick Law Olmstead and Calvert Vaux. At the end of a long day, it's a pleasure to stroll through one of the meadows or stop off and just relax at one of the lakes. In the summer, you can enjoy free Shakespeare in the park at the Delacorte Theater. Top directors give new renderings of classic plays in star-studded productions, like that of *The Seagull*, starring Meryl Streep and Kevin Kline and directed by Mike Nichols.

Upper West Side

The Upper West Side is located between 59th Street and 110th Street, between the Hudson River and Central Park. Because of the closeness to Central Park and the many neighborhood services and conveniences, it's a very desirable living area. Columbus Avenue has many trendy shops, restaurants, and bars.

For you, museum buffs, there's famed American Museum of Natural History between 77nd and 81st streets on Central Park West.

Some theaters on the Upper West Side are

- the Promenade Theater, 2162 Broadway, New York, NY 10024, (212) 580-1313;
- the Vivian Beaumont Theater, 150 West 65th Street, New York, NY 10023, (212) 362-7600;
- the Mitzi E. Newhouse Theater, 150 West 65 Street New York, NY 10023, (212) 362-7600.

Upper East Side

Some of the world's most expensive designer boutiques can be found on Madison Avenue on the East Side. There are also many terrific restaurants and bars, some quite old, some new and trendy. And then, of course, there are the museums, some of the most famous in the world. Both the Metropolitan Museum (1000 5th Avenue at 82nd Street) and the Guggenheim Museum (1071 5th Avenue, between 88th and 89th Streets) are located on what's been called the Museum Mile. You'll also find the Whitney Museum of American Art there (945 Madison Avenue at 75th Street).

On 89th Street and East End Avenue (in Carl Schurz Park) is Gracie Mansion. This is the home of the mayor of New York. If you're interested in visiting this 1779 Federal-style mansion, you can take a tour any Wednesday.

Some theaters on the Upper East Side are

- the Mazur Theater, 555 East 90th Street, New York, NY 10028, (212) 369-8890;
- St. Bart's Playhouse, 109 East 50th Street, New York, NY 10022, (212) 751-1616.

Harlem

Harlem is located between the rivers, from 97th Street to 168th Street. It is the largest residential area in the city, covering some six square miles. Originally, it was a Dutch settlement called *Nieuw Haarlem* (New Haarlem) back in 1658. The row houses and apartment buildings on Strivers Row (West 138th Street) were built in the 1890s by some of the top architects of the time. In the twenties, Harlem became the cultural hub of black America. At one time, you could go uptown to the Apollo Theater on 125th Street and catch the likes of Billie Holiday or Ella Fitzgerald. Unfortunately, social and economic factors led to the neighborhood's drastic deterioration, so that by the 1970s, Harlem was reputed to be one of the most dangerous, crime-riddled, and drug-infested parts of the city. Now, however, it is on the upswing. There are Starbucks and Gap stores slowly coming into the area. Many of the incredible brownstones are getting facelifts, and the area is becoming home to students, yuppies, and realty investors. Former president Bill Clinton now has his offices in Harlem.

One theater to check out in Harlem is the National Black Theater, 2031 5th Avenue, New York, NY 10035, (212) 722-3800. Other theater in Harlem is

- the Classical Theatre of Harlem, 520 8th Avenue, New York, NY 10018, (212) 564-9983.

Safety First: Know How to Protect Yourself

As you may know, New York City has had a dramatic reduction in its civilian crime rate in the last few years. There are a great number of police officers on New York City streets these days, especially since the World Trade Center disaster. But even with all the police out on the streets, you still must always provide for your own personal safety. There are two basic rules to keep in mind: try not to make eye contact with strangers, and don't be too friendly with strangers. I know that for some out-of-towners, this kind of behavior might seem very unsociable. Walking around, carrying a camera, and constantly looking at street maps can make you look like someone new to the city. Tourists are easy marks for scam artists and pickpockets.

Public bathrooms, if you can find any or that are open, are generally not well-kept and are potential crime scenes. Generally, hotels, department stores, and restaurants (pretend you're a customer) are safer for those times when you've "just got to go."

While walking around the city, you should not keep your jewelry on display (especially if you find yourself on the subways or in dangerous neighborhoods). If you're wearing expensive jewelry, simply conceal it under your clothing. That expensive diamond ring that you're wearing should be turned around on your finger, so that only the band is showing. Handbags should be gripped tightly, and wear the strap diagonally.

Central Park is a wonderful place to walk through during the day, but can be somewhat dangerous at night. If you must go through the park, walk on the main thoroughfares, not in any of the woody areas. After dark, it's generally safer to walk on main thoroughfares—that is, avenues—rather than streets. And if possible, go in groups rather than alone.

Don't carry too much money; there's always an ATM around somewhere. Speaking of ATMs, always make sure of who else is near you when you're taking out cash. Make your cash pickups during daylight hours and check the mirrors. Don't count your cash in public, tuck your wallet in a discreet pocket, and always hide some emergency money in a shoe or sock.

A Brief Introduction to the Four Other Boroughs

I am not going to devote a lot of space to the rest of New York City here. The Metropolitan area is colorful and various, from the historic seaport community of City Island (off the Bronx) to the factories-turned-galleries of DUMBO (in Brooklyn). During your downtime (when you are not studying and working), you can explore the many sights and communities. Here is a brief overview of what is out there.

Brooklyn

Brooklyn is the largest of the five boroughs of New York. It is the one-time home of Woody Allen, Mae West, Neil Diamond, Barbra Streisand, and recent Tony winner Mel Brooks, among many celebrities. It has more than 2.9 million residents. Many people consider Brooklyn to be a city within the city. There are many different cultural communities scattered throughout the borough, such as Brighton Beach, which has more than three hundred thousand people from the former Soviet Union.

Sights to see in Brooklyn include the Brooklyn Heights Historic District, (especially Montague Street). This lovely fifty-street area is filled with charming restaurants, cafés, and brownstones. While there, you can take in a lovely view of Manhattan from the Waterfront Promenade.

Also in Brooklyn is the Brooklyn Museum at 200 Eastern Parkway, near Park Slope. This is the second largest art museum in New York. And of course, there's the world famous Brooklyn Botanical Gardens (900 Washington Avenue, at Eastern Parkway). The Brooklyn Academy of Music has some of the most exciting theater in the world. This 145-year-old theater is home to the New Wave Festival of music, dance, and theater. You can catch some interesting international and avant-garde theater here from October through December.

Some theaters in Brooklyn include

- King's County Shakespeare Company, 138 South Oxford Street, Brooklyn, NY 11217, (718) 398-0546;
- St Luke's Lutheran Church Theater, 259 Washington Avenue, Brooklyn, NY 11205, (718) 622-5612;
- Heights Players Theatre, 26 Willow Place, Brooklyn, NY 11201, (718) 237-2752;
- Harry Warren Theatre, 2445 Bath Avenue, Brooklyn, NY 11214, (718) 996-4800;
- Outreach Theatre Inc. Theatre of Dreams", 1219 77th Street, Brooklyn, NY (718) 680-3319;
- Impact Theatre Company, 190 Underhill Avenue, Brooklyn, NY 11238, (718) 390-7163;
- Gallery Players, 199 14th Street | Brooklyn, NY 11215, (718) 595-0547.

The Bronx

The Bronx was named after the Dutch settler, Jonas Bronck, who claimed this area as his farm back in 1636. For many years, this borough has been given a bad rap. The truth of the matter is, there actually are beautiful residential areas to be found in the Bronx, especially in the northern part.

The Bronx Zoo (Bronx River Parkway and Fordham Road) is the largest urban zoo in the United States. Check out the Congo gorilla forest. It's a re-creation of an African rain forest. Also, try to get to the New York

Botanical Garden (200th Street and Southern Boulevard), a National Historic Landmark. Here, you'll see everything from rainforests to desert plant life in the garden's glass conservatory. And of course, there's "The House That Ruth Built," Yankee Stadium (161st Street), for all you baseball fans.

While in the Bronx, check out the Pregones Theater, 575 Walton Avenue, Bronx, NY 10451,(718) 585-1202.

Staten Island

Like the Bronx, Staten Island is often put down and known primarily for the Fresh Kills garbage dump. But there are large areas of protected wilderness on Staten Island that are unlike anything else in any of the other boroughs.

It wasn't until 1964, when the Verrazano-Narrows Bridge was built, that there was a connecting land link between Staten Island and Brooklyn. The Staten Island Ferry departs from Battery Park, and it's a scenic ride, as well as the best way to get there.

Theaters on Staten Island include

- Go Forth Productions, 8 Remsen Street, Staten Island, NY 10504, (718) 987-4939;
- Sundog Theatre Inc., 370 St. Mark's Place, Staten Island, NY 10301, (718) 816-5453;
- Staten Island Shakespearean Theatre Company, 460 Brielle Avenue, Staten Island, NY, (718) 390-6616.

Queens

Queens was named in 1683, after Queen Catherine of Braganza, the wife of Charles II of England. Until the nineteenth century, it remained primarily a rural area. Today, Queens is made up of many working-class and middle-class neighborhoods. There are more than seventy-five cultural groups living in Queens. Jamaica, Queens, is largely made up of Caribbean families, Astoria has many Greek families, and Flushing has a very large Chinatown. Queens was once the home of Jerry Seinfield, Marvin Hamlish, and Paul Simon.

Flushing Meadows-Corona Park was the location of not one but two world's fairs. The Unisphere, a sculpture of the Earth, still remains standing from the 1964 World's Fair. For sports enthusiasts, there's Shea Stadium (home of the Mets), the National Tennis Center (the location of the U.S. Open), and Belmont and Aqueduct Racetracks.

And of course, there are Kaufman Astoria Studios and Silvercup Studios, home to many film and TV productions. Some of the great films of the 1920s and 1930s were shot in Queens, including films with Marlene Dietrich, the Marx Brothers, and Edward G. Robinson. The American Museum of the Moving Image at 3601 35th Avenue (in Astoria) is a unique museum that pays tribute to films and TV series. Opened in 1988, and built in what was once an old Paramount studio, it contains three floors of fascinating movie and TV history exhibits. For more information on this important actor-must-see museum, call (718) 784-0077 or (718) 784-4520.

Some theaters in Queens are

- Thalia Spanish Theatre, 47-17 Greenpoint Avenue, Sunnyside, NY 11104, (718) 729-3880;
- Queensborough Performing Arts Center 22205 56th Avenue, Bayside, NY 11364, (718) 631-6311.

Getting Around

Unlike most of the cities in the rest of the world, New York City has public transportation twenty-four hours a day. To ride the subway, you must purchase a MetroCard. You can buy these MetroCards at subway station booths, as well as many locations around the city that show a "MetroCards Sold Here" sign. At this printing, the following rates apply: the flat fare for a ride (on buses and subways) is $2.25. With a Pay-Per-Ride MetroCard, you can buy as many rides as you want from $4.50 to $80. If you put $8 or more on your card, you'll get a 15 percent bonus—for example, a $20 purchase gives you $23 on your card. The seven-day unlimited-use card costs $27, or you can purchase a one-month unlimited-use card for $89. If you want to get an unlimited-use card for one day, that'll cost you $8.25.

Thousands of people use the trains to commute to work and school each day. Signs indicating the route of the line are sometimes found inside each car, and there are maps in each car showing the whole subway system. The subway is usually the fastest way to shuttle from one borough to another.

The five boroughs have extensive bus systems, and routes and schedules are posted at many bus stops. The Metropolitan Transit Authority produces a separate bus map for each borough; unfortunately, it is difficult to obtain copies of many of these maps. You can try to pick them up from subway token booths, but forget about trying to get them on the buses.

For more information on MetroCards, call (212) 638-7632. For the MTA status information hot line, call (718) 243-7777, which is updated hourly from 6 a.m. to 9 a.m.

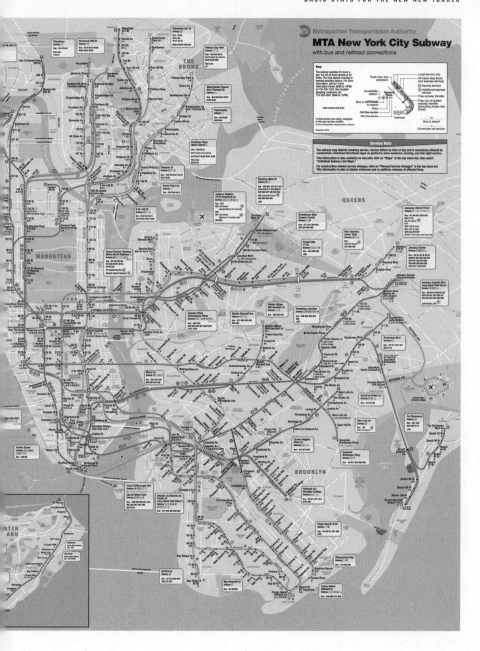

OKAY, YOU'RE HERE. NOW WHAT?

New York City is one of the most expensive places to live in the United States. Now that rent control is slowly being eliminated, those great little low-cost rent deals that you used to be able to find are practically extinct. One possible way to help cut the cost of high rentals is to get a roommate (or roommates). There are many reputable roommate services in New York that will be happy (for a fee) to help you either find people who already have apartments and are looking for a roommate or match you up with someone like yourself, looking to find a place.

There are several ways to find an apartment in New York. The *Village Voice*, a free weekly newspaper, comes out on Wednesdays and can be found in many locations throughout the city, from groceries to libraries to major chain drugstores. A second great source is the *Sunday New York Times*. Also, on the web try *www.craigslist.org*, another great resource for apartment hunters. Other recommendations include local newspapers throughout the city that have classified sections.

Many people turn to realtors to help with their search for an apartment. Never pay a realtor money up front. You only pay when they find you the apartment you decide to rent. Generally, their fees are 15 percent.

Rent Costs, Neighborhood by Neighborhood

These figures were current when this book went to press.

- Greenwich Village: studio/one bedroom, $1,500 to $4,000; two bedrooms, $4,100 to $7,500
- Chelsea: studio/one bedroom, $1,700 to $4000; two bedrooms, $4,100 to $6,500
- Hell's Kitchen, now known as Clinton: studio/one bedroom, $2,000 to $3000; two bedrooms, $3,200 to $4000
- Upper West Side: studio/one bedrooms, $1,900 to $3,000; two bedrooms, $3,500 to $5,000

- Morningside Heights/Above 96th Street: studio/one bedroom, $1,300 to $2,200; two bedrooms, $1,800 to $2,800
- Harlem: studio/one bedroom, $1,100 to $2,000; two bedrooms, $1,500 to $3,000
- East Village: studio/one bedroom, $1,400 to $2,500; two bedrooms, $1,900 to $3,000
- Noho: studio/one bedroom $1,900 to $5,000; two bedrooms, $4,000 to $8,000
- Soho: studio/one bedroom, $2,000 to $4,500; two bedrooms, $5,500 to $10,000
- Lower East Side: studio/one bedroom, $1,750 to $3,000; two bedrooms, $2,300 to $3,000
- Tribeca: studio/one bedroom, $2,200 to $4,400; two bedrooms, $4,000 to $10,000
- East Side (Midtown): studio/one bedroom, $3,000 to $4,500; two bedrooms, $4,500 to $8,200
- Union Square/Gramercy Park Area: studio/one bedroom, $1,600 to $3,000; two bedrooms, $2,600 to $4,000
- Queens/Astoria and Long Island City: studio/one bedroom, $1,000 to $2,000; two bedrooms, $1,500 to $2,000

Interviews with New York Realtors, Sandy Reilly and Bill Massof

Aside from up-to-the-minute book stats, I felt that a couple of interviews with New York City realtors would also be helpful in your search for that perfect apartment. Much of the following information is totally subjective, based on the realtor's experience. Sandy Reilly is a full-time real estate broker. Bill Massoff is an actor and part-time real estate broker.

Sandy Reilly (SR)
Reilly Associates
211 East 43rd Street, Suite 1008
New York, NY 10017
(212) 490-2003
reillyassoc@netscape.net

How has the apartment rental situation changed in the last decade or so? How would you describe the marketplace now?

SR: The obvious thing is that the prices have gone up tremendously in the last decade. It's been a seller's market. As a matter of fact, people have been bidding on apartments. Sometimes, if you're buying, or even renting, and you put a deposit on it, it doesn't mean that you're going to definitely get it. If someone comes in at a higher price, there's a good chance that you'll lose it, even a rental.

Now, the economy has changed, and you can already tell that it's getting bad for the sellers. It's getting better for the renters. It's happening slowly, but it's happening. All of a sudden, buildings are getting apartments to rent.

In what areas of the city (or outside of the city) do you think you can still find "reasonable" housing?

SR: Areas like Greenpoint in Brooklyn are good to look at. Greenpoint is only ten minutes away from the city. A lot of the homes there are renovated. Astoria, Queens, has gone up in price, but you can still get a good price. Jackson Heights, Queens, is also still good, as is Bedford-Stuyvesant in Brooklyn. Forget Brooklyn Heights; it's very expensive over there.

Roughly, how much are studio and one-bedroom apartments renting for in the different sections of the city, and how hard are they to come by?

SR: You can find alcove studios on the Upper East Side, in good buildings with doormen, for $1,800 to $2,300. (An alcove studio, by the way, is bigger than a regular studio.) That's a lot of money for a young actor coming to New York. One bedrooms in these same doorman buildings are $2,500 and up. Now, in not-so-elegant buildings, the prices obviously are lower for both one bedrooms and studios. If you go uptown, in the 90s, you can get good prices. But they're building new luxury high-rises up there, so the prices for those spaces will not be low. The 50s through the 80s are prime on the East Side. I'm talking the area closer to Central Park. You can still find something reasonable if you rent in a three- to five-floor walk-up. You have to really look, but they are there.

What is expected of a first-time tenant in New York City (security deposits, references, etc.)?

SR: One month's rent, one month's security. The potential renter will have to have a job, a bank account in the city, a Social Security number, some form of references. Actors are not exactly the most desirable tenants. For the most part, actors come here without a job and relatively little money. If buildings can get a parent to cosign for the young actor, it might not be so hard.

Specifically, can you think of anything a first-time tenant should know before renting an apartment in New York?

SR: Don't come in with great expectations. Don't think you'll find exactly what you want in square footage. Not right now, not in this market. People who live out of New York pay much, much less for much, much more room. Ask yourself if you can really afford to live in the city. My advice is take a first apartment that isn't exactly what you want, live there for a year so that you can learn the lay of the land. During that time, you can be looking around for more of what you're looking for. You'll have much more time to search and network.

Including using realtors, what are the best ways to find apartments in New York?
SR: The *New York Times*, the *Village Voice*.

Any apartment rental scams that actors need to know about?
SR: There are many things that go on that are "unethical," but they are not illegal. People promise you things but don't come across, and you're left with no apartment. The one good thing about using good brokers in New York is, they can protect you from some of the scams out there. They know the buildings they represent, and they know the management of the buildings. There is usually a relationship between the broker and the management of the building. The broker knows how the maintenance in that building is.

Any other advice that you have for actors looking for housing in New York?
SR: My best advice for actors thinking of moving to New York: don't live in Manhattan unless you have a good amount of money. Right now, it's just too expensive, and you won't be getting your money's worth.

Outside of the city, you won't go through such heavy reference checks. Here, as I said, you may have to have someone sign for you since you don't have a job, a bank account, or references.

One of the very compatible jobs actors take to supplement their careers is that of real estate agent. Aside from what could be a lucrative income, the flexibility of hours is very conducive to an actor's schedule. What follows is an interview with successful actor/model/realtor Bill Massof.

Bill Massof, actor, realtor at Custom Brokers
Custom Brokers
Real Estate Brokerage
361 West Broadway, Floor 2
New York, NY 10013
T (212)-334-3011

Being a musician, I came here initially to be a part of the vibrant music scene. But in my first year in the city, I met many people who introduced me to other activities I had never considered trying before. I took an acting class, did a test shoot with a photographer for modeling, and began working part-time as a waiter. Eventually, I started working as an actor and model on a regular basis, making a living doing commercials, TV, film, and print ads. I never stopped pursuing my music, writing, and performing with various bands over the years. Now I am practicing real estate sales in conjunction with my acting and modeling, working with Suzanne Brose at Custom Brokers, a friend from my early days in the city.

How did you come to be interested in working in real estate?

BM: I became interested in doing real estate sales through other actors and models I knew, who recommended it as a good second career. The flexible schedule allows you to go on auditions and castings and to be available for acting jobs, most of which tend to book at the last minute.

The fact that it is a people-oriented business, where you are dealing with customers face-to-face, also appealed to me. I already had some experience in sales from having worked in several New York City department stores prior to my acting career.

What does the work entail?

The practice of real estate entails many aspects as a sales person primarily, facilitating the buying, selling, or renting of a home on behalf of a client or customer. You are essentially the person who orchestrates the process of finding the right match between buyer and seller, tenant and landlord. To this end, the more you know about the market, the better you are able to inform the parties involved and point them in the right direction. Your job is to provide all relevant and pertinent information useful to the client reaching his goal. This means getting to know your customer's wants and needs, asking questions, finding and viewing viable options, and refining the search until the customer is satisfied.

How did you prepare for this kind of work? Were there tests involved?

The state of New York requires that you take a seventy-five-hour course at an accredited school of real estate. You must pass both the school exam and a separate New York State exam. This qualifies you for a license. However, any prospective licensee must become affiliated with a brokerage agency who is willing to sponsor you. In effect, you agree to follow the rules and guidelines of the New York State Real Estate Board, and your broker is responsible for making sure you understand and follow these rules. The course can be taken in a concentrated ten days or spread out over four months.

Given the present economic crisis, how has the real estate market been affected? How does that affect your work on a day-to-day basis?

The real estate market is currently in the process of recovering from an economy in severe recession. Buying and selling of properties has been at a low ebb, but is starting to show signs of improvement as the economy grows and the stock market rises. Investors have been cautiously waiting on the sidelines, looking for a sign that we've hit bottom and that the risks of a worsening downturn are outweighed by the positive signs for a recovery.

For the real estate salesperson, this means more activity as buyers venture out to take advantage of the low interest rates and home prices. Rentals remain a strong market due to landlords offering incentives, such as a free month's rent, payment of the broker's fee, or both.

Where do you work?
I am licensed to work anywhere in the state of New York, but I tend to work mainly in Manhattan, where I live, and occasionally in Brooklyn and Queens.

What are the present prices (general) in your marketplace (rental rates, to buy rates, etc?)?
There is a wide range of prices for rental units, condos, and co-ops in my marketplace, from full-service luxury buildings on Park Avenue to prewar six-floor walk-ups on the Lower Eastside. The prices vary at any given time, however, depending on supply and demand, and the overall health of the economy.

What kind of real estate do you primarily deal with (rentals, condos, etc.)?
Primarily rental, since that is currently the most active market. I do have clients who are looking to buy—one who is selling and a condo owner who is planning to rent out his apartment.

How have you managed both an acting career and a career in real estate? Are they compatible?
I have found a way to do both by organizing my time according to the demands of each business. Practicing real estate is very time sensitive, a process that requires complete attention and focus on the needs of the client from start to finish. Every step of this process is as important as the next, and one misstep can easily turn into a lost customer. It is important that everything happen in a timely fashion, according to the needs of the client and the client's schedule. The acting business is very similar in many ways. You need to be available to make the audition during the time allotted and be available for the shoot on whatever days you are needed.

Initially, I struggled with this conflict being jerked back and forth between obligations to my clients and responding to acting and modeling opportunities at the same time. My broker, Suzanne Brose, and her office manager, Tom Bohan, at Custom Brokers, helped me solve this problem by pairing me with another agent who could step in and take my place whenever a conflict arose. This allowed the agent-customer relationship to continue seamlessly, never missing a beat, so that when I returned to my customer, it was like I never left.

Any suggestions for actors who might think of coming to New York?
Network, network, network. This comes naturally for many people but is very difficult for others. It is necessary, however, for both acting and real estate. It is also true for finding an apartment on your own. For someone coming to New York for the first time, it is important to come prepared for the reality of the high living expenses here, especially rent. Prepare ahead of time by visiting the city, getting to know people, and establishing relationships, so that when you are ready to move, you have a network and you know the lay of the land.

Places to Shop

There are thousands of places to shop in New York. Since this isn't a book on tourism, I'm just mentioning a few of each, just to start you out. You can't beat New York for some of the best bargains around. Sure, there are the high-end designer stores in Soho and on the Upper East Side, but there's also Orchard Street on the Lower East Side, where great bargains were born. I'll be listing the best shopping neighborhoods and streets.

Lower Manhattan / Financial District

You should check out the South Street Seaport (Take the 2, 3, 4, 5 subways to Fulton Street). There you'll find stores like Abercrombie & Fitch and Ann Taylor. There's a lovely ambience in this area that makes shopping even more fun.

The great store in this area is Century 21. This has been called "the king" of discount department stores. Perfect for the actor's budget—you can find unbelievable bargains here, as well as camera and computer equipment.

Chinatown

Here you'll find knockoff sunglasses and watches, leather goods, and backpacks. As you walk along Canal, Mulberry, Mott, and Elizabeth streets, you'll find all kinds of inexpensive items. Do not purchase bootleg DVDs, software, and videos as these are stolen goods. I personally advise you not to buy answering machines, radios, and things like that in this area. I've been told that if you absolutely must purchase these items here, be sure to open the box first before you buy.

Lower East Side

This area runs from Houston to Canal, along Orchard, Allen, and Ludlow. Years ago, you could find all kinds of bargains in this area. Not anymore. You can find some bargains here, on things like luggage, shoes, leather goods, and linens. Because many store-owners in this area are Jewish, shops are closed Friday afternoon and Saturday. You can find hip, edgy clothing south of Houston and north of Grand Street, between Allen and Clinton.

Soho

There are many trendy stores here, from Banana Republic to A/X Armani, J. Crew, Guess, H&M, Bloomingdale's, and Prada. This area runs from Broadway west to 6th Avenue and from Houston Street to Canal Street. Broadway is the most commercial strip in this area. Stop off at Dean and Deluca's for coffee or a quick lunch.

Nolita

This area near Little Italy has become a very hot shopping area in the last few years. Elizabeth Street and nearby Mott and Mulberry streets have many interesting ethnic shops, including Indomix (232 Mulberry Street) and Tracy Feith (240 Mulberry Street).

The East Village

To many, this area is where the truly hip shoppers get their clothes. The best way to get here is to take the number 6 train to Astor Place. Designers like Jill Anderson (331 East 9th Street) and Janice Huminska (315 East 9th Street) have stores here. There are many boutiques in this area. Don't miss St. Mark's Place—8th Street turns into St. Mark's from 3rd Avenue to Avenue A.

Greenwich Village

There are tons of great shops and boutiques in the West Village. You can also find antique shops, gourmet, crafts, and affordable, trendy shoes.

Bleecker Street, west of 6th Avenue, offers great gourmet food shops like Amy's Bread and Murray's Cheese. There are also many trendy clothing stores in this area, including Ralph Lauren, Marc Jacobs, and Intermix.

The Meatpacking District / Chelsea

This area goes from 14th Street to 29th Street and from 7th Avenue to the West Side Highway. You'll see many art galleries here as well as top designers like Stella McCartney (West 14th Street) and Christian Louboutin (59 Horatio Street).

The Flatiron District / Union Square

Here you'll find everything from a giant Whole Foods to Filene's Basement to Barnes & Noble. Don't miss the great Greenmarket, which is the biggest farmers' market in the city. The lower 5th Avenue and 6th Avenue area offers Victoria's Secret, T.J. Maxx, Kenneth Cole, and Old Navy.

Herald Square

Yes, here is where you'll find the world's largest department store, the Macy's on 7th Avenue and West 34th Street. Also, don't miss the Manhattan Mall, which has a stunning array of stores (West 33rd Street).

Times Square

More and more stores seem to be populating the Times Square area these days, selling everything from clothing to athletic goods, and don't forget beauty retailer Sepoera. The great Virgin Megastore, which was a popular tourist destination, closed a few years ago. Forever 21 is now in that location (1540 Broadway) You'll also find Toys "R" Us (1514 Broadway, West 44th Street and Broadway), and nearby, the Diamond District (West 47th Street between 5th and 6th Avenues).

Fifth and Madison Avenues from 57th to 79th Streets

Here you'll find Tiffany & Co., Niketown, Louis Vuitton, Banana Republic, and many upscale retailers as well as less pricey options. Stores range from Saks Fifth Avenue, Henri Bendel, and Barneys New York to Versace to the NBA store. This area is a shopper's dream, the quintessential "shop 'til you drop" location.

THE DRAMA BOOK SHOP
250 West 40th Street
New York, NY 10018
(212) 944-0595 or 1-800-322-0595

The Drama Book Shop is unquestionably New York's best place to find plays, anthologies of plays, biographies, theater- and film-related works, videos, etc. The store has a lounge that's used for readings, book signings, and presentations. In addition, there is an intimate basement space used for play readings and small play productions. A must-go for all actors!

The Upper West Side

Aside from being a wonderful area to live, the Upper West Side is a great place to shop. The stretch of Columbus Avenue from West 66th Street to West 86th Street offers all sorts of stores, from small boutiques to national chains. Nearby Amsterdam Avenue also has some boutiques, and over on Broadway, there seems to be an increasing number of new stores. But Broadway on the Upper West Side is a gourmet haven, featuring stores like Zabar's and Fairway.

You Gotta Have Friends: Nightlife in New York

After a week of making the rounds and auditions, it's nice to go out on the weekends. New York is the city that never sleeps. There are thousands of night spots in New York, from the sophisticated cabarets uptown to the grungy East Village clubs and bars; there's something here for everyone. Again, I'm just mentioning a handful here.

Main Sources of Information for What's Happening

Here are some periodicals that can tell you what's happening in New York:

Paper Magazine's "P.M. 'Til Dawn" and bar sections list the latest trendy hot spots.

Time Out New York offers more diversified listings (by category) for the hip and, well, not so hip.

The *New York Press* is another reliable source of nightlife information.

The *Village Voice* supposedly contains more ads for nightclubs than any other weekly newspaper. What's great about the *Village Voice* is that it's absolutely free. It comes out on Wednesdays.

Next Magazine comes out weekly and lists many gay and lesbian events that are going on in the city. It's free and you can get it at all gay bars and gay businesses.

Dance Clubs

Webster Hall, 125 East 11th Street, (212) 353-1600. A four-story disco club with something for everyone of every persuasion and musical taste.

Pacha, 618 West 46th Street, (212) 209-7500. "The crown jewel of European nightlife brings jet-set decadence to NYC," according to their Web site.

Cielo, 18 Little West 12th Street, (212) 645-5700. Well-designed, fun, but it can sometimes be a bit difficult to get in.

Marquee, 289 10th Avenue, (646) 473-0202. Located in Chelsea, with a chic and trendy clientele.

Grunge and Rock Clubs

Arlene's Grocery, 95 Stanton Street, (212) 358-1633. As of this moment, this is the latest cutting-edge, live rock club in the city. And what's best about the place is that there is no cover—perfect for those actors on a budget.

Revolver, 210 Rivington Street, (212) 505-7625. Rock and roll joint; hipster hot spot.

Folk, Country, and Rock

The Bitter End, 147 Bleecker Street, (212) 673-7030. Some of the rock music greats started out here: Stevie Wonder, Arlo Guthrie, and Billie Joel, to name just a few. The cover is usually $5.

Kenny's Castaways, 157 Bleecker Street, (212) 979-9762. Another Village club that's maintained its sixties atmosphere since, well, the sixties.

Latin Music

Copacabana, 560 West 34th Street, (212) 239-2672. If you're into live Latin music, you can't beat this spot. You can catch live salsa and merengue in one room and the ever-popular disco in another.

China Club, 268 West 47th Street, (212 (398) 3800. After-work Latin parties are very popular.

Jazz

Sweet Basil, 88 7th Avenue, (212) 242-1785. Another Village jazz institution, where such legends as Dizzy Gillespie and Wynton Marsalis played at one time.

Birdland, 315 West 44th Street, (212) 581-3080. If you want to hear the up-and-coming groups, they say that this is the place to go.

Village Vanguard, 178 7th Avenue South, between 11th and Perry streets, (212) 255-4037. This legendary jazz club, open since 1935, has featured many of the greats (and sometimes still does). If you like jazz, this must be the place for you. Very expensive.

Blue Note, 131 West 3rd Street, DVD(212) 475-8592. Opened in 1981, the Blue Note is arguably the world's most popular jazz club. World renowned musicians take the stage for six-day runs, with Mondays usually reserved for excellent local talent.

Comedy Clubs

Today's comics may be tomorrow's sitcom stars. There has been a trend in the last decade or so for talent agents and TV producers to scout the comedy clubs for new sitcom talent, so you never know if that comic you're watching will be the next Jerry Seinfeld. You can expect to pay about $15 per person on a weekend (on top of a drink minimum). At most comedy clubs, reservations are required.

Caroline's Comedy Club, 1626 Broadway, (212) 757-4100. Many of the top comedians have appeared here and still do.

Chicago City Limits, 1105 1st Avenue, (212) 888-5233. As all actors know, familiarity with improv can be indispensable to their work. Here, you have an opportunity to learn from some real pros.

Dangerfield's, 1118 1st Avenue, (212) 593-1650. This world-famous comedy club has been around since 1969.

Gotham Comedy Club, 34 West 22nd Street, (212) 367-9000. You can catch some of today's hottest comic headliners at this club.

Bars/Restaurants

Here are a few places where people in the business are known to stop off for a cocktail or two:

The West Bank Café, 407 West 43rd Street, (212) 695-6909. This trendy theater restaurant also offers a popular theater cabaret, where you can catch comics, revues, and theater pieces.

The Film Center Café, 635 9th Avenue, (212) 262-2525. This theater/film hangout offers a relaxed atmosphere with good hamburgers and a 10 percent discount to showbiz union members.

Bar 89, 89 Mercer Street, (212) 274-0989. This hot spot in Soho offers monster martinis and a very classy (and pseudoclassy) crowd.

Whiskey Bar, 1567 Broadway, (212) 930-7400. Located at the exclusive W Hotel. Very fashionable hotel. For those who consider themselves "cool."

Hogs and Heifers, 859 Washington Street, (212) 929-0655. This Southern-style, down and dirty biker bar has been a hot spot for years. On any given weekend, you might catch Drew Barrymore, Harrison Ford, or Julia Roberts there.

B Bar, 358 Bowery, (212) 475-2220. A very trendy spot in the East Village.

Barrymore's, 467 West 45th Street, (212) 391-8400. One of the popular theater hangout bar/restaurants in the theater district.

Joe Allen's, 326 West 46th Street, (212) 581-6464. Another very popular show business bar/restaurant hangout in the theater district. There's a "flop wall," which displays posters of Broadway musicals that flopped.

Sardi's, 234 West 44th Street, (212) 221-8440. The legendary theater bar. There are caricatures of stars on many of the walls. A place you should certainly stop off for a drink.

Splash Bar, 50 West 17th Street, (212) 691-0073. A popular Chelsea gay men's bar, which on most nights, features male go-go dancers.

The Monster, 80 Grove Street, (212) 924-3558. A West Village favorite for gays. Upstairs is a piano bar, downstairs a disco.

Henrietta Hudson, 438 Hudson Street, (212) 924-3347. A mainly lesbian bar that has a regular crowd and also attracts professionals and out-of-towners.

Gym Bar, 167 8th Avenue, (212) 337-2439. New York's gay sports bar.

Boxers NYC, 37 West 20th Street (between 5th and 6th Avenue). (212) 255-5082. Another popular gay sports bar.

PART II

An Actor Prepares

"BRUSH UP YOUR SHAKESPEARE": ACTING SCHOOLS IN NEW YORK

One of the most surprising things I learned in my interviews with casting directors and agents is that the first thing they look for on an actor's résumé is their training. Think about it, if you were going to have surgery, wouldn't you prefer it if your doctor had trained at a respected medical school rather than some place you've never heard of? Diversified training with well-known teachers and schools is not only a smart way to grow as an artist, but is also a résumé builder. There's Meisner training, the Method, the British technique, and the list goes on. Open yourself up to new ways to grow as an artist. You need a foundation, a technique that you can depend on, a way to approach the work. I'm not a major proponent of one system of acting over another. I believe all actors develop their own way of working based on their own sense of truth, who they've studied with, and on-the-job training.

Another thing is that as you develop as an actor, different problems arise that you might want to address in a classroom situation. The classroom is the place to attend to such problems. It's a place to stretch, overcome fears, try out roles that you might be right for. Most good acting classes are safe, supportive environments. I strongly suggest leaving any acting class where the teacher is in any way abusive. Always trust your instincts if you feel uncomfortable with a teacher. Make sure that you are given enough classroom time to perform. Yes, you can learn from observing others, but remember that this is a performance art; you grow from experience.

Just because a teacher is one of the "name" teachers in New York does not mean that he or she is the best teacher for you. You must believe that what he's teaching is accurate and truthful. If you think he's full of it, leave.

In New York, there are many acting schools and private acting coaches. Many schools here are connected with theaters, such as the Atlantic Theater School, the Ensemble Studio Theater Conservatory, the Roundabout, etc.

Some prestigious summer theaters, such as the Williamstown Theater, offer internship programs. Colleges in New York (and everywhere else) offer summer workshops for actors.

Acting Schools: Things to Look For

Here are some things to keep in mind before selecting a theater school, acting class, or acting coach:

- Would you want this school or teacher listed on your résumé?
- Has anyone recommended this school to you? Referrals are one of the best ways to find acting schools. Ask around.
- What well-known actors have studied in this school, with this teacher?
- See if you can audit a class before deciding to commit to a school.
- Where is the school or teacher located? Will you feel safe if you have to take class at night there?
- How many students are in each class?
- How often will you get to work in the class? Remember, this is a "performing art."
- How expensive is the class? Are there work-study programs?
- Learn about the technique that is being taught at the school or by the teacher. Is it mainstream training, such as Meisner, the Method, or a combination of methods?
- What is the background of the teacher? Where was he or she trained? What has he or she done professionally?
- Will you be able to interview or audition for the teacher?
- How are the classes divided? How will the level you will be placed in be determined?
- How long is the commitment to the school? In some cases, you have to commit to a two-year program. If you don't have any prior training, you might seriously consider enrolling in one of these programs, which can be very comprehensive and thorough (although such programs can also be expensive). But make sure you find out what is the policy if you have to discontinue studying for a period of time.
- Does the Better Business Bureau have any complaints about this teacher or the school?

Interviews with Acting Teachers

Michael Howard (MH) has been active professionally as an actor, director, and teacher for more than fifty years. During the last twenty years, he has been teaching full-time, and in 1986, he expanded his studio to include teachers from other disciplines, because of what he perceives as a growing need for actors to work in a wide variety of theatrical styles. He has directed on

Broadway for the Theatre Guild, was a pioneer of the Off-Broadway theater movement, and has directed at regional and stock theaters around the country, including four years in Atlanta, where he was the founder of the Alliance Theater. Mr. Howard taught and directed at the Juilliard School Drama Division for eight years, at the Yale School of Drama with Robert Brustein, and at Boston University where he was a visiting associate professor. He is a graduate of the Neighborhood Playhouse, a member of the Ensemble Studio Theater, and a member of the Actors Studio since its inception.

William Esper (WE) has been the head of his own studio since 1965, as well as director of the Professional Actor training at Mason Gross School of the Arts at Rutgers University since its inception in 1977. He is a graduate of Western Reserve University, as well as the Neighborhood Playhouse School of Theatre, where he was trained as a teacher by Sanford Meisner, with whom he worked closely as a teacher and director for fifteen years. Mr. Esper was on the staff of the Neighborhood Playhouse for twelve years and associate director of the Playhouse's Acting Department from 1973 to 1976. He is a past member of the National Board of the National Association of Schools of Theater and a former vice president and board member of the University Resident Theater Association. The professional actors Mr. Esper has worked with include Jeff Goldblum, Paul Sorvino, Christine Lahti, Jennifer Beals, William Hurt, David Morse, Peter Gallagher, John Malkovich, Glenn Headley, Kim Bassinger, Tonya Pinkins, Sam Rockwell, Callista Flockhart, Richard Schiff, Daphne Rubin-Vega, Aaron Eckhardt, and Patricia Heaton.

Terry Schreiber (TS) was an actor prior to 1969. He toured with the ATA and the Portable Phoenix. One of the early places that he taught acting was the Clark Center for the Arts. In 1969, he began teaching classes twice a week to twelve actors in a converted loft on the Upper East Side. Enrollment increased, and the group began mounting productions in what were the early beginnings of New York City's Off-Off-Broadway movement. The studio continued to grow, adding more faculty to its staff, including, most recently, Betty Buckley. In 1996, the studio moved to its newly renovated multiuse space at 151 West 26th Street in New York. Aside from his teaching accomplishments, Mr. Schreiber is an accomplished director, having directed plays on Broadway and abroad.

What did you do prior to teaching acting?

> MH: Prior to teaching, I was an actor, but I also taught while I was acting. I went to the Neighborhood Playhouse before I started teaching. Then I went into the army, and then came back around 1945. I was looking for work, and some friends said, let's start a class to "work out." That was really the beginning. They asked me to do it, and I found that I really liked it.

Aside from the High School of Performing Arts, I also had my own class. I really enjoyed teaching at Performing Arts. They had some interesting people there. There was this woman, Marjorie Dyke, Dr. Dyke. She was the head of the department and was very supportive of me and my work. I realized that I was really good at it and found that it was very satisfying.

I was also a director. I directed a few things on Broadway, in stock, and worked on several tours. I went down to Atlanta and opened up the Alliance Theater with a company of actors that I brought down from New York.

WE: I started out as an actor when I was about fifteen. After high school, I went on to study at Western Reserve University. At that time, Cleveland was a wonderful town in terms of theater. There was the Cleveland Playhouse, one of the earliest regional theaters in America where they did a lot of wonderful plays. A lot of the national touring companies came through Cleveland back then. If plays were successful on Broadway, the following year, they'd go on national tours and would pass through Cleveland. My mother had a kind of artistic bent, and she was the one who took me to the theater. I wanted to be in the theater ever since I could remember.

After I got out of Western Reserve, I went into the army for two years. After the army, I came to New York and went to the Neighborhood Playhouse, which at that time was probably *the* place to study acting. Sanford Meisner was head of acting there, Martha Graham taught movement. It was a tremendous faculty. When I got out of there, I made my way as an actor-director. I really fell in love with directing. One of the reasons: as a director, you had a lot more control than as an actor. Also, I love to rehearse, even perhaps more than to perform. And directing was about rehearsing. At that time, I was also coaching actors with audition scenes and monologues. When I actually began teaching, I fell in love with it.

TS: I was an actor. I did a lot of work before I came to New York, in summer stock while I was in college. Then I came to New York and started teaching in 1969, with no intention of giving up acting. I got tired of going out of town to do acting work. I toured with the ATA and the Portable Phoenix, and we started to play theater games at schools. And I really enjoyed the theater games. My wife at the time knew that I loved it and suggested that I look into teaching.

When and why did you start teaching?

MH: Sidney Lumet was a friend of mine, and he had just started teaching at the High School of Performing Arts. This was in the late 1940s. He said I should also teach there. They hired professional people to teach the seniors. Sidney left—he got a job in television—and I took over. I did this for a number of years, stopping and starting, depending if I got an acting job or not.

WE: I started teaching in 1962. Right after I graduated from the Neighborhood Playhouse (1958), Sandy Meisner left the Playhouse. He went to Hollywood for the next few years. He came back in '62 and helped set up a new school called the American Musical and Dramatic Academy. The vision of the school was to prepare actors for legitimate theater and film and TV, as well as for musical theater. That's where I apprenticed as a teacher, and I got my first class there and started teaching in earnest. Shortly after that, I set up private classes. The first class I had had two people in it, two friends of mine. One of those people was Paul Sorvino. And there was also Karen Black.

TS: One of the places that I ended up teaching was at the Clark Center for the Arts. After a year of teaching there, I felt it was ridiculous. I mean, here I was putting in all these hours, but I'm not getting the salary I should get. So I started out on my own, with twelve students, in 1969. I think 1970 was the last time I acted. I also was directing at that time. I found it much more fulfilling than acting.

What do you think actors should know before signing up with any acting teacher?

MH: I studied with Lee Strasberg and Sandy Meisner. I don't believe it's a matter of what system is good. They are all systems of teaching actors, rather than teaching acting. I think the important thing is finding a person and a place that you feel is responsive and supportive, where the concerns are your concerns. A place where the concerns for truth are the same as yours, where you can use yourself creatively.

WE: Before people come to see me, I think it's really important that they've done their research. They should be aware of the work I do. They should know something about me, perhaps know people who have studied with me. They should talk to my former students in depth about the work I do. Perhaps they should become familiar with the work of actors I've trained. If people are just "shopping," I tell them to go away and find out what I do.

TS: I think that they should interview with everybody in the city. They should go from a feeling, if they are comfortable with the person. If the teacher is going to shift them to another teacher in the studio, I think the studio should set up an interview with that teacher. I think classes should be separated from beginning to intermediate to advanced.

Do you feel that all actors should study acting before auditioning/working?

MH: Certainly, there are some brilliant people who have never studied. I think that the reason to study is twofold. One is to develop for yourself some rock to stand on for those days when your intuition is not responsive. If your intuition is so free that it's always there for you and you're always responsive and truthful and alive, I'm not sure if you need a class. But there are not many people like that. Most of us need a beginning place to develop our own method. Because the final thing is, I must tell you, I don't believe there is any actor who does just the Meisner method or the Strasberg method or whatever. They develop their own method.

WE: All of the successful actors that I've worked with, and without exception, put their primary focus on training, secondarily on seeking work. Once they had mastered the craft, they put their primary efforts into seeking work. There is such a thing as being self-taught, but a good teacher can show an actor shortcuts that can save him a great deal of time. What a talented actor might come to on his own after eight or ten years' work, a good teacher can accomplish in two. The problem with trying to learn on the job is that in a professional work situation, the focus is not on teaching the actor their job. The focus is in the enterprise, in getting either the play or film done.

TS: I feel that all actors should study before going out there to audition, because they just don't know what they're doing. They have to learn a technique somewhere. Even if they're the best-looking person in the world, they need to study. If there is nothing there but a quality, that'll wear out.

What, specifically, do you look for when you interview/audition actors?

MH: First of all, I look for ambition, fire in the belly. Something that will push them over the enormous hurdles and difficulties that all of us face in getting work and creating a career. I think I can see that. Also, commitment. People who know what hard work is, don't have stars in their eyes. I don't audition people. I taught at Juilliard for eight years and Yale for two years, and I did a lot of auditions. I learned it was very hit-or-miss. It isn't a matter of talent. It is sometimes, a matter of temperament. I really care about how committed they are, how anxious, how much they need it.

WE: At the studio in New York, I interview (not audition) students. At the Mason Gross School, I audition. What I look for is seriousness of purpose. I look to see if they're really ready to make a commitment, if they're committed to their own growth and development. I want to make sure that they're not just "dabbling." I sometimes ask people, "If you had to make a choice between being very good and being very successful, and you couldn't have both, which would you choose?" I'm also interested in hearing them tell me why they want to act. I want to know what they think it is within them that makes them want to be an actor. You're always looking for personality, some depth. They must catch your interest; there should be a certain complexity in their personality. You need to sense that they are artistic, have an artist's sensibility.

TS: We do an orientation twice a month for everybody who is interested. Out of that, I do individual interviews and auditions. At the interviews, I want to know background information: where they studied, what kind of acting exercise work they've been exposed to. Also, their acting background. If they've done musicals, even Broadway musicals, but have never taken an acting class, I need to know that. In that case, you can't just put them into an advanced class. They shouldn't be in over their heads and intimidated. We have a Monday night class that is nothing but technique, and that is for the actor who has just had maybe one acting class, musical theater people, or for reentry people (people who've been away from acting for a number of years).

Is there a certain emphasis or technique that you use in your classes?

MH: A lot of it comes from what I found works over the years. For instance, I do a lot of clown work now, a lot of mask work. I still think that sensory work, at least an idea, a sense of it, is important. I think working without strain is important. Some people use the word "relaxation," but I feel that that's an overused word in this work. The big joke in anybody's work is when they tell you, "Just use 'yourself.'" Well, the truth is, there are about forty-six Michael Howards. They are very different. And some of them are very secretive and don't want you to know anything about them. And some of them I use all the time. A part wants you to choose. You know what I think craft is? It's the ability to choose which self to bring to work. Our job is to illuminate the material. The way to do it is to reveal some aspect of yourself.

WE: I worked with Sanford Meisner for a total of seventeen years. He was my mentor, my artistic father, a tremendous influence. And that, combined with the twenty years since creating and running the conservatory at Rutgers, has been influential on my work. I'm still kind of the leading authority on the work of Sandy Meisner, but in my work, you're always operating from your most personal self, so the work evolves in its own way. I still use a lot of the basic improvisational exercises that Sandy developed over the years that I was with him. But I've also gone on in my own way. At Rutgers, I've gone much more deeply into classical work. That work has led me to a lot of perceptions and sensibilities in terms of developing an actor.

Meisner was very interested in language, and style and theatricality. He did a lot of experimenting in style. He had a Shakespeare workshop for about four years in New York, and he was very good at it. I worked with him in certain aspects of that work, and it inspired me to go on.

TS: We teach a good American style of acting. It's based on Strasberg, Meisner, and Bobby Lewis, the people who went over and studied with Stanislavski. It's a combination of working from your own reality and working with the creative "as if." I was in a group once, and we invited different teachers in to teach, and I found that very interesting.

Can you describe the format of your classes?

MH: Class meets only once a week for five hours. The first hour or hour and a half is exercise work. Some of it is clown work, some of it is animal work, some of it is mask work—different kinds of exercises.

WE: I work with actors twice a week for about three to three and a half hours. People work in every class. They have to be prepared to work in every class. I'm very demanding and strict about outside work. Every actor in my class knows that he's got to get together with his partner at least once between each class and rehearse in a serious way. I only allow up to twenty-two students in each class. From my point of view, it takes at least two years to get a real understanding of the working craft of acting. For realistic work, where you're going into things like language and such, it goes beyond two years.

The work breaks itself down into two major parts. The first year of work is all work on the instrument. We work with a basic improvisational exercise, which takes about five or six months to put together. You have to work on one element at a time. The finished exercise has in it all the elements of a finished scene, except for the dialogue. It would consist of the actor's dialogue, not a writer's dialogue. These exercises work on a number of issues in the actor's instrument: their sense of truth, their ability to craft themselves and be spontaneous all the time, their aliveness and vulnerability to the other actors, and the ability to allow themselves to be affected in every moment by what the other actors are doing. The work also gives them the ability to emotionally prepare, to work on concentration, to be able to go from one unanticipated moment to another unanticipated moment. The first year, it's all about straight acting. We don't do much character interpretation until the second year. What I mean by "straight acting" is, the actor is the character in the imaginary circumstances, without any adjustments. The first year is not about you, it's about what the other actor is doing to you. The second year is about character and interpretation.

We also offer voice and speech to actors who need that kind of work. If people have physical issues with their instrument, we make sure that they address them. There are also supplemental things, like script analysis, mask work, physical class work, the business of acting, auditioning, etc.

TS: It's a combination of exercise work and scene study. The first class of every month, I do a group exercise that includes some bioenergetic work as a warm up, then we do a group sensory task or a group physical condition. I just teach the advanced classes now. There are six specific exercises that I do with people. Then there is a Friday class, which is a scene study class where we zero in on a specific playwright. For instance, we've been working on Tennessee Williams for the last few months. I'm trying to get actors to read more plays and then see overlapping themes.

Are there times when you feel that a student should not continue in your class? When should an actor stop studying?

MH: Just last week, I told a student, "You should not go on with me, because you're not getting it." I said, "What you did today has no relationship to what I wanted from you, what you're capable of." It was a painful session, and I don't know what he'll do. It was quite rash, quite painful. Sometimes, I take the person aside and say, "You've been here a long time, and I'm not helping you." I think it's always the teacher's fault, never the student. The hard part of being a teacher is taking those very difficult people and not being able to get them to drop the shit. You must let the student know, "I'm not getting to you, you're not getting me. You may need someone else."

I think the actor should stop intuitively. They should stop when a) "I'm not getting this guy, this is not what I want," or b) "I got this guy." I think they should leave when they've heard it all, when they think they have. But also, when they feel that the energy that they're getting, their desire to be there, their excitement to be there is no longer present, they should get out of there. It should add to their lives, make them excited to be in theater.

WE: Yes to the first question. I'll discontinue with anyone who is unprofessional, who is not reliable or not responsible to other students by collaborating with them. If they miss too many classes, I'll drop them. If, after six months, I feel there's no real talent or actor's temperament, I'll suggest that they leave.

An actor should stop studying when his heart tells him to. There's a time to focus on training and there's a time to focus on getting the next job. If, when an actor is working, he feels that he's lost something or that something is missing, he might want to return to class again to deal with it.

TS: When they've been there too long, and there's no progress being made, no acting problems being solved, they should leave. If they are using the class just as a crutch, they should go. Use the class as a gym, especially when you're not active during different periods. But they must get out there and audition, they must apply what they've learned to the real world. Also I should mention, don't study acting in two different places at the same time. That can only end up being confusing. I think it was Meisner who said it takes twenty years to learn the craft. That certainly doesn't mean that you shouldn't be working during that time. You should be learning and working. As the actor goes on to work, they'll develop their own method.

What advice do you have for actors who are thinking of coming to New York to pursue an acting career, to study acting?

MH: I think research is very important. It means reading what you can about the teachers with whom you're thinking about studying. It means going on the Web and seeing what you can learn. It means coming and seeing the teacher in person. When they come down, they get to look at the place, see the other actors who are studying here. They'll get a feeling about the teacher and the school. And they should trust that feeling. When I meet with prospective students, I remind them that we are interviewing each other. Even though I'm asking all the questions, I recognize that you're evaluating me. I remind them that they're doing that, and that they ought to be doing it. Find out about the teachers that you're thinking about studying with and go with your instincts.

WE: I think that New York is the place to study. When you're studying, it's important to be in a place such as New York, with a real cultural center. I don't think it's good to be in a wasteland someplace when you're training. I also think that it's important, when training, to see live acting on stage with really, really good actors. I honestly think the best teachers are here.

TS: Again, I feel that they should interview with everybody in the city. Keep their eyes and ears open. Check out the place, make sure that you feel comfortable with the person that you're thinking of studying with.

List of New York Acting Schools

Here is a list of some other respected teachers and schools in the New York City area. This is by no means a complete listing of every acting school and coach in the city. Schools and coaches come and go every year. What I've decided to list here are the more popular ones, according to a consensus of actors that I've interviewed.

Robert McCaskill
McCaskill Studio
336 West 37th Street
Room 340
New York, NY 10018
(212) 777 6050

Acting Studio Inc.
29 East 19th Street
New York, NY 10003
(212) 228-2700

Actors Institute
159 West 25th Street
New York, NY 10001
(212) 924-8888

Actors Workshop
65 West 55th Street
New York, NY 10019
(212) 757-2835

Stella Adler Conservatory
of Acting
419 Lafayette Street
New York, NY 10003
(212) 260-0525

The Glenn Alterman Studio
400 West 43rd Street,
Suite #7G
New York, NY 10036
(212) 769-7928

American Academy of
Dramatic Arts
120 Madison Avenue

New York, NY 10016
(212) 686-9244

American Musical and
Dramatic Academy
2109 Broadway
New York, NY 10001
(212) 787-5300

Circle in the Square
Theatre School
1633 Broadway
New York, NY 10019
(212) 307-0388

William Esper Studio Inc.
261 West 35th Street
New York, NY 10001
(212) 904-1350

Harlem Theater Company
473 West 150th Street
New York, NY 10031
(212) 281-0130

HB Studio
120 Bank Street
New York, NY 10014
(212) 675-2370

Roger Hendricks Simon
1501 Broadway
New York, NY 10036
(212)-841-0204

Michael Howard Studios
152 West 25th Street

New York, NY 10010
(212) 645-1525

Kimball Studio
60 East 13th Street
New York, NY 10003
(212) 260-6373

Ed Kovens
20 Dongan Place
New York, NY 10040
(212) 567-6761

New Actors Workshop
259 West 30th Street
New York, NY 10001
(212) 947-1310

James Price
29 East 19th Street
New York, NY 10003
(212) 228-2700

The New York
  Conservatory For
  Dramatic Arts
39 West 19th Street

New York, NY 10011
(212) 645-0030

T. Schreiber Studio
151 West 26th Street
New York, NY 10001
(212) 741-0209

Lee Strasberg Theater
  Institute
115 East 15th Street
New York, NY 10003
(212) 533-5500

Ward Studio
145 West 28th Street
New York, NY 10001
(212) 239-1456

Weist-Barron School
  of Television and
  Commercial Acting
35 West 45th Street
New York, NY 10036
(212) 840-7025

Dance Schools

Broadway Dance
  Center
221 West 57th Street
New York, NY 10019
(212)582-9304

Steps on Broadway
2121 Broadway
New York, NY 10012
(212) 874-2410

Broadway Dance
  Center
322 West 45th Street
New York, NY 10036
(212) 582-9304

New Dance Group
254 West 47th Street
New York, NY 10036
(212) 719-2733

Movement and Dance Techniques For Actors the Latsky Method

www.heidilatskydance.net
(917) 929-6985

Improvisation Classes

Upright Citizens
  Brigade
307 West 26th Street
New York, NY 10001
(212) 366-9176

Chicago City Limits
318 West 53rd Street
New York, NY 10019
(212) 888-5233

"ARE YOU TALKIN' TO ME?": THE IMPORTANCE OF SPEECH AND VOICE

Some actors come to New York with very distinct speech regionalisms or speech defects. This can be a problem and a hindrance to a successful acting career. In a profession where the way that a character speaks may be of major importance, having any kind of speech impediment will only make your chances of landing a role more difficult. A Midwestern or Southern regionalism, although totally okay in your hometown, will not help your acting career. You may be the best actor in the world, but if that regionalism gets in the way of the role that you're trying out for, you won't get work.

There are many speech teachers in New York who can help you eradicate the problem. To find the best teacher for you, I suggest going through the ads in *Back Stage* listing speech teachers (especially in the classified section). Many of these teachers will require some money up front for a number of sessions. Before you commit to this, make sure that this is the right teacher for you. Meet with the teacher and see if you feel that she or he can help you solve this problem. Try to find out who else has studied with her and what the results were. Do you feel comfortable with her? Remember, in most cases, you will be working with the teacher one-on-one.

Interview with Speech Pathologist Sam Chwat, Founder of New York Speech Improvement Services

Sam Chwat is one of New York's leading speech teachers. His celebrity speech makeovers include Julia Roberts, Marcia Gay Harden, Willem Dafoe, Robert De Niro, Kate Hudson, Olympia Dukakis, Kathleen Turner, Gregory Hines, among many others. Chwat also spends part of his fifty- to sixty-hour week working with executives, broadcasters, diplomats, and politicians. "People discriminate based on speech," Chwat has said, "and no more is this more true than in show business." Careers can be sidetracked indefinitely if an actor has an obvious speech problem.

Describe the way you work with an actor, and what is a typical session like?
During the initial consultation, we carefully analyze the needs and goals of a performer. The performer may come to us with one or more of these issues:

- My accent is so dense and different from American English that people do not understand me.

- I have such a distinctive regional or foreign accent that people are constantly ignoring what I say and are commenting on how I say it. As a result, I am not considered for many roles in the acting world.

- I don't necessarily want to lose my accent, as I may need it for an unusual audition in the future. However, I need to acquire Standard American speech as a specialty skill to use on auditions and when networking with people in the entertainment industry.

- I definitely want to lose my accent, but I want to learn to do Standard American English at will, switching back and forth as I please.

- I need to learn a special foreign or regional accent for use in a particular audition. Marcia Gay Harden, who won the 2001 Oscar for Best Supporting Actress, learned her Brooklyn accent from us for her role as Lee Krasner in *Pollack*. Willem Dafoe learned his Transylvanian accent from us for his 2001 Oscar-nominated role in *Shadow of the Vampire*. And, of course, one of our most notable achievements was teaching Robert DeNiro to trade his New York accent for an Appalachian one in *Cape Fear*.

- I have a physical or medical problem that causes my voice to sound strained or harsh or limits my professional potential as an actor.

In the initial session, we determine whether the actor's goal with us is long- or short-term. This is, if he or she needs to learn a specialty accent for a particular role, we will first determine how many sound changes need to be made by measuring the client's normal accent against the target accent. We will also evaluate the client's aptitude for what we call "imitability," his or her ability to hear sounds or imitate different sounds. We will then teach him or her a written coding system for his or her script and demonstrate how the new accent can be used throughout the script and in script changes. We will also provide an audiotape demonstrating the accent in terms of the script. Sessions for the longer-term client, who needs to use Standard American English across spontaneous conversations, will include a great deal of improv assignments and intense conversational skills.

Clients may see us one to three times a week for up to six months, and results are seen very rapidly.

Is that process very different from creating an accent or regionalism for a role?
The process is fairly similar. Our work always starts with analysis of the difference between the native and the target accents. We then teach the client to imitate the new sounds in different parts of words and show the client

how to link words with the new sounds. Although we focus more on script work for the performer who has a specific audition or script in mind, we use a great deal of conversational drill work, improv play, and tape-recorded assignments for the speaker who wants to permanently adopt a new manner of speaking. We also carefully guide the speaker through conversational assignments, at first with low-pressure conversations, and finally, in more stressful speech situations where it might be difficult to think before you speak.

In preparation for using a specialty accent for a particular role, we can carefully plot where an actor may need to make the accent lighter or heavier. For example, when a person is more excited or exhausted, an accent is expected to be more pronounced.

Does the acting of the role come into play during your work, or is that worked on separately?
Speech therapist instructors are phoneticians, not acting teachers. We are very careful to stay away from interpretive line readings, which are really in the province of the actor and his or her director or acting teacher.

Generally, how many sessions does it take for an actor to learn a new accent or acquire Standard American English speech?
We've had enormous success in teaching an accent in one to three sessions. However, these results are optimal when the focus is on learning the accent in terms of a particular script, and it is much like learning a song with particular sound changes, lyrics, tempo, and beat. We've had actors who've insisted on staying in character off-set and on-set, between takes, and in all aspects of daily living, and these performers have had an easier time learning the accent than the actor who learns the accent only in terms of the script.

The length of our instructional program actually depends on three elements: the imitability of the performer, the willingness to practice, and the number of sounds necessary to change.

When working with an actor who is shooting a film, do you go to the set?
Depending on the budget, or whether the production studio or the actor is paying, we can see an actor from the preproduction period through the duration of the film. When I coached Robert DeNiro for his Appalachian accent in *Cape Fear*, we did marathon three-hour sessions five to six days a week for three months before production, and I cued and coached him every day on set in Fort Lauderdale for the three-month duration of the shoot.

Most performers will receive considerable coaching line by line before shooting. We've even had handheld telephone prep sessions before each shooting day begins. We always supply the performer with tape recordings of the accent, tapes of the actor performing the lines, and considerable notes helping him to remember what he needs to do.

You've seen hundreds of clients over these many years. What continues to hold your interest?
I'm intrigued by the motivations that drive people to change or improve speech patterns. Most of our clients are driven by straight business decisions—that is, people need to acquire skills to advance their ambitions or careers

Any other advice for actors regarding this work?
Actors should not limit their self-definition. An actor should learn as many accents as possible to avoid typecasting and to make him or herself eligible for as many roles as possible. An actor should enable himself to be seen in as many ways as possible by agents and directors, and this involves refining speech skills to suit any characterization. Finally, the Standard American English accent has been proven to be the most marketable and lucrative manner of speech for voice-over and dramatic acting, and an actor should explore every possibility of mastering this skill.

HEADSHOTS

Three things that are of major importance when you're ready to start looking for acting work are your *headshot,* your *résumé,* and the right *audition monologue.* They create the first impression that casting directors, agents, and directors will have of you. It's important for you to put a lot of time, thought, and energy into making sure that these three things represent you and your talent well. It is for this reason that I'll be discussing them in detail in the next few chapters.

Simply put, the headshot is your calling card. As I just mentioned, it's the first thing that introduces you to "them"—the casting directors, agents, everyone. As you get to know people in the industry, it's also a means of refreshing memories, reminding people about you. Needless to say, getting just the right headshot that sells you in the best way possible is very important. You'll want a photographer with whom you feel comfortable, whom you trust, whose work you find impressive. Below, I have listed some suggestions that will help make this important chore less confusing and time consuming.

The goal here is not merely to razzle-dazzle them with a drop-dead photo that makes you look like Jude Law or Julia Roberts, but to get a good photo that looks like you "on a good day." It shouldn't be dramatically altered to hide every flaw you feel you have. Some slight retouching is certainly okay, but a major overhaul that gives you a "Stepford Wife," characterless, too-good-to-be-true look is a definite no-no. Fortunately, here in New York, we have a abundance of excellent headshot photographers. Here's what you should look for before you begin the trek:

Price of the Photo Session (and Reproductions)
The price of headshots varies quite a bit in New York City. You can expect to pay between $200 and $1,250 for the session. By the way, don't think that spending top dollar will necessarily yield the best result. There are many variables that go into a winning headshot (see below). You can also expect to pay

about $65 for reproductions. That's the cost of the photos plus the negative. Although you want something that you're proud to send out, you needn't pay a premium for these. More information about finding a place for photo reproduction is given below.

Finding the Right Photographer

Begin with actor friends whose headshots impress you. If none of their headshots blow you away, look around at headshots of actors you meet at auditions or in class. Don't be shy, just ask, "Who took that great shot of yours?"

After they tell you the photographer's name, here are some other questions you might want to ask:

- Did you feel relaxed during the shoot?
- Did you feel a rapport with the photographer; that is, did you feel comfortable about making suggestions?
- Was the studio clean and comfortable?
- How much time did he allow for the shoot? Did you feel rushed?
- How long did you have to wait to get your headshots?
- How many headshots do you get with the initial fee?
- How much does he charge for the shoot? For extra photos?
- Did he help you select photos from the contact sheet?

After you've found five or six photographers, call them and set up an appointment to meet with them and look at their portfolio. Be aware of that first phone call, how you are dealt with on the phone.

Your Interview with the Headshot Photographer

When you go to the studio, it's very important that at some point, you actually meet with the photographer. Quite often, he'll be doing a shoot and his assistant will show you his portfolio. It's very important that before you book a session with any photographer that you have some sense of him. The interview need only be a few minutes, but you should be able to tell if this is someone you trust, that you like, that you want to collaborate with. Don't allow him to give you a hard sell or try to impress you with some of his "name clients."

Headshot Shopping

When looking through photographers' portfolios, take your time, don't rush. Study the details of the pictures. There are certain key elements that you should be looking for:

- Does the lighting in the headshots have a naturalistic look? Does it seem too extreme, too dramatic, calling attention to itself? Does the lighting flatter the actor?
- Look at the actors' skin in the photos. Does their skin look natural? Is there a washed-out quality? Are there shadows on the face?

- Does the photographer use back lighting, and if so, does it work effectively for the actor?
- Does the photographer use natural lighting? If so, does he use it well?
- Does the photographer have variety of styles in his book? Does he take three-quarter body shots? Ultratight shots (letterbox shots)? If not, feel free to ask if he does do them.
- Does the photographer shoot outdoors? Realize that weather can be unpredictable, especially in New York. But if the opportunity presented itself, could this be a possibility?

The Photo Shoot (and Preparing for It)

When you've selected the photographer, set up an appointment when it's most convenient for you. There is a certain amount of preparation necessary before any photo shoot. The most important things are to get a good night's sleep for a few days before the shoot, drink a lot of water (helps make the skin look good), and try not to drink alcohol or smoke cigarettes (I know, it can be hard if you're a smoker) for a few days before the shoot. The difference will be well worth it. Here are some important recommendations to keep in mind prior to your shoot:

Market Yourself Well

Give a lot of thought as to how you want to market yourself. Are you a young mom type? A business exec type? Your wardrobe, hairstyle, makeup, accessories should all reflect the image that you are trying to create. Think of your wardrobe as the "suggested" costumes for your character. That's not to say that if you're getting sent up for doctor roles, you should wear a stethoscope to "indicate doctor" at the shoot. All you really need to do is suggest the type. It'll also limit the kinds of roles agents and casting directors might see you for. Remember, your type begins with your physical appearance, what you were born with. If you're not a model type, don't try to make yourself look like one in your photos. Use TV commercials, magazines, and newspaper ads to get a sense of what your type is wearing today.

According to photographer Arthur Cohen, "The most common mistake that actors make is not knowing how to market themselves. If you don't know what type you are, then you can't make the right decisions as to what to wear, your hair, your look, etc."

Types of Headshots

There are two major types of photos you should prepare for. First is the *commercial shot*. This shot is primarily used in TV commercials and for print work. It should have a wholesome feel. Generally, people casting in these industries look for a smiling shot with teeth visible. This shot should exude a warm confidence. If you fit into the all-American category, wear light colors, shirts with open collars. If you're a business type, wear more tailored, conservative clothes. I always feel you should wear the entire outfit: wear the entire suit even though the camera will only see the top half of you, the reason being, you'll *feel* different if you are fully dressed a certain way. Your expressions, however subtle, will also reflect it.

The *legit* shot should be somewhat more dramatic. These photos are used primarily for TV, film, and theater. There should be a certain intensity to the photo. The lighting should be more subtle or moody than the commercial shot. The *corporate* shot is for those actors who are interested in doing industrials. Obviously, you're going to have a corporate look for these shots. The clothing should be conservative and tailored. Hairstyles should not be too excessive.

Wardrobe

Color can play a vital factor in your shoot. Although your prints will be in black and white, the color of the clothes you select has a definite energy that will affect your mood and behavior in your photos. Speaking of blacks and whites, some photographers say yes, others say no. The photographer's lighting will play a key factor as to how well they work for your shoot. It's okay to have one or two black and white choices, but certainly look for variety of color in your clothing. And make sure the whites aren't too bright or the blacks too dull.

Be careful of selecting patterns that are too busy. They, along with stripes or plaids, are real attention-takers, stealing the focus from the star of the show—you. Make sure all your garments are well ironed (bring the iron with you) and that there are no stains on them. It only makes sense to try on any outfits you're planning on bringing to the shoot before you leave.

Photo Mood

Be in the best, most open mood you can be. For the couple of hours that you'll be shooting, it's imperative that you project a warm and friendly feeling. The photos must project confidence and self-assuredness. Remember, everyone will be looking at your eyes first. Make sure that they are open and alive. But don't work too hard, or you'll come across as overeager, hyper, or desperate. Your photos shouldn't seem stagnant or posed. They should come across as active, as if you were in the middle of something. If you are too concerned or worried about how you look, the photo will reflect that.

You and Your Photographer

Allow the photographer to be your director. You selected him; believe in him. The two of you should collaborate. Trust any instructions that he gives you. If you have questions or concerns, feel free to ask about them.

According to photographer Jinsey Dauk, "You have to be willing to allow the photographer to direct you. The more you can play with his or her directions, relax, and just go with the moment, the better your pictures will come out. And remember, the casting director wants to feel the life, the spirit, come through in the photo."

That Smile

Your smile should be natural and relaxed. Most commercial shots are smile shots. They should be friendly, sincere. You shouldn't look like you are frozen or, even worse, wearing a fixed grin. Think good thoughts. Think about things that genuinely make you happy. If the smile comes only from the surface, it'll show to seem to be frozen.

Makeup

Makeup can make a big difference in the shoot, especially with women. It's well worth the extra expense for women to hire a makeup/hairstylist to get the best look for each shot. Professional makeup people know all the little tricks, from covering a blemish to emphasizing your best features. Makeup used for photos is different from everyday makeup. Some actors have their makeup done prior to the shoot (generally less expensive); others bring the hair/makeup person to the shoot. If you do decide to do your own makeup, use a high-quality base that won't cake up during the shoot. The idea is to have natural skin tones in your photo, not something artificial looking. Remember, when color is added to the face, it will often come across as shadow. Use the color to your advantage, say, to contour an area. Eye shadow, if used too excessively, will darken the eye sockets, giving you a raccoon look.

Men should use a cream base to cover a too heavy beard. I suggest shaving at the shoot, or right before it. If you occasionally wear a beard, you should come with the beard grown in, take some shots, and then fully shave for the balance of the pictures. Don't forget to have makeup ready for the area that's been covered by a beard. Also, you should have an exact beard copy of your beard that you can put on if someone prefers you in the beard. Now, with the digital cameras, you can see the photograph right there at the shoot.

Making the Best of It

I know, sometimes photo shoots bring on all kinds of fears and stress. The secret, aside from trusting the photographer you'll be working with, is to do anything you can to help relax yourself. Bring along music that you like; do deep breathing before the session; leave yourself more than enough time to get to the shoot. I've heard of actors that have a few drinks before the shoot to relax them. This is not a good idea. The eyes will seem sleepy, and the face will be too relaxed. One thing you can do before settling down to doing the actual shoot is spend a few minutes with the photographer. Make sure that you're both on the same page as to what you're planning to do.

What Are They Looking For?

When asked what she looks for in a headshot, casting director Ronnie Yeskel said, "The soul. Sexuality. You can tell a lot about somebody in a photo. What makes me go absolutely ballistic is when I call someone in from a photo and she doesn't look anything at all like her photo."

Casting director Risa Bramon Garcia says she looks for "an intensity and a focus. I want to see confidence."

After the Shoot

As with auditions, the best thing to do after a photo shoot is "let it go." The session is over, and there's nothing left to be done. In anywhere from a few days until a week later, you'll see the contact sheets. The contact sheets are tiny prints of all the photos you took. Try to get as much input as you can as to which ones are the best for you. Casting directors, agents, or directors that you know can be of real help in this process. It's sometimes very hard to see ourselves objectively. The photographer can also be of some help in your selection of the best photos. Be sure to use a loupe or a magnifier while looking over the contact sheet.

Retouching

In a nutshell, do as little as possible. Sometimes, facial lines need to be softened because there is an unnatural hardness due to the freeze quality of photography. Or there may be a temporary blemish that arrived just in time for your shoot, which now should be banished from your headshot. But you must leave all your little imperfections just as they are, since they will always be with you.

Reproductions

Your photographer will give you the DVD of the shoot or, in some cases, a contact sheet from which to select your shots. Hopefully, if the session went well, you'll have two or three different options for making reproductions. Aside from your headshots, you'll need picture postcards, and I also suggest getting photo business cards duplicated. If you have to, you can use the same photo for all three. But if you've found several good photos, use different ones.

You can find a duplicating service one of several ways. First, your photographer might recommend one that he feels does quality work. Another way is by checking ads in the trade papers. And finally, check with actors you know and see which of their photo repros you like. Get the specifics (cost, dependability, service) from your friend.

You should expect a good photo similar to the original. Sometimes photos are too dramatic, lightingwise. Photo reproductions of these tend to look more unlike the originals than those with less lighting.

Cameron Stewart, the owner of New York–based photo reproduction lab Reproductions says, "You must scrutinize the original photo before giving it to a lab. Too often, actors will select a photo without looking at the photos' details. Then after you've made up a hundred copies, you realize that there are little distracting things that you've never considered. Look carefully at those atmospheric features in the background. Something might be more distracting than you realize."

Your 8" × 10"

I recommend the semi matte finish for your headshots. It is the most popular and generally is problem-free. Be sure to have your name printed on all your photos. I can't tell you how often a photo becomes separated from the résumé. Depending on your budget, I'd order between one and three hundred to start.

Generally, reproductions increase the contrast of the original photo (which is why photographs with very dramatic lighting may not reproduce so well). You should make sure that the photos you get from your photographer are in good contrast. Things like your skin and hair should have good texture and detail.

Picture Postcards

Picture postcards are an economical and handy way to keep in touch with casting directors, agents, and directors. Be sure to have your name and contact numbers printed on them (beneath the photo). Again, depending on your budget, I'd start with between one and three hundred. They can go very fast, especially if you're out there auditioning and interviewing. Don't waste these cards on constant "just writing to say hello" correspondence. Limit to once a month if you just want to keep your face in front of them and as often as you need to inform them of any significant, work-related news.

Photo Business Cards

Photo business cards are handy, economical, and a great marketing tool. You never know when you'll meet a casting director or agent. Since you're not always carrying a picture and résumé with you, this small photo business card, carried conveniently in your wallet, is an excellent way to give out your contact information.

Samples of Good Headshots

Photograph by Robert Kim. Pictured: Drew Carey

Photograph by Robert Kim. Pictured: Cassandra Creech

Photograph by Robert Kim. Pictured: Angeline Jolie

Photograph by Robert Kim. Pictured: Glenn Alterman

INTERVIEWS WITH HEADSHOT PHOTOGRAPHERS

Robert Kim

Robert Kim began his show business career as a child actor, starring with Rock Hudson in his first feature film. Since then he has worked in virtually all aspects of motion picture and television production, serving with distinction for four years on the SAG Minorities Board. He is a recipient of the Southern California Motion Picture Council's Golden Halo Award for his many contributions to the entertainment industry.

After he opened his first photo studio, he quickly became the preeminent headshot photographer in *Back Stage* (formerly *Drama-Logue*) for fifteen consecutive years, his work forming the basis of what has been called "The LA Look" in headshot photography. Since then, he has opened two more studios in Chicago and New York, specializing in actors and launching the careers of many of Hollywood's most well-known celebrities.

How important is having a good headshot to an actor?

RK: Ninety-nine percent of the time, the actor gets the audition from their headshot. So the importance of getting a good one cannot be underestimated. Some believe that simply having an extensive résumé and a good agent will get them the job, but when I think about how many potentially great careers have been sabotaged by submitting bad headshots, it staggers the imagination. A great headshot can often be the start of a successful career, but a bad one can ruin a career before it's even begun.

Is there any difference between a New York headshot and a Los Angeles headshot? Any difference between headshots for the theater and headshots for motion pictures and television?

RK: Back in the day, before the advent of cheap air travel, there were dramatic differences between New York and LA. headshots. This grew out of the relative isolation between New York and LA. actors. However, with the advent of cheap air travel and the phenomenon of the bicoastal actor, New York headshots began to imitate the "LA. Look" in photography, forever blurring the distinction between the two. The introduction of the Internet made the world even smaller, morphing both styles into one. Today there is virtually no difference between a New York and an LA. headshot. I have never noticed any difference whatsoever between headshots for motion pictures and television and those used for theater submissions. They are identical in every way and interchangeable for use in either application.

What kinds of things should actors be looking for when they're searching for a headshot photographer?

RK: Things like experience, length of time in the business, reputation in the industry—all are important.

Actors come in all shapes, sizes, and colors. Always insist upon viewing a wide assortment of headshots consisting of a diverse sampling of actors—with all nationalities, sexes, ages, and types represented. Be sure to look for substantial variety and depth in a photographer's portfolio. Cookie-cutter or "assembly line headshots" (photos that all look exactly alike) may be fine for high school yearbooks, but not for a field as competitive and demanding as acting.

How does the actor find a competent headshot photographer?

RK: I notice you said "headshot photographer." That's a very important distinction. There's a dizzying array of different photographers in the marketplace, all claiming to be headshot experts. However, just owning a fancy camera doesn't make them "experts." Headshots for actors are extremely specific, designed with one purpose in mind—to get actors more interviews. I routinely see actors going to photographers who know next to nothing about what the typical actor requires. Begin your search by compiling a list of photographers experienced in working with performing artists, then ask fellow actors, agents, managers, acting coaches, and casting directors for their recommendations. The Internet is one of the most convenient and valuable tools for researching photographers today, and one of the most effective methods of narrowing down your choices. In addition, always, *always* visit the photographer in person before deciding whether you want to work with him or her. This is absolutely essential. If the photographer doesn't offer personal consultations prior to your shoot, look elsewhere.

Which is better, natural light or studio light?

RK: There seems to be an ongoing debate over which is better, but ultimately, it all boils down to personal preference. I believe studio lighting is considerably better than natural lighting. From the blinding sun and insufferable heat of summer, to the biting wind and bitter cold of winter—the list of reasons is endless. I vastly prefer shooting indoors, where I can completely control the light and moreover provide a private, comfortable studio environment for the actor, free from the challenges of having to rely on Mother Nature to "get the shot." Does a headshot actually look *better* when taken with studio lighting? I believe that the answer is an unqualified yes. Studio light can do everything natural light can do, and do it better and more consistently.

What about cropping? Which is a better format, a standard headshot or a three-quarter body shot? A vertical or horizontal presentation?

RK: I don't believe that there is any one right way to crop a photograph today, any more than there is one right way to approach an acting performance. That's why I always shoot every client in all of these formats, allowing each actor to select the best style for their particular needs. One note, however: when submitting online, often a horizontal (or landscape) crop can alter the final electronic image significantly. That's why it is generally better to use the standard vertically cropped photo online.

What are the best ways an actor can prepare for their photo session?

RK: A little advance planning can go a long way in enhancing your headshot experience. Don't wait until the last minute to prepare for your photo shoot! Follow the advice and suggestions of your photographer. Select your wardrobe carefully and always discuss your grooming concerns (hair styling, etc.) well in advance of your session.

What kind of clothing do you suggest actors bring to their shoot? Anything they should not wear?

RK: There's a time-honored adage: "clothes makes the man." Never has this saying been more relevant than in regard to your headshot session. The photographer you choose should have an extensive knowledge of color, style, and wardrobe as well as how they apply specifically to an actor's special needs. They are the building blocks of your session. Understanding proper clothing selection is a crucial element in composing a great headshot and should not be overlooked.

One final note: never wear anything in a headshot that is more interesting than you.

What should women know with regard to proper hair and makeup for a shoot?

RK: Hair and makeup are integral parts of getting a successful headshot and should be decided upon in advance by you and your photographer. Makeup for headshots is entirely different from daily-wear makeup, and unless you are a seasoned expert, is better left to a professional. Always hire a competent, seasoned makeup artist prior to your shoot, preferably one with experience working with your photographer, who will understand his special needs as well as yours. When determining which specific hairstyle you wish to use, remember to choose a hairstyle that is not only age-appropriate but helps define the precise look and image you want to express. It should be simple enough so you can repeat it on your own—it will serve you no good to have a fabulous hairdo in your headshot that you simply cannot duplicate on the day of your audition.

What is the best way an actor can prepare for their photo shoot? What do you recommend they do in order to relax during the session?

RK: Everything about your photographer and his studio environment should be conducive to a relaxed and pleasant headshot experience. I use music extensively to help achieve this end and always encourage my clients to bring their favorite DVDs or iPod to the session. And on the subject of relaxing, never drink alcohol prior to being photographed, not even "a little one." Even one glass of wine can adversely affect your eyes to an obvious degree. Better to rely upon your photographer's ability to direct you and make you feel comfortable. Save the celebrating until after the shoot.

What are the ingredients for a successful headshot?

RK: In my estimation, a great headshot should be both flattering and appropriate for the role that the actor is submitting for. It should look like you do on your best day, but never so overproduced that it no longer resembles you. The bottom line is, a successful headshot is one that consistently gets you in the door.

What is the most common mistake you see actors make in regard to getting headshots?

RK: Going to a bad photographer.

What about price? How much should an actor reasonably expect to pay for a good headshot?

RK: On the subject of price, I have a saying: if you paid a fortune for headshots and all your acting dreams came true, it was a bargain. If you paid nothing and it didn't help your career at all, you overpaid.

So before you ask a photographer what he charges, you should ask yourself this question: how much is my career worth?

I've seen literally thousands of actors spend a king's ransom on expensive acting classes, books, health clubs, and seminars, only to have their headshots taken by the cheapest photographer they could find. A headshot is the most important marketing tool an actor can have. It is the first arrow in your promotional quiver. It is your calling card. Would you rather be represented by a cheap, unflattering photograph or one that makes you already look like a success? Simply having a "decent" headshot has never been good enough. You need a powerful image to realize your full potential, something that will make you stand out from the masses.

You've probably heard the adage, "You get what you pay for." Not always. I've seen scores of actors waste exorbitant amounts of money on so-called superstar photographers, only to have their overpriced headshots end up in a casting director's trash can. Going to a "bargain basement" photographer is certainly no better. Using headshots like these will virtually guarantee you a lifetime of waiting tables and doing extra work.

Choose carefully.

How often should an actor get a new headshot?

RK: The only time you should get new headshots is when
1. your old ones are no longer working;
2. you've dramatically changed the way you look (gained or lost weight, changed your hair color or style). Arbitrary answers like, "You need a new headshot every year" are usually the advice of photographers seeking more of your hard-earned money.

Any other advice for actors regarding getting headshots?

RK: Never choose your photographer based solely upon price. Very low prices often indicate poor quality and service, but extremely high prices offer no guarantee of ability either. I generally tend to look for photographers in the mid-price range. Second only to going to an incompetent photographer, the worst thing an actor can do is to choose a photographer based upon how much they *like* them. Often the most convincing con men have the best personalities. Naturally, no one wants to use someone with terrible people skills, but remember: this is not a personality contest. In my opinion, quality and industry reputation eclipse all other considerations when selecting an outstanding photographer. If their work is on a consistently high level, you can automatically assume that they know what they're doing.

Don't ever totally rely on the advice of your agent or actor friends regarding who is "the best photographer." They may (and often do) know less than you. Remember the three magic words when it comes to selecting a good photographer: compare, compare, compare! Never take anyone's word for it; always conduct your own research. Your career depends on it.

Arthur Cohen (AC) has been a photographer in New York City for about twenty-five years. He has photographed many celebrities but prefers to keep his client list private. He also works for a number of different magazines, shoots album covers, and does photo editorials.

What would you say are the most common mistakes actors make at a photo session?

AC: The most common mistake is the one they make before the photo session: their marketing plans, their types. Not knowing how to market themselves is major. If you don't know what type you are, then you can't make the right decisions as to what to wear, your hair, your look, etc. Other mistakes include coming in for a shooting after getting a bad haircut, bringing the wrong clothes, or getting headshots before you're ready.

What criteria do you feel actors should use when selecting a photographer?

AC: You should ask yourself, do you like this photographer's style? Do you like the photographer? Are you comfortable in the studio? Does the photographer come highly recommended? Bottom line—it should be a visceral, gut feeling that this photographer is right for you.

How can actors prepare for a shoot?

AC: Again, marketing is the best way you can prepare. Be in as good a shape as you can be. Know who you are and what it is that makes you unique.

What type of and how much wardrobe do you recommend actors bring to the shoot?

AC: I like to do four or five really good changes. They should be clothes you love and are really comfortable in. The clothes should reflect both your type and personality.

Any cosmetic tips for men and women at a shoot?

AC: Don't have a heavy tan or you'll photograph muddy. Make sure your hair is exactly the right length and color before the shoot. At some times of the year some people's skin is drier and flakier— don't shoot then (unless you've taken care of it with humidifiers and moisturizers). If your hair is damaged in the summer, make sure to take care of that before the session. I like people to be close to their ideal weight. If you're going to have any cosmetic dental work, make sure you're comfortable with how it feels before you set up a photo session.

How often do you feel actors should get new headshots?
AC: Not until you've changed substantially from your last headshot.

What should actors be thinking during the shoot? Is there something that they can focus on to help make their pictures look more alive?
AC: I work very easy when I shoot, very conversational. If they want some more dramatic shots, I'll ask them to run a little monologue in their brain. I'm not a real "coacher," I'm more relaxed in the way I work.

How much time does each session take?
AC: I allow several hours, but generally my male sessions are two hours, my female sessions are three.

The Photo Reproduction Studio

Below is an interview with Reproductions owner Cameron Stewart (CS). He's been in the photographic field for thirty-one years and at Reproductions for seventeen.

In selecting a photo reproduction studio, what things should an actor look for?
CS: Quality, service, and a willingness of the lab to work with them and help them. Pictures are, in a sense, an advertising piece. They should ask the photographer they're working with to suggest a reproduction lab. Since they've hired the photographer as a technical professional, they should trust his advice. Also in the theatrical community, there is a tremendous amount of word-of-mouth going around.

What are the most common mistakes actors make when bringing in their photos?
CS: I think that the most important thing actors should realize is that this is a business. Many actors come in and go at this in sort of a halfhearted sense. Consequently, we have actors come in and buy, like, fifty copies of their photos, something like that. In a sense, they're wasting their money. Fifty copies aren't going to get you very far. You need to work with extensive mailings, get your name out there. In order to do that, you need to work with a greater volume of pictures, which also consequently goes to a lower per

unit value. Look at it as an investment in copies as an advertising venture in a business.

The second mistake is bringing in a photo that is of poor quality (bad focus, smaller than 8"×10" size). I've encountered problems with some photographers supplying their clients with "InkJet Quality" photographs. Inkjet paper is very delicate to scratches and if it is not printed properly, you can see the inkjet dots on the original.

Any other photo items actors can use for self-promotion?
   CS: Photo reproductions are also used for voice-over cassette covers and opening announcements for plays and nightclub acts. One thing I always suggest is, know your audience—that is, know who you're targeting and find the best tool, be it a photo or whatever, to get their attention.

Other Recommended Photo Labs:

Precision Studios
36th Street Studio
260 West 36th Street
New York, NY 10018
(212) 302-2724

Modernage Custom Imaging
 Labs
1150 6th Avenue
New York, NY 10036
(212) 997-1800

List of Popular Headshot Photographers in New York City

There are literally hundreds of professional headshot photographers in New York City. The ones that I'm listing here are ones that have been recommended to me by fellow actors. The information listed is the way the photographer prefers to be contacted.

Arthur Cohen Photography
56 West 22nd Street, 8th
Floor
New York, NY 10011
(212) 691-5244

Nick Granito
35 East 28th Street
New York, NY 10016
(212) 684-1056

Joe Hensen Photography
236 West 27th Street, Suite
10RW

New York, NY 10001
(212) 463-0575
Fax: (212) 463-0608

Hoebermann Studio
281 6th Avenue
New York, NY 10014
(212) 807-8014

Robert Kim
320 West 37th Street
Studio 1101
New York, NY 10018
(212) 645-5788

www.robertkim.com
kimfoto@earthlink.net

Blanche Mackey
526 West 26th Street, #909
New York, NY 10001
(212) 633-6869

Chia Messina Photography
15 West 24th Street
New York, NY 10010
(212) 929-0917

Peter Hurley
134 W 26th Street
#1203
New York, NY 10001
(212) 627-2210
www.peterhurley.com

Barry Morgenstein
   Photography
135 West 26th Street
New York, NY 10001
(212) 647-1288
www.barrymorgenstein.
   com

Studio Babaldi
333 West 39th Street
Room #603
New York, NY 10018-
   1379
(212) 253-8795
www.babaldi.com

Bill Strong Studio
315 West 39th Street,
   Studio
1608
New York, NY10018
(917) 687-4669

EVERYTHING YOU NEED TO KNOW ABOUT
A GOOD RÉSUMÉ

Hopefully, after seeing your terrific headshot, the casting director or agent will be curious enough to want to learn more about you. The place they'll look is your résumé, on the flip side of your photo. Your résumé is a very important marketing tool. You should put a lot of thought and energy into creating it. It is a business card that can help get you interviews, auditions, and work.

The actor's résumé should only be one page long. It should be stapled to the back of your picture. Several of the casting directors that I spoke with said to tell actors to not have their résumés printed on the backs of their photos The photograph may bleed through the résumé and make the résumé illegible in the fax. Make sure that résumés are trimmed to fit the 8" × 10" size of the photo, without protruding. While there are several differences between the format of the New York and Los Angeles actor's résumé, obviously, all résumés should be well organized, neat looking, and very readable. You want to accentuate the positives of your career so far.

I suggest that you start out by creating a list of all your acting credits and training. If you're young and haven't done too much professionally, it's not a horrible thing. Young actors are often apologetic about their sparse résumés. Don't be. And don't try to fudge it by creating imaginary work that you've never done. Believe me, someday, somewhere, someone will call you on it, and it can be a very uncomfortable moment. After catching you in a lie, the casting director/agent will lose some degree of respect and trust for you. This is not the best way to start a new relationship. If you haven't done much professional work, emphasize the training you've had. If you haven't had much training, well duh, perhaps it's time to go out and get some, and with well-respected teachers if at all possible. List the "representative roles" that you've done in classes. That means, let them know some of the scenes that you've worked on in your classes. Don't try to pretend that you've done the entire play if you really haven't.

As for classes, remember, acting is a craft; your priority should be to prepare as best you can for the potential work ahead. Many casting directors that

I've spoken with mention that they're very interested in seeing with whom an actor has studied. This is especially true if there aren't a lot of professional acting credits on the résumé. (See the interviews with agents and casting directors in chapters 15 and 17, respectively.)

Your credits should appear in the order of their importance, not their chronological order. Don't list the dates of the performances, which is something I've been noticing on many résumés lately. It really doesn't matter if you did the play last year or three years ago.

The Heading

Your name should be at the top of the page. It should be in the largest print on the page. You may want to have a slightly different font for your name to call attention to it.

Beneath your name should be all union affiliations. Obviously, if you're not a member of any show business unions, you'll leave that area blank. I've actually seen résumés list unions that are in no way connected to show business. Don't do this. Beneath your union affiliations should be contact numbers where you can be reached: an answering service, a cell phone or beeper or your answering machine. I don't suggest listing your home phone number (or address) on your résumé. You never know into whose hands your résumé might fall.

Your Vital Statistics

Your height, weight, and eye and hair color should be listed together. If you're uncomfortable about listing your weight, women should list their dress size, men their jacket size. The reason this information is necessary is that people's headshots can at times be misleading. Sometimes people's faces aren't in proportion to their body types and sizes.

At one time, actors used to list their age or age range, but this is no longer necessary or appropriate. Some actors play younger, some play older.

If you sing, don't forget to state your voice range. As to whether you should list your social security number on your résumé, I suggest that you don't. I know there are some agents and casting directors who want you to, but once again, you never know where your résumé may end up. And that information floating around may get into criminal hands.

Your Acting Credits

This section of your résumé should be broken down into several subtopics: "Theater," "Film," and "Television." In New York, the "Theater" section is generally listed first. If you've had significant theater experience, you may break down the theater section into "Broadway," "Off-Broadway," "Regional Theater," and "Stock."

If, on the other hand, the only theater work you've done is in showcases, and you've done significant film and TV, hit 'em with your best shot first. Remember, accentuate the positive.

With theater credits, you should name the play, the character you played, and where it was done. As to whether you should also list the directors, there are two thoughts I have about this: If you have worked with some impressive directors, I'd certainly let that be known. But whether you should list *all* the directors you've worked with should be determined by the overall "look" of the résumé. You don't want it to appear cluttered. Listing impressive directors you've worked with is certainly a plus.

Training

This section is more important than most actors realize. Nearly every casting directors and agents I interviewed said that the training section gives them insight into how serious the actor really is about his career. This section is especially important if you don't have many professional credits.

Special Skills

Do you speak a foreign language or do a dialect? This is the place you can let them know it, and it may help get you a job. This is also the section where you inform the readers if you can play a musical instrument, can do gymnastics, horseback riding, or rollerblading, are trained in the martial arts, can do impressions of celebrities, can do American Sign Language, whatever. Any skills that you excel in should be listed here. You'd be amazed at what may be needed for a character in a film or television commercial. Also, interesting special skills can grab the attention of the agent or casting director and begin what may turn into a great conversation. I've also seen things like "own tuxedo," "can drive a standard shift," "taxi driver's license," "expert waiter," "European passport."

Sample Work Stills

Something that is becoming increasingly popular these days, and that I recommend to all of my students, is to exhibit small photos of you taken from shows, films, or sometimes even commercials you've done (if it's very "character") right on your résumé. These half-inch or so photos are scanned through a computer and line up down the right-hand margin of your résumé. You can fit perhaps five or six of them on a résumé, but if you only have a few, that's also fine. They should show you in different acting situations. They should show your range. There is no sense in showing similar characters on the résumé.

Make sure the photos are of a high quality and specifically feature you. There is computer software now that can freeze a still from a commercial or film you've done. Most plays have a still photographer who takes publicity photos. You'll want to contact that photographer and see if you can get a copy of at least one good shot where you are actively engaged in a scene. The idea here is "a picture is worth a thousand words." When they look at your résumé, their eyes will immediately go to the photos first. When the casting director sees you playing four or five different characters, two things will go through his mind:

- this actor books, is a working actor;
- this actor is versatile, can play several different types of characters. It may give the casting director some different ideas about how you can be cast.

Another thing about having the picture on the résumé is that while the casting director or agent is interviewing you, the photos will catch their eye. They don't have to scan the résumé looking for information.

Listing Review Excerpts (Blurbs)

Another attention-getter appearing on résumés is the addition of a few short blurbs from reviews of you (not the show) on the left-hand side of the résumé. You'll want to list the most impressive lines from the most acknowledged critics (*New York Times, Village Voice,* and such) if possible. If not, Joe Schmoe from Idaho will do just as well. Things like, "John Stevens did an incredible job, making Hamlet totally believable," or "Roberta Wheeler played Blanche with honesty, vulnerability, and passion" are the kind of things you'd like listed on your résumé.

I know it might seem like you don't have much room on your résumé for your credits if you have both photos on the right side and reviews on the left, but I've seen it done attractively, and it doesn't have to use up too much space. Vary the font sizes, so that it's attractive and easy on the eye. Again, the name of the game is whatever sells you best.

Résumé Layout

Unfortunately, too many actors just plop their credits down on their résumé without too much concern about how it looks to the reader. But what so often happens is, impressive credits are lost among some not very impressive credits. You want your headshot to show the very best "you" possible; the résumé should be just as impressive. Look at a bunch of résumés. Notice which ones catch your eye and which ones you barely glance over.

Generally, a casting director or agent will quickly scan the résumé for just a few seconds. Unless something pops out at them, they may very well miss the most important credit you have. You can do a very attractive layout on your own computer. This kind of work is best done on a high-quality or laser printer. If you prefer that someone else does it for you, there are many companies out there that do high-quality résumé graphic work. Check out *Back Stage* for ads offering these services. Make sure that the company has a storage service for your résumé so that you can update it whenever the need arises.

Updating the Résumé

Hopefully, your résumé will need constant updating. That means that there is ongoing activity in your career, obviously a good thing. It's okay to temporarily handwrite a new recent credit or two. But sometimes you end up with too many write-ons, and the résumé begins to look sloppy. A more attractive solution is to have section on the bottom of your résumé specifically titled "Most Recent Credits." Beneath this title, leave some room so that you can describe recent events in your career. If you have a reading coming up or a workshop you'd like industry folks to attend, here is the place to let them know about it.

Making Copies

You can make copies cheaply at a Staples or Kinko's or any copy center. I suggest that you don't try to get too gimmicky by using flashy-colored paper. For one thing, it usually makes what's on the résumé difficult to read; for another, it really seems like an unnecessary bid for attention. Use a white, ivory, or subtle pastel tint. Make sure that the paper isn't too lightweight. Also, be sure to crop the paper to 8"×10" so that it fits properly with your headshot.

Résumé Pet Peeves

There are several things on résumés that irritate casting directors and agents.
- First, misspellings. You should know the correct spelling of the theater, the play (or movie), and the character and director that appear on your résumé.
- Don't list special skills that you really don't have. Saying that you're an expert at rollerblading or horseback riding, aside from being dangerous to you if you get a job that requires these skills, can cost a great deal of money to a production company when they find out at the very last minute that you can't deliver the goods. You will embarrass yourself and enrage the casting director.
- Don't lie, plain and simple. It's not a fib, it's not a gray area, it's a lie.

SAMPLE OF A NEW YORK RÉSUMÉ

Joe Smith
AEA SAG AFTRA

(Cell phone, Answering Machine)
Height: 6'1"   Weight: 188   Hair: Blond   Eyes: Blue

Theater

Off-Broadway

| My Group | Harry | Manhattan Class Co. |
| Renegades | Steve | Roundabout |

Regional

Snake Oil	Carl	Long Wharf
South Pacific	Lt. Cable	Kansas City Rep.
Sweet Bird of Youth	Chance	Barter Theater

Television

One Life To Live	Ronald (recurring)	ABC
All My Children	Steven Holden	ABC
As The World Turns	(recurring)	CBS
	Mr. Jackson	

Commercials

Principal on-camera (national and regional usage)
(reel available on request)

Training

Acting	Terry Schreiber
	Michael Howard
Dialects	Sam Chwat
Commercials	Joan See
Special Skills	Yoga instructor, marathon runner, all athletics, can drive standard shift, speak fluent Italian and Spanish, own tuxedo

A sample of Review Blurbs that can be added to the resume (on the bottom of the page):

Critical Praise

"Intense and mercurial, Cynthia Cook brings a real sense of danger and longing to her portrayal of the Girl."

—Margaret Stokan, *The Monitor*

"Ms. Cook has a tender quality to her acting which helps bring the Girl's longing and suffering to light.

—*OOBR*

"Ms. Cook makes a sprightly Rosalind."

—Leslie Wood, the *Upper Eastsider*

THE SECRETS TO GIVING SUCCESSFUL INTERVIEWS
AND WINNING AUDITIONS

Every working person in the country has probably had to face the dreaded job interview at least a few times. Actors are unusual in that appearing at job interviews is a constant, recurring part of their lives. Add to this the fact that New York actors are interviewing (and auditioning) in one of the most competitive, talent-filled cities in the world. As a New York actor, you will need to develop the confidence and the strategies to put across your best self: communicative, interested (not desperate), informed, positive, and authentic. This chapter will help you discover how to do just that.

Common Sense for Interviews

A talent agent's time is valuable. As an actor, so often you will be instructed to "tell me something about yourself." Make your answer concise, interesting, personal, and yet to the point. The agent isn't interested in your personal life, but in your professional life. Always keep your interview with the agent businesslike. You can be cordial and friendly, but always maintain a professional demeanor. Some questions that may be going through his mind are

- Will I be able to get this actor work?
- Do I get calls for his type?
- I wonder what his range is?
- What types of roles would he be right for?
- How would he do in film, television, on daytime serials?
- Does he have enough training, or should I suggest some coaches or schools to him?
- Will I feel comfortable working with him, or will he be a problem?
- Will he be reliable, show up to auditions, and be professional?
- How serious is he really about his career?
- Is he shopping around with many other agents?
- Is there anything in his past that I should know about?

Confidence is crucial in the interview. You must muster up all the confidence you can *before* you walk in that door. How you present yourself is very important. You can't just "wing it." Be able to give a clear, intelligent response to questions like:

- Why are you interested in show business?
- What does your career mean to you?
- Why would this agency be right for you and your needs as an actor?
- What are your career goals?
- Do you plan on living just in New York or are you thinking of being bicoastal?
- Where do you primarily want to focus: film, theater, or television?
- Besides your career, what other things do you do?
- Have you worked with other agents before? Have you ever been signed before?
- What kind of things have you been doing on your own for your career?

Prepare a loose script of answers to all these questions. Don't memorize your answers, but be ready to call upon the information in an impromptu manner.

"So What Have You Been Doing Lately?"

This is the question that you're guaranteed to be asked at almost every interview. Your answer for this one must be prepared well in advance. Again, you don't want to recite a memorized script, but the information should be at your fingertips. How you deliver your answer is almost as important as what you've got to say. There is a thin line between arrogance and confidence. Arrogance is usually a sign of underlying insecurity. Agents are very aware of this. You must come from as positive a place as possible when being interviewed. You must seem genuinely enthusiastic about your future. Enthusiasm is contagious. If you are honestly enthusiastic about your career, there's a good chance that the agent or casting director or director will feel it too and want to work with you. This is not the time for shyness, hoping that the interviewer will draw you out. Be forthcoming, and have a smile that emanates from inside.

Much of the information that you'll be discussing will already be on your résumé. Be sure to bring to the interviewer's attention anything of importance that you've done that might not be there. If you've been a day player on one of the daytime serials recently, let him know. If you've just had a callback for a play or movie and are still waiting to hear from them, let him know. Let him know about any positive, recent activity. Attitude is everything. He doesn't care about the problems in your life. He's not your father, shrink, or best friend.

The Audition Monologue

Before I get into the specifics of auditioning, I'd first like to spend some time discussing the all-important audition monologue. As I've worked with thousands of actors on monologue and audition coaching, I feel that I have a substantial personal and practical knowledge in this field that I'd like to share with you.

First of all, all actors should have several monologues worked on, memorized, and ready to go. The monologues should be appropriate for the many types of material that you'll be auditioning for. Also, it's good to have a repertoire of monologues so that you don't get bored doing the same one or two over and over again.

Many actors don't have a clue as to what are the ingredients of a good audition monologue. Actors spend years training, and then when it's time to show their wares, they select material that doesn't display their talent. Here are some of the main mistakes actors make when selecting audition material.

Monologue Mistakes

- *Selecting material that is too old or too young for them.* It's very important to find material that is somewhere in your age range. It only makes the casting director's job more difficult if you've selected a monologue with a character that's not in your age range.

- *Editing several bits of a character's dialogue from the play, and then trying to force it to work as an audition monologue.* You must remember, the playwright did not write this material to be performed for auditions, so your slicing and dicing of his dialogue should be done carefully and judiciously. Also, certain playwrights write their dialogue with a poetic musicality. In some instances, editing their dialogue breaks their rhythms and the material looses that something special that worked so well as dialogue in their play.

- *Selecting material that doesn't have any dramatic (or comedic) impact.* Remember, this is an audition; you want to show your wares, but you also want material that will engage the casting director, make him want to watch.

- *Selecting monologues that are too heavy on exposition.* I really don't care about a character's entire background; I want to see characters who are alive and active right now in front of me.

- *Selecting a monologue that doesn't have any transition.* You don't want to do a monologue that only expresses one emotion over and over. In the short period of your audition, you want to be able to express some emotional variety.

- *Selecting monologues that can't stand on their own, without having to know the rest of the play.* So often, an actor will select a monologue from a play that he's worked on. The advantage is that he knows the character very well—a good thing. But you also have to look at the monologue as audition material. It's important that it be able stand up on its own. If the monologue is mostly expositional, or if everything you're speaking about can be understood only if you've read or seen the rest of the play, this is not a good audition piece. Also, what might have been a magic moment when you performed the entire play might not be so special as an audition piece. Remember, the audience watching the play got to see how everything built to that moment of the monologue. The auditors at the audition only see the monologue as it stands at the audition.

- *Selecting material that has been "done to death" by other actors.* Yes, some of those great monologues really move you, excite you. Well, guess what? They move and excite thousands of other actors, who do them every day, at countless auditions. It can only work to your advantage to find material that is new, original, and engaging.

- *Doing the same monologue so often that it becomes stale.* Yes, you loved that monologue when you first started doing it three years ago. But after you've done it a few hundred times, you'll notice that you seem to go on automatic pilot every time you do it. Rotate your material.

- *Choosing material that is inappropriate for the play that you're auditioning for.* For instance, if you're auditioning for a new Neil Simon play, doing dramatic material from Sam Shepard or Eugene O'Neill is not a smart choice. No one says that you should only use other Neil Simon material for your audition, but it behooves you to find material that's in the same ballpark. Try to find things that are similar in genre and sensibility.

- *Selecting material that runs too long.* If the casting breakdown says two minutes, don't bring in material that runs over four minutes. And don't cut that four-minute monologue that you sometimes do down to two. More often than not, you'll cut the life, the muscle out of the monologue.

- *Selecting inactive, past tense monologues.* Remember when you were a child, how your parents used to read you those fairy tales that were mostly told in a narrative form, and mostly in the past tense? If you'll recall, they told you those stories to put you to sleep. Doing past tense, narrative, expositional monologues will have the same effect on a casting director. Try to select emotional, present tense, active, conversational material.

- *Choosing material that is offensive.* Curse words, offensive language, and sexually explicit material is rarely appropriate for most auditions. There are some plays for which such material is appropriate—some David Mamet plays, for instance. But by and large, you'll only lose points by offending the casting directors with off-color language.

- *Selecting material that "stretches" you.* Auditions are not the time to show your range. Actors should select material that best shows off their strengths right now.
- *Selecting material that is strongly identified with a star performance.* If you select material from films, try not to select monologues or scenes that have the lead actors' stamp on them. If the material is strongly identified with a certain star, you'll be working against the handicap of comparison.
- *Selecting a monologue that's written in a very distinct dialect.* Generally, it's not too smart to do an audition piece in a dialect. There are exceptions. If the play that you're auditioning for is written in that dialect, and you are adept at it, it's okay. Time and again, I've seen talented actors ruin a good audition because their dialect kept slipping and calling attention to itself.

If possible, try to find monologues where a character overcomes some adversity. Finding monologues like this is not always easy, but if you have a choice between playing a self-pitying, whining loser or someone who has triumphed over a major trauma, go for the latter. Everyone loves a winner.

Basic Monologue Preparation

How you work on and develop your audition monologue is very important. If you rush the process and memorize too soon, you'll be missing out on a vital part of discovering what the piece is about. Even though it is an audition to get work, you should be preparing the piece in a craftlike way. Try to approach this as you would rehearse for any role in any play. Even though it may only be two minutes long, it is still a piece of theater and you should rehearse it the same way you'd prepare for any other role. I know sometimes you find out that you have an audition in two days that may call for a specific kind of monologue you don't have. The panic sets in, and you memorize something that seems appropriate almost overnight. You've given little or no thought as to what the material is about. You may be a good enough actor to pull it off, to do a good audition, but you've missed out on a vital part of the process of preparing a monologue for an audition.

It's for that reason that I always suggest to my students that they have many monologues (of all kinds) ready for auditions. For many actors, there is a lot of downtime—time that could be used for this kind of preparation. At the least, every actor should have at least two contemporary dramatic monologues, two contemporary comedic ones, one or two classical pieces, and perhaps one surreal monologue. The more of each that you have, the better prepared you'll be for any occasion. When I ask some of my musical theater actors how many songs they have in their repertoire for auditions, they generally tell me they have many. When I ask them how many monologues they have prepared for auditions, they quite often get embarrassed and admit they have very few (if any at all). You should always be adding new monologues to your audition repertoire all the time. Monologues get stale very soon, especially if you're out there auditioning all the time.

Rehearsing the Monologues

If the monologue you are working on is from a play, it is important that you read the entire play before your initial work on the monologue. You should know at what point in the story this speech is being delivered, have an idea of why the character is saying it, where the character is, to whom he's talking, and, basically, what the monologue is about. If you select a monologue from a monologue book and depend only on the brief synopsis the book offers, you will generally not have enough information to create a successful audition monologue for yourself.

The best way to approach your work on a new monologue is to simply say the words, without trying to act or perform them. What you're looking for at this beginning stage are any initial impulses, feelings that begin to register. Obviously, you're also trying to understand what it is you're saying, the meaning of the words. Most actors, eager to get the thing going, rush through this step. The idea here is to discover, not to perform.

After you've done the initial read-through, put the piece down and see what remains with you—what feelings, ideas, impressions, impulses. This is an important phase of your relationship with the monologue. Those initial feelings and impulses are the foundation for how you will develop the monologue, how it will grow.

As I mentioned, if the monologue is from a play, you will want to know where this piece fits into the tapestry of the play. Be aware of the moment before and after the monologue that you've selected. Knowing where the material fits in can only help you in your preparation. But you are NOT doing the play. Always remember, this is an "audition." Sometimes you have to adjust the material slightly. That doesn't mean be dishonest in your performance. Always keep in mind that an audition is the time for you to show your wares (i.e., your talent) as an actor. Some actors are so concerned about "doing that actual moment from the play" that they play down down their audition too much.

If it's an original piece—a "what you see is what you get" type of thing— you may want to start making simple decisions such as:

- Where are you?
- To whom are you speaking?
- Why are you talking to this person (people)?
- What time of day is it?
- What do you want from the person (people) to whom you are speaking?
- What are you talking about? What do you mean?

After reading, investigating, and making decisions, take a short break then pick up the monologue again. Once again, there should be no expectations and no need to rush to performance. See what comes up—what feelings, what thoughts, what impulses. After that read-through, put it down for a bit. By this point, you'll notice that you've developed some feelings about who the character is and what's going on.

Many actors like to do improvisations in the time between the readings. The improvisation should be an attempt to express the monologue's thoughts in your own words. With this technique, you may get a deeper understanding of what the piece is about.

I am a strong believer in the actor's imagination. I think that many actors become too dependent on acting tricks to help get them connected to material. When working on new monologues, always trust your instincts. As you work on the monologue, try to encourage your childlike sense of play, of discovery. If you allow your instincts to guide you, you'll come to many realizations about the monologue, the character, and the scene.

Next, read through the monologue several times. Notice I didn't say recite or perform. Each read is still done with the intention of exploring, seeking to discover more. What does the character really mean by this word, that phrase? Notice how the thoughts are strung together, their sequence. You should be constantly reexploring the basic questions: Where is the character? To whom is the character speaking? Why is he saying what he's saying at this particular time? Is he really saying what he means? Is he just fooling himself with his own words?

As you say the words of the text, attempt to say them as *you* would say them. Find your own sense of truth, your own reality—make it your own. Don't try to go to the character; have the character come from you.

Here is a concept I use with my students that they seem to find effective. In life, when you really communicate with someone, there are imaginary arrows that carry your words and thoughts (intentions) to the listener, the person that you're speaking to. When these imaginary arrows (the information) "hit," they are received by the listener, and the listener, hopefully, comprehends what you're saying. At that point in the communication, he responds in some way—a verbal response, perhaps a look in his eye—indicating that he has received the communication. Partially based on his response, you continue on with your communication, continuing to say what you have to say. His response can flavor what you'll say next and how you'll say it. You can imagine the arrows going in a circle, from you to the listener, and then back to you, ongoing.

When performing a monologue, although there is no one actually there, you must create the impression that there is. Unless it's an inner monologue, you must create the impression that this is a scene occurring and that the other person is very present. The more you make it your intention to communicate to that imaginary person, the more effective and dynamic the monologue will be. It will have a stronger sense of reality. I see so many monologues that are done with great passion and emotion, but so little of the actor's energy is spent trying to communicate that to the imaginary person. There is a slight flatness or self indulgence in the performance when there is no attempt being made to communicate with the (albeit imaginary) scene partner. Always remember, most monologues are, in actuality, duologues; the other person just happens not to be saying anything at the time. Also, as you begin to stage your monologue for audition, remember to place the imaginary character that you're speaking to out front, above the heads of the people you're auditioning for.

As you continue working on the monologue, try *not* to repeat the exact line readings each time you go through it. Fool yourself; let each read-through be fresh, as if you've never said these words before. Memorizing too soon sets up verbal patterns that give the impression that you are reciting the words, rather than experiencing the intentions. When we were children, we were all taught the pledge of allegiance. We memorized it the same way, by rote: "I pledge allegiance . . . to the flag . . . of the United States of America," and so on. Actors working incorrectly on monologues develop similar rote verbal patterns. When it comes time for the audition, they end up reciting the words the same way that they memorized them. You can sometimes hear the exact way an actor memorized his monologue.

To give a knock-out audition, you must be willing to "dance on the edge of the sword"—that is, to take risks, sometimes big ones. Sure, it's far safer to recite a monologue than it is to go into an audition and just let it fly, whatever happens, happens. If you've worked on the monologue well, there will be an inner landscape of the material inside of you, which developed as you rehearsed the piece. It will be a creative source, a point of reference that will allow you to do the monologue spontaneously and in the moment. Auditions, by their very nature, are stressful and anxiety-provoking situations. It's understandable that any actor would want to make himself feel as safe as possible. But believe me, there is so much more joy for those brave enough to use the audition room as a place to take chances, risks.

We've all experienced those auditions where we delivered the monologue *exactly* as we rehearsed it. Every phrase, every movement, every moment performed exactly as we worked on it, with nothing left to chance. We leave the audition room feeling somewhat accomplished, because we "hit every mark." But somewhere inside, there will be a feeling that perhaps we were too safe, too rehearsed; we weren't that personally engaged.

But then, there are those auditions where (perhaps by accident) we threw ourselves into the material, wholeheartedly, fully; we did it like we've never done it before, and discovered an essence to the character, the material, and ourselves that we never quite knew existed. That is far different, far more exciting than just being safe. At the end of those auditions, you feel like you don't want to leave the audition room. You want to hold on to the moment, to the aliveness that you're feeling. You want to remain because you've just experienced why you wanted to be an actor in the first place. You have just "danced on the edge of the sword," and you loved it.

Much of what I've just discussed about audition monologue preparation can be applied to all auditions, not just monologue auditions. Actually, when you think about it, most of what I've just discussed is pertinent to effective acting in general.

Approaching the Audition

Most actors that I know say that they don't like to audition. Some are terrified of auditions; others resent them. No matter how you feel about them, auditions can be stressful, anxiety-provoking experiences. We've all experienced the tight-throat, cottonmouth, clammy-hand feelings that come right before the audition. Once you become aware of the tension, it seems to be the only thing you can focus on. The good news is that there are things that you can do to help reduce the stress. The bad news is that, until they find a better way to cast a role, auditions are something you'll have to learn to live with.

Theater Auditions

Try not to think of the audition room as a place where you are going to be judged, but rather as a place where you are going to perform. After all, you are an actor; you love to perform. Try to find a way that you can actually enjoy the experience, embrace it. I know that might seem impossible, but try to make it a pleasurable experience. Sometimes, actors like to impress the casting directors with how "hard they are working." This usually leads to a self-conscious, tension-filled audition. Relax rather than push!

Don't spend time worrying about what they're looking for. More often than not, they don't really know. They may think they know, but believe me, their minds can quickly be changed when an actor gives a strong, personalized audition, when an actor makes material his own. I remember when we were casting my play, *The Danger of Strangers*. I was looking for a good-looking, Michael Douglas type for the male lead. James Gandolfini (*The Sopranos*) came in and auditioned. When I first saw him, I thought, "Boy, is that guy wrong for the role!" But his audition was so personal, so convincing, that I immediately gave up my preconceived idea of who I thought the character was. Remember, I wrote the play, I thought I knew my own characters. But in his audition, he showed me things about the character that I'd never realized. Needless to say, he got the role and ended up doing it brilliantly.

Before the actual audition, try to visualize how wonderful an experience it will be. You've probably heard this before, but visualization can play a major part in winning auditions. Many top athletes say that visualization is a key component in their success. The more you can see yourself doing a good job at the audition, the more likely it will happen.

Be mindful of what you wear to an audition. Yes, it should reflect the character that you're playing, but it should also reflect who you are as an actor. And certainly don't wear clothing that is too tight and inhibits movement or relaxation.

When auditioning with comedic material, don't push for the laughs. Some actors feel that comedic monologues or scenes are a time for them to show off their stand-up comic capabilities—wrong! You are recreating a moment from a play. Always keep the reality of the play in mind.

If you've been asked to do a scene in an agent's office, find a scene partner whose work you respect. Many insecure actors feel that if they pick a good actor to do the scene with them, the other actor may steal the limelight from them. Choosing a weak actor to do your scene with will only throw your own timing off and bring down the quality of your work.

Make sure that you can be heard. Even if the material that you've selected is delicate and sensitive, they must hear you! Be aware of where you are physically in the audition room. You want to be neither too close (right in their faces) nor too far back. You want to use the space in a comfortable manner appropriate for the material. Don't get frozen in one spot or remain seated for the entire audition (unless that's what the scene calls for).

If you've been asked to prepare two scenes for the audition, make sure, in your rehearsal process, that you create an ample and appropriate transitional moment. How you want to go from one selection to the next is all part of the audition performance.

Try to have two songs ready for all auditions, even if you're not a singer. If they ask if you're a singer, tell them that you can carry a tune. The songs, like your monologues, should be part of your audition arsenal.

As I've mentioned, your audition begins the moment you enter the room, so how you enter that room is very important. The casting directors start to form their first opinions of you within the first ten seconds. How you say hello, connect with them, and introduce yourself is very important. Like the material you have selected to perform, the entire entrance should be prepared. I'm not suggesting an actual scripted entrance, but one where you know specifically just how you want to present yourself. In your preparation, you should envision your entire audition. In your mind's eye, you should see yourself entering the room in a relaxed and confident way. You should also imagine yourself doing an excellent audition, exactly as you've rehearsed it. And finally, you want to imagine yourself totally relaxed and able to talk comfortably with the director and casting director if they choose to have a discussion after the monologue. All of this preparation is part of the monologue preparation (the acting) that you're doing outside of the audition room. With all this mental work to be done, you can see why chatting with other actors in the waiting room area is a total waste of valuable time.

When reading from sides, try to make eye contact with the person you are reading with. Don't hide in the script; take it off the page. Try to say the words that appear on the page; don't ad lib a lot. It'll infuriate the playwright (if he's there) and won't win you any points with the director either.

Don't upstage yourself. Try to keep your energy and focus downstage, in the area of the auditors. Don't keep looking down at the floor; that's where your energy and good work will be going.

If you make a big mistake during the audition and you feel you can't go on, politely ask them if you can start over again. Don't let the mistake throw you so badly that you can't go on. Rise to the occasion, and do the best you can during the second go-round.

Always bring extra pictures and résumés to the audition, even if you believe they received them in advance. After you've left the audition room, write down the names of all the people that you've just auditioned for. Keep an ongoing record, a database for future reference.

The Ten Steps to Successful Monologue Auditions

1. The first step begins before the actual audition. Before you leave home, try to get yourself in the right frame of mind. Relax, perhaps do some breathing and stretching. Some people use the visualization described above.

2. Arrive at the audition at least twenty minutes early. Make sure that you are relaxed and ready to work. Sometimes, it's good to go off in a corner and do a quick speed-through of the monologue(s), followed by a run-through. Don't waste valuable time chatting with other actors or socializing.

3. As part of your preparation, you want to be in character for the first monologue. Enter the audition room in a confident and professional manner.

4. Smile directly at the people auditioning you, say hello, and find the playing area that you will be auditioning in. If they wish to engage you in conversation, you must be willing to talk with them. Most casting directors save conversations for after you perform.

5. Announce what the monologue is from and the character's name. There is no reason to give a description of where in the play the monologue takes place.

6. Give yourself a moment, and then, perform it as best you can.

7. When you've completed performing the monologue, if they've requested a second one, prepare to make the transition from the first character to the second. Once again, give yourself a moment before you begin.

8. After you've finished, smile, let them know you're through, say "thank you." If they wish to talk with you, you must be ready and willing to converse in a friendly and professional manner. They may want to get a sense of you as a person, as a potential actor in their

play or company. They may ask you what you've been up to lately. You should have the answer to this question prepared in advance.

9. When you've finished talking with them, tell them it was nice meeting them, again say "thank you" and leave in a confident, unhurried, professional manner.

10. Once you leave the room, the only thing left to do is to let go of that audition and move on to the next thing in your day.

The Secrets to Giving a Good Cold Reading

A cold reading occurs when an actor is asked to perform material from a play, screenplay, or monologue that he hasn't had a chance to read through at least once. If at all possible, try not to do a "totally" cold reading in a professional situation. At the least, you should be given time to read through the text once to become familiar with it. Sometimes, however, actors are asked to do ice-cold readings at an audition. If you have no choice in the matter, if it's what the casting director has instructed you to do, then just do the best you can. Trust your instincts, go with what you feel as you read through the material.

Sometimes, a playwright will ask an actor to do a totally cold reading of his new play, although most playwrights agree that there is little value in hearing work read cold. If you've had a chance to read through the play in advance (anywhere from a few hours to a week or so), but have not rehearsed it, you might call this a "warm" reading, although to some, technically, it is still a cold reading. If you find yourself being asked to give a cold or warm reading, here are some things to keep in mind.

Don't lock yourself, head down, in the script. Try to look up. This is known as "scanning." To scan properly, you must try to relax yourself while reading, to stay loose. Your eyes scan from the text to the person that you're talking to, and then back to the text, and so on.

Don't be overly concerned about losing your place on the page. As you learn to scan the text, you'll notice that you can actually look up and communicate, then back down again, grab some lines, a phrase or two, and then look up again and communicate. The more you practice this, the more you'll notice you're able to retain. To keep from losing your place, keep your thump in the margin, and allow it to slide down as you read.

As you read the words, give yourself time to understand and identify with them. Try to make sense of what the character means, what she's trying to say. There is no way you can commit to a piece if you don't know what ideas are being conveyed.

When you look up at the person that you're talking to, try to communicate the meaning and emotions of the text. In all scenes, cold scenes included, relationship is what's important. Listen to what the other actor is saying; don't rush back down to the script for your next lines. However, it's not necessary to stay locked on the other actor when you don't have lines.

In both monologue and scene cold readings, try to take risks. If you feel an impulse to do something a bit outrageous, go for it. Don't try to be safe or subtle—it's boring. The more you trust yourself, allow yourself to be free with whatever you feel and think in the moment, the more fluid (and honest) the read will be.

I recently finished two books on these subjects. For monologues, *The Perfect Audition Monologue* (Smith and Kraus), and for cold readings, *Glenn Alterman's Secrets To Successful Cold Readings* (Smith and Kraus). If you'd like more information on either of these subjects, be sure to check out these books.

VIDEOTAPES AND DVDs: DO YOU HAVE A REEL?

Once you've met an agent or casting director, it's not unusual to hear them say, "Have you got a reel?" or "Do you have film on yourself?" What they're asking for is a DVD that has samples of past work you've done. This is another invaluable tool for an actor, and you should work your hardest to have a professional-looking reel. If you've had speaking parts on a soap opera, done some episodic television work, on-camera commercials, or worked in film, you must always get copies of your work. I know that sometimes this can be a pain; it's not always that easy to get a copy of from the producer. You must be persistent in your attempts, but always polite and professional. Generally, most producers or ad agencies will give you a copy of the work (in some cases, you may have to pay for it). And there are companies that, for a fee, will professionally record your show or commercial for you. Although you can record it yourself, most home video equipment doesn't always produce the best quality.

Once you've gathered the material, you have to edit it down to a six- to eight-minute reel. I advise getting professional opinions (casting directors, agents) of which material you should use.

Inside the Editing Studio: For the Actor Who Has Worked Professionally

You'll need to find a reputable studio that will help create your reel. The best way to find studios is by word of mouth; ask around. If you're impressed with someone's reel, ask where it was produced. These days most actors have a DVD of their work. Some actors, however, still use videotape. For the most part, I'll be referring to the reel as a DVD. The original DVD that you make up is called "the master reel." From this, you can make up as many copies as you want. Generally, editing a DVD will cost between $250 and $600.

DVD

Keep these things in mind when editing your DVD:

You should not be totally dependent on the studio engineer to create your reel for you. Come in prepared, do all your work at home beforehand. Know the order you want your material to appear in and time each segment you want on your reel *beforehand.*

All DVDs should start out (and end) with your name and contact information. After your initial name and contact information, it's smart to have a headshot of you on the reel. Keep the intros to each segment on your reel simple, not too fancy. If you have it, I suggest that you start out with a prime-time scene or a soap opera scene where the emphasis is primarily on you. It's preferable to have a scene where you are in a relationship situation.

The scenes that follow should show variety both in range and in locations. You want to make your reel as entertaining as possible. Unfortunately, in this business, many actors are typecast, and your work may have a certain sameness in terms of the characters you're portraying. Just do the best you can with what you have. Scenes that include close-ups of you are golden.

As for showing your commercials, there are two schools on this. Many casting directors feel that you should have a separate reel for commercial and dramatic material. I somewhat agree, unless you don't have enough quality material to make up your dramatic reel. If not, then just add your commercials at the end of the dramatic/comedic scenes.

For the Actor Who Doesn't Have Professional Material

If you haven't done much professional on-camera work, don't despair. There are a few things you can do to start a reel.

Perhaps you've worked in one of the many student films that are always shooting in New York. You may be able to find material there. Make sure that the quality of the film is good.

If you haven't worked in high-quality student films, there are production houses in New York that will tape scenes for you to put on your DVD. Again, quality here is very important. You don't want it to look like you taped it with your own video camera (which, of course, you'd never do). Select material that you are very comfortable with, that you've worked on before. This is neither a time to stretch nor to try out new material. I feel that the best choices for the DVD should be contemporary, rather than classical material, and scenes that don't require too much movement. The material should be within your age and emotional range. The emphasis in the scenes should be on you and your character, and there should be close-ups of you. Make sure that the quality of the studio's work is totally professional. If you've had someone videotape a live performance that you've done in a theater, be careful. Quite often, the quality is not good enough for a video reel; it comes out too grainy. Generally, the shots taken of a play don't emphasize the actor, but rather the production. Also, make certain that the sound quality is good.

Ben Bryant, a freelance video editor, says, "Remember, the purpose of the demo reel is to show as much range as you can in as short a time as possible. Casting directors can tell within fifteen or twenty seconds whether or not you have what they're looking for. Make sure, if you hire a videographer to shoot your live performance in a play, that he is adept with lighting or sound; neither of these things can be fixed in an editing studio. The videographer should use a wireless radio mike or an omnidirectional mike for scenes with several actors in them."

Johnathan Perry, at Video Portfolio Productions, says, "Actors waste a lot of time in the editing studio. They should do all their decision making at home before they get to the studio. Otherwise, it's going to cost them."

Perry also says, "In regard to actors who wish to shoot their monologues or scenes with a professional video photographer, don't try to do things that are too elaborate. Don't get caught up in props. Don't act as you would on the stage. Video acting, like film acting, should be honest, but much smaller than on the stage. Usually, I'll get in close with the camera. If you're too big, it won't look real. Don't do too much physical stuff. Don't wear bright red, it bleeds. An actor who has dark skin shouldn't wear bright white shirts. All the light goes to the shirt, which makes it very hard to get your face to expose properly. Striped or checked patterns don't come out well on video (they shimmer)."

Sending Out Your Reel

Check in *Back Stage* and ask around for the best duplicating studios in the city. Quite often, the studio that made up your master reel will have a duplicating package. But check around for the best buy for your buck.

As to where you should send your reel, start with the *Ross Reports* for the names of the casting directors and agents that might be interested in seeing your work. Never send out a DVD to anyone unless they say you can. Otherwise, there's a good chance it'll never be looked at. Make sure that every DVD you send out has a label with your name and contact info. Quite often, the DVD is separated from the box it came in. The box should also have your contact info and perhaps a picture of you on it.

Keep accurate records of all the people to whom you sent a DVD. Include a stamped, self-addressed box to get the reel back. A couple of weeks after you've sent it out, check back with the casting directors or agents and ask if they've had a chance to view it. You may have to follow up couple of times before they actually view it. Always be polite, cordial, and businesslike in your phone conversations with their office. In some cases, they may never watch it; you'll just have to accept that.

Try to keep your DVD as current as you can, updating it with new work as it comes along.

One way to let casting directors and agents know of your DVD is by mentioning "DVD available on request" on your résumé. You'd be surprised how many casting directors will request your DVD after seeing that.

DVD Duplications

After you've gathered your TV, film, and/or commercial material, you'll want to bring it to a professional to create the DVD and make copies. These companies can also help you in creating your voice-over CDs. Here are a few people who can help you with this next phase:

Chromavision
49 West 27th Street
New York, NY 10001
(212) 686-7366

Editors Hide Away
219 East 44th Street,
8th Floor
New York, NY 10017
(212) 661-3607

ESPY Duplication
611 Broadway,
Suite 708
New York, NY 10012
(212) 353-0362

MARKETING YOURSELF AS AN ACTOR

Marketing is a crucial part of this business and should not be passed over lightly, especially by aspiring actors. It is called, after all, show *business*. So get with the program. The people with whom you will be dealing on a daily basis—the talent agents, the casting directors—are all businesspeople. You must be able to communicate with them, hold your own, and play the game.

Lee K. Bohlen, a professional life coach who holds workshops for actors, stresses how important it is for actors to become aware of the business they are in. "Actors must think of themselves as a product. Once they do, they must then figure out the marketplace to which they want to sell their product (themselves). They must figure out the way that they can do this most effectively. One of the problems is that many actors think successful marketing is simply developing your craft. They take acting classes, dance classes, singing classes, etc., and feel that if they're well trained, they'll just be 'discovered.' That, quite often, is just a myth. They forget that this is a business, an industry. They leave out the part about being a businessperson."

Ms. Bohlen feels that actors can move along much further if they "specify where they really want to go in their careers." There are several marketplaces covered under the umbrella of show business. There are commercials, film, television, radio, and theater.

I can't begin to tell you how often I have consultations with actors who tell me that they "kind of want it all—TV, film, commercials, and theater." They believe that they can be all things to all people in the business. Underlying this notion, I believe, is a sort of desperation, a willingness to sell out, no matter what it costs, just to get ahead in the business. Why go to musical auditions if you know that you're really not a good singer and can barely dance? Why waste your time going to auditions for classical productions if you've never had any classical training and never done a classical production in your life? What I'm talking about here—what is crucial to an actor's career—is focus. Certainly, talent and luck cannot be overlooked, but you only have so much time in a day, in a life, in a career.

Make a Decision

What I suggest to my students is to make a list of what they really want careerwise. It might be movies or theater or commercials, whatever. Prioritize, choose. You came to New York with a dream of what you wanted, hoped for. Now, it's time to be specific about that dream.

For instance, your list might look like this:

1. Motion pictures
2. Television (episodic)
3. Daytime dramas (soap operas)
4. Commercials
5. Theater
6. Voice-overs

Once you've actually listed the order of priority, you now have a place to start. You can now investigate which talent agents and casting directors are strongest in those areas. For instance, when looking through the *Ross Reports*, you won't be pursuing talent agents whose strongest area is theater, since you've listed theater next to last on your list. You'll begin your search with agents strongest in film and television. Same thing for casting directors. Why spend all that time and money on mailings to voice-over production houses if that's at the bottom of your list? Efficiency of this sort will allow additional hours to take classes, work on monologues, and network.

Defining Your Type

The more specific you can be in the marketing of your product (yourself), the quicker the sale. According to Ms. Bohlen, "Actors tend to stay in the place where casting directors and agents identify them. They are categorized as young mom, young leading man, business exec, etc. We all have qualities that are beneath these surface labels. For example, think about Jack Nicholson. You can think of all the roles that he's played, but there's one thing that he brings to everything he does. That one thing is his 'real type.' In Nicholson's case, that real type can be described as 'dangerous and violent.' It's something you see in all his work. He brings these qualities to everything he plays."

When an actor can identify his real type (the type that he is even when standing still), then he can really begin his self-marketing campaign. Everything you do after you figure out your type should reflect that message about yourself that you want the world, specifically the world of show business, to know. From your headshots to specifically targeted mailings to the auditions you go to, everything should be part of your career game plan.

I'm very aware that, to some degree (especially at the beginning of a career, when "they" don't really know who you are), you will be typecast. It's a way of identifying groups of actors. I'm not saying that you should avoid that, just that you shouldn't work so hard always adjusting to their categories. Be creative; find the balance between the way that they need to categorize you and your need to specify who you really are.

Specifically in the fields of television commercials and print work, I realize that the categorizing of actor by type is very specific and distinct. Once again, I suggest that you adjust to their predetermined categories, book the job, and then find ways to express your individuality within the confines of what is appropriate. Think of great television commercials that you've seen. Yes, the actor in the commercial was specifically typed, but then, he found a way to shine. Every time you'll see that actor after that, you'll notice, in the more successful cases, that that actor had made a mini niche for himself in the industry. These actors become "identifiable."

Image Consultants

Finding your specific type and discovering which marketplace you'll be pursuing is just the starting point. You'll need to know how to dress appropriately and how to groom yourself in the most appropriate way. This is where an image consultant may come in useful. Generally, image consultants charge between $400 and $1,000. They will help you assess where you are and where you need to go, as far as the type that you're trying to project. They can help you discover which colors are flattering for you and which are not. Men, as well as women, can find some value in an image consultant. Today, many image consultants are much more than just stylists. They will work with you on things like your body language, posture, how you project on camera, even how you communicate with others.

The consultant will interview you and try to discover exactly which image you're trying to project about yourself. Think of the old Hollywood system. Image consultants worked for the studios full-time. Clark Gable, Bette Davis, Joan Crawford—when you think of these stars, there is a specific image that still comes to mind. That image was carefully created by image consultants who were hired to bring out something very specific in the stars' personalities. The way they wore their hair, their clothes, and their makeup was very calculated.

The image consultant will go through your wardrobe and see what you presently own that can be of use in selling your image. They'll make suggestions about different outfits, different "looks." They'll go shopping with you to find the clothing that is most suitable for the look you're trying to project.

Laurie Krauz, an image consultant, feels that she is like a teacher to her clients. "I give my clients information about their body types and how to translate that information into merchandise they can find in the marketplace. If you take Katharine Hepburn at one end of the continuum and Marilyn Monroe on the other end, you'll notice that one is very angular, and one is soft and curvy. What I try to do is help actors find where they are on this continuum. The world views you in a certain way, and because the world looks at you a certain way, you develop a certain personality. With actors, type is all physical, it's all body line. The actor playing Dracula is not someone short and delicately boned. Generally speaking, the more angular people are cast in the more dangerous kinds of roles. It's almost like we are all in agreement about what type is and the psychology of the impact of bone structure. It's important for actors to come up with the best type for themselves—a type that is totally them so that they can embody it with every inch of their skin."

Accentuate the Positive

Working with an image consultant can be of great value, but there are things you can do to improve your image on your own. If you're too heavy, go on a diet, go to the gym. If your teeth are crooked, have them fixed. There are many things that you can do to improve the way you look. Do everything you can that will not only project the type that you're trying to create, but to give yourself the inner confidence necessary for this business. I've seen careers take off after thirty years when the actor or actress, finally fed up with how he or she looks, takes charge and corrects an image that has gotten sloppy.

Your Business Office

Before you begin your mailings, I suggest that you create a well-organized office area where you'll be doing the business part of your work. In order to work efficiently, you'll need this office area to be well stocked. Aside from the sheer practicality of an office area, it gives you that business sense that, as I mentioned, is very necessary for actors to get used to. Your office space should include the following things:

- a desk and chair
- an appointment book
- a computer
- message pads
- stamps, stapler, stationery
- Scotch tape, Post-it notes
- a mail scale
- pictures and résumés
- a calendar
- reference sourcebooks.
- a place to keep accurate records of expenses, photos, résumés, taxis, phone calls, anything that pertains to the business
- anything else that you might need to run a successful business

Your Preliminary Game Plan

You should have a well-thought-out, meticulous marketing campaign. As you progress in your career, the marketing plan will inevitably change. You must be flexible as to how you'll proceed. There are many variables that affect a show business career: things like luck, auditions (good or bad), contacts that you'll meet in your daily career, etc.

Here are some basic things to keep in mind when planning a career strategy:

- At the beginning, keep your game plan simple.
- Make goals realistic and within your grasp.
- Have a set of short-term and long-term goals.
- Set out what you want to accomplish each day, each week, each month, and even each year for the next few years.
- Write out how you plan on accomplishing each of your goals. Be as specific as possible.
- Keep your goals realistic, but always just a bit beyond your each. This way, you'll never settle and be satisfied. You should always be a little hungry for the next goal.
- On a weekly and monthly basis, check to see how you did. Did you meet the goals that you set up for yourself? If you didn't, try to understand why not.
- Try not to blame others, the world, or luck for all your failings. Learn from what you didn't accomplish, and then move on to the next goal.
- Keep very up-to-date files on everything that goes on in your career.
- Keep notations about every audition you go to. Who did you meet there (casting director, directors)? How did you feel about what you did? If you didn't do well, ask yourself why not (and try to correct it at the next audition).
- Keep records of everyone to whom you send a photo and résumé. If you receive a response from any of them, be certain to mark it down.
- Keep a record of all follow-up phone calls that you make. Jot down the name of the to whom person you spoke. If it's a receptionist, jot down her name if possible (she may be a new agent there next month).

Targeted Mailings

Actors do mailings to get their photos and résumés to agents, casting directors, and in some cases, to directors and producers. These days, large mass mailings are cost prohibitive and mostly ineffective. You should do your research and find the select group of industry professionals that might be interested in your type and mail them your pictures and résumés. I'll be discussing networking facilities later on in the book. They are the most productive way to contact industry professionals. That being said, I'll now discuss what you'll need to know for small, targeted mailings.

Each picture and résumé you send out must have a cover letter attached. It's just rude (and foolish) to send a picture and résumé and not include a brief note introducing yourself. The body of the letter can be the same to all the people (depending on category, i.e., agents, casting directors, producers) that you send it to; just change the names and addresses. Obviously, this entire process is much simpler if you have access to a computer (especially for follow-up letters).

The cover letter should be professional, friendly (but not too!), and succinct. Make sure that there are no typos and that all names are spelled correctly. Always personally sign each letter. If someone has recommended that you contact an agent or casting director, this is pure gold; don't forget to mention it in the letter. This is a business of contacts and connections. Always ask around; actors you know can be your greatest ally in making contacts. Even better if they'll make a phone call to their agent recommending you.

Hal Hochhauser, the owner of Shakespeare Mailing Service, says, "The headshot shows what you look like, and the résumé lists related background and experience. Very important items, but on their own, they can create a somewhat impersonal appearance, considering the personal nature of our business and importance of this introduction. It's the cover letter that gives you a voice, a personality, and a chance to convey your thoughts."

Ingredients of a Good Cover Letter

- It should be direct and professional.
- It should be cordial and succinct.
- State what you want, why you're writing the letter.
- Inform the recipient of recent events in your career that are not listed on your résumé.
- Try not to get too personal; this is, after all, a business letter.
- Briefly let them know about what your future career plans are.
- If you've made some positive contacts with casting directors, let them know about it.
- If at all possible, you should use a printed letterhead in your correspondence; if you don't have printed stationery, be sure to include your contact information at the top of the cover letter.
- At the end of the letter, tell them that you'll contact them in the next week, and be sure that you do. By doing this, the ball will be in your court; you're not left sitting waiting for their call. You may say something like, "I look forward to meeting with you soon."
- Always end your letter with something like, "Sincerely" or "With warm regards."

Sample Cover Letter

Ann Actress
43 West 83rd Street
New York, New York 10024

January 7, 2011

Contact Name
Name of Agency or Office
Address
City, State, Zip Code

Dear Contact Name,

I am seeking new representation and would like to meet with you to discuss the possibility of working with you. I am presently freelancing commercially with several agents in New York.

There are two important issues I would like to mention that are not apparent on my résumé. First of all, I have been making my living as an actor for the last three years. In addition, in the short time that I've been in New York, I've been developing contacts. Many of the interviews and auditions I get are through personal sources. Ninety percent of the work that I book is through my own efforts. I don't say this to downplay the need for representation, but rather to express to you my personal motivation and aggressiveness. I firmly believe that, with your representation, I would be able to book many more jobs. There are simply too many audition opportunities passing me by.

On that note, and for your reference, I have attached a list of the casting directors/offices that are familiar with my work.

I will follow up with a phone call next week to arrange an appointment. If that is inconvenient, or if you would like to meet sooner, please don't hesitate to contact me. I look forward to speaking with you in person.

With warm regards,
Your name

One of the main sources you can use to do your mailings is the *Ross Reports Television and Radio*. If an agent or casting director says, "Don't mail pictures" or "Don't visit"—don't!

Place your photo and résumé, with cover letter attached, in a 9" × 12" manila envelope. There's no reason to include a cardboard stiffener. I suggest that you write "Do Not Bend" on the envelope.

Address the envelope to the agent or casting director, and don't forget to put your return address on it. Make sure that the cover letter corresponds to the recipient on the envelope. I can't tell you how often actors put the wrong letter in an envelope.

If you're presently appearing in a play or cabaret, be sure to enclose a flyer. Highlight your name on the flyer.

Go the post office and make sure that you have the correct postage. Self-adhesive stamps are smarter to use than licking them one by one.

Always keep very accurate records of who you've mailed to and when. Make sure that this information is always kept up to date.

Picture Postcards

About a month or so after you've done your mailing, you should follow it up with a picture postcard. If you've had *any* activity in your career (under-five on a soap, callback for a play, shot a commercial, etc.), be sure to mention it. Keep records of when you mailed out the postcards and continue mailing them monthly or if some advancement happens in your career. It's all about persistence! Actors get more work from their postcard mailings than from headshot mailings.

Hal Hochhauser says that postcards "cost less to mail than 8" × 10"s and are less expensive to reproduce. You save on envelopes and postage, and they're easier to prepare—no gluing, stapling, stuffing, or sealing. But most important is the way they're handled by agents and casting directors.

"Offices get so much mail, they cannot physically save and file pictures/ résumés that aren't used. Compared to postcards, 8" × 10"s are cumbersome. Postcards are small and can easily be stacked on a shelf or stored in a drawer. Some agents/casting directors keep categorized card files on their desks. When a specific type is sought, they just thumb through the cards, pulling out many that may be appropriate. Postcards stand a better chance of being saved than 8" × 10"s, thereby increasing your chance of being called at some future date from a picture you send today.

"Regular mailings, with messages that highlight your qualifications and experience, keep your face familiar and phone number handy, increasing the chance of being called when someone of your type is needed."

Ingredients of a Good Picture Postcard Mailing
- Make sure that the address is correct.
- Be sure of the spelling of the casting director's or agent's name.

- Be sure of the sex of the person. A name like Pat or Terry, for instance, could be either a man or a woman.
- Use "Ms." for women you don't know.
- Make sure that your handwriting is legible. Sometimes, it's better to do only a few postcards at a time. If you notice that your handwriting is getting sloppy, stop.
- Make sure it's brief. You don't need to cover every inch of the card with your information.
- Be businesslike, but cordial.
- Make sure to always say, "Best wishes," "Sincerely," or "All the best" at the end.

Sue Henderson's Labels, Publications, Consultations

According to Sue Henderson of Henderson Enterprises Inc. (*www.hendersonenterprises.com*), "actors need to do mailings to build credibility with people. Actors should do an initial mailing just to get themselves in the files of the powers that be, be it casting directors or agents. But it doesn't end there. You must constantly be doing follow-up mailings to maintain credibility, to let them know what you're doing. Mailings are something that you can do to connect with these people. It is one of the most important parts of an actor's marketing campaign. Actors can't just make rounds, walk in anymore.

"The best way to start any marketing campaign is to do a major mailing campaign. Before you can target any specific area, it's best to let everyone know about you. Many of the casting directors cover different areas—commercials, musical theater, legit, like that. At least once a year, I'd hit every casting director. There are about three hundred casting directors in New York who keep active files with actors. There are commercial agents, film and TV agents, theater agents, children's agents. You can target the specific type of agent you want.

"As for targeted mailings, be specific in your field. If you don't do musicals or television commercials, they are certainly a group you don't need to follow up with. Another thing: after your initial mailing, keep a file of anyone who has responded to you. You should do a targeted mailing every month. Actors pursuing work should be sending out at least one hundred postcards a month."

Please note: Several listings in this book (talent agents, personal managers, etc.) were compiled from The Sue Henderson Labels. For the most updated listings, please go to *www.hendersonenterprises.com*

Networking Facilities

In the last decade or so, the networking facility has become one of the most effective ways to meet casting directors and talent agents. Actors select the casting director or agent they wish to meet from a list, pay a small fee, and have a five-minute, prearranged audition with the casting director or agent where they will perform a monologue, read from sides, do commercial copy, or sing. Although it is stressed that there are no guarantees of employment, this is an effective way to make initial contacts.

Meeting an agent or casting director in person is certainly better than just a picture and résumé sent through the mail. The hope, of course, is this might be the start of an ongoing relationship. You still have to follow up with postcards and invitations to let them know which shows you're performing in and any career activity of note.

If you're just starting out in the business, with no training, this is not the best venue for you. You'll need to have some training. You don't want to meet the right people at the wrong time, i.e., before you're ready. Many of these casting directors and agents have great memories, so you don't want to blow a good opportunity before you're ready to be seen. Patience will serve you well here.

Interviews with Owners of Networking Facilities
Tony Nation, Actors Connection

As a professional actor, Tony Nation (TN) has thrilled audiences from Off-Broadway to numerous regional theaters across the country, to film and TV, concerts and recordings. In 2000, Tony had the opportunity to become a partner in Actors Connection. Currently, he is the president of Actors Connection in New York City and has been a partner in the business for ten years. In that period of time, he has had the opportunity to personally meet and get to know eighty to 90 percent of the agents and casting directors in New York City.

Paul J. Michael, (PM) owner of The Network

Paul J. Michael, Executive Director of The Network, has personally met with more than seven thousand actors in career consultation over the past three and a half years to help coach the business savvy of New York actors. He is a speaker on the business of acting for all Acting Success Now seminars on the East Coast and teaches his "Business of Acting" course at the Barrow Group's summer program. Paul has been a featured speaker at New School's MFA program, The Neighborhood Playhouse, HB Studios. and Steve Perlmutter's Acting Studio, as well as Actorfest and SAG and AFTRA panels.

Todd Etelson, (TE) president, Actors Technique, NY, Kids, Teens & Adults

I came to New York as an actor from a nice regional market called Washington D.C. I did stage, TV, film, and regional commercials, gaining my SAG Union Card in a regional market, and built a nice résumé over the course of a few years. I decided on New York over LA, and started cold, needing contacts and continued guidance. I've been on numerous daytime soaps, network TV series, film, national commercials and print. Actors Technique NY specializes in kids and Teens Acting and Casting Director Audition Technique On-Camera Classes, but we also have adult classes.

Marc Isaacman, owner of One on One

MI: After pursuing an acting career here in New York City, I took on an assistant position at an LA. talent agency. There, I learned

a) how difficult it is for an actor to get seen. One of my responsibilities was to throw away all of the headshots that came in the mail.

b) agents were totally spent at the end of a working day, and they would not want to travel to risk the chance of seeing theater that might cause them to slit their wrists.

What type of actor needs to work with a networking facility?

TN: Any professionally trained actor who is currently seeking talent representation and looking to meet and showcase to agents and personal managers. For the actor who is already represented, we provide an excellent arena to showcase to casting directors in all areas of the business.

PM: Actors wishing to build a presence in the New York entertainment industry can benefit greatly from using an experienced, knowledgeable, and top-notch networking company. Established personal relationships with leading industry professionals are essential when trying to be noticed in a sea of hardworking actors. The Network events offer invaluable opportunities to meet one-on-one or in small, focused groups with leading casting directors, agents, and managers.

TE: Most actors need to work with a networking facility. Youth or adult, if you're an actor, you need to be seen, period. You can't meet too many people in this industry, and this industry is always changing. All actors should consider taking casting director classes or workshops, or attending industry meet and greets at a credible networking or educational facility. We bring in New York's top agents, managers, and casting directors to either teach our youth and adult classes or watch talent through industry meet and greets. If signed, you still need casting directors to know you, as they can request an actor to audition. For those with no representation, there's no better way to show industry the goods than to be in front of them.

MI: An actor who has a good, solid foundation with training.

What services do you offer actors?

TN: Besides our networking seminars, audition technique classes, and special events, we also offer free seminars on a wide range of topics, including the business of show business, how to find talent representation, taxes for actors, health and fitness, financial advice, and more. We also offer thirty-minute complimentary program consultations for actors who are new to Actors Connection. Our program consultants are here to provide advice in matching the actor's career goals into the right seminars, classes, and special events. We also have two programs, LA. Connection and N.Y. Connection, which are designed to help actors decide if they want to make the big move to either city to pursue their acting career.

PM: The Network provides free, ongoing career guidance for actors trying to break into the ever-changing market of film, television, theater, commercial and voice-over work. An actor is his or her product. A clear, direct, and plotted business method for how to sell that product is essential. The Network also invites industry luminaries to join The Network for our seminars and classes. They bring with them the wisdom and depth of knowledge to demystify "the process," as well as allow the actor to deepen his or her personal relationship with industry professionals.

TE: We offer on camera, commercial, TV, film, scene, improvisation, musical theater, and other classes for young actors tp hone their skills. All actors have the choice of op coaching class for acting technique or casting director audition classes. We provide Industry meet and greet days, where we bring in a variety of agents and mangers to view your work. New York casting directors teach all our on camera audition technique kids and adult classes. We also provide abbreviated agent, manager, and casting director greets, where you can pass along a headshot and audition for industry professionals without sitting through a lengthy Q and A session. Our classes always have an agent day in the final class.

MI: We offer private appointments with agents, managers, and casting directors, one-day/night workshops, and multiple-week on-camera classes where actors have their on-camera work e-mailed to them for their convenience. Additionally, if an actor needs cinematic footage of herself so a casting director/agent/manager/filmmaker can get a taste of her work, we have an amazing service. We also offer auditions online, where an actor can have their audition beautifully shot in our professional studio, edited, and e-mailed to a casting director in LA. within minutes.

How does an actor go about deciding which agents' and casting directors' seminars are best for them? Do you offer guidance in making their selections?

TN: It's the responsibility of each actor to educate themselves on who they should meet, which agencies they are right for currently, and which casting directors they should be focusing on for their acting career. Talent agencies and casting offices provide totally different services; it's not one-stop shopping. Actors who aren't sure who they should be showcasing to can meet with our program consultants for guidance on which industry guests are right for them.

PM: Our highly experienced career counselors work directly with each of our clients through ongoing career consultations to help determine the best course of action for our actors. Our knowledgeable staff is always ready to assist with a bevy of information about our guests and their classes. Each client's profile is updated regularly with typing information and pinpointed areas of focused interest so that we may notify them directly when we've scheduled a guest who is looking for their type or skill set.

TE: We offer continued guidance to all our actors and help them make the best decisions relative to their goals and needs. If you are signed to an agent or manager, you should consult them as to whom they work with and which industry professionals are the right ones for you to meet. Fellow actors can help, but we work with agents and managers in New York all the time, so we would have a better idea which companies are worth your time and focus. If you're new, you'll want to hone your skill before you attempt gaining representation.

What kind of monologue material do you recommend actors prepare for their auditions? Any advice on how they can be best prepared for these meetings?

TN: Just as a singer has a book of audition songs, I recommend that each New York actor have at least five monologues ready to go at any time. Your monologues should be one or two minutes long, no longer. For our seminars and for all first meetings with an agent, the first monologue should be what I call a "calling card monologue." It should be contemporary material that is comedic or serio-comedic in nature, and shows who the actor is without any type of accent. Again, first you want to show them who you are, and then from there, you can show them more levels. Do not do a dramatic, screaming-crying-cursing monologue as your first monologue to an agent. I hear this feedback from agents all the time. They are in very busy, stressful jobs. Make them laugh, show your personality and charm. Also, unless the agent has requested it, do not do a classical or Shakespearean monologue as your first piece. The second monologue should be the dramatic monologue, which simply shows a different side of who you are. Again, just because it's dramatic doesn't mean it has to be a screaming-crying-cursing monologue—in fact, none of your monologues should be this type, in my opinion.

PM: When preparing for an introductory career consultation, the actor should prepare a contemporary monologue under two minutes in length. If a musical theater performer, a short 16-bar selection is requested in addition to the monologue. In regard to our classes, events, and seminars, each of our industry guests has specific requirements. In many cases, the guest will preselect sides based on actor submitted headshot and résumé which are then e-mailed to each actor individually. In other cases, prepared film/TV/theater sides or commercial copy are requested (The Network has an expansive library from which to select sides). When choosing copy or a monologue, choose something that speaks to you, a piece to which you can bring your individuality and uniqueness. Try to find underused or more obscure material to avoid using the same material as your competition.

TE: It takes time to find the right monologue that fits you. You should have several diverse monologues in your stable, ready to go. I'd consider having a serious, comedic, serio-comedy, contemporary, and classical monologue. I've seen actors pick monologues out of plays, monologue books, and attempt to write monologues themselves. Unless you're an established writer, I don't recommend actors writing their own monologues. The bottom line is that an actor should "own" her monologue and know it solidly. A monologue coach will help you take your monologue to the next level. It's in your best interests to find a coach or class that you feel comfortable with to help you hone your monologue skills.

MI: Do something that's close to your personality as possible.
We do offer guidance by offering individual consultations free of charge.

Any advice for the cold reading scene and commercial copy auditions?

TN: I think it's important for every actor to make sure they have specific training in both of these areas. The auditioning techniques that are proven for both cold reads and commercial auditions can vastly improve both an actor's callback and rate of bookings. We offer a wide variety of audition technique classes in both of these areas here at Actors Connection.

PM: Cold readings are a perfect opportunity for an actor to bring his or her individual personality to the forefront. When performing a cold read, scan the scene quickly, determine the focus of the scene and characters and then launch. Make bold choices, make strong decisions, and most importantly, be your original self. Everyone present is aware that this is a cold read, so step up to the plate and swing. This is a great chance to show what you innately bring to the table.

When auditioning with commercial copy, it is essential that you understand that casting directors are looking for you to fit a very specific type. Dress for the role that you are reading. Be that individual "to a T." You are there to do one thing: sell a product. The framework of that character must be evident not only in look, but in essence; voice and take on the material. Understand the product and understand who you need to be to sell that product.

TE: Here's where preparation counts. You will receive the copy once you get to the audition and have just a few minutes to feel comfortable with it. You need to know what to look for and be able to see the copy quickly. Cold reading is a skill. From an agent's point of view, they really want to see who you are, your inner qualities and emotions, what makes you unique and marketable. With that said, take chances with your audition choices and commit to them. Right or wrong, you've committed. Commercials are interesting. It's about looks and personality. It's getting to be less and less about talent, but with that said, the hard part is booking the job, so you need to be prepared. A lot of energy and creativity is important and good improvisational skills are a must.

MI: The more you practice this, the better you'll get. Of course, attending cold reading classes will only help exercise this muscle.

What are the most common mistake actors make at the seminars?

TN: Actors not being prepared to meet the caliber of guest they are meeting, or even not knowing who they are meeting in a seminar. You would also be surprised at the number of actors who don't bring in their picture and résumé to give to the guest for our seminars. From there, it's about how the actor is marketing and branding himself. If you don't know what you are selling, the industry won't know what to buy. It's all about doing one's homework, and then talent, training and timing.

PM: Actors who come unprepared, late, underdressed, or underrehearsed to any type of call or class should re-up with their commitment to their craft. Casting directors and agents are assuming that when you walk in the door, this is your best self. This is the impression you imprint on their minds for the longevity of your stay in the industry. First impressions are hard to rewrite. Additionally, nerves are your worst enemy and are easily combated. Always remember that these professionals *want* you to be good. This only makes their job easier.

TE: Industry professionals work with people they like. Don't try to become their best friends or be obnoxious. Be professional. That includes having an up-to-date headshot and résumé With the audition itself, actors tend to "act." It's the biggest complaint I've heard. Take your time and be real. Learn to live in each moment and not anticipate. Don't try to be something you're not or show them what you think they want to see. Lastly, memorize your monologue or audition material. Know it cold. Too many actors bring in material they've picked up a day or two before and really haven't honed it yet. It's your big chance to do well, and first impressions count. If you're bad, they won't remember you, but if you're great, they'll never forget you.

MI: Believing that all they need to do is show up. Success only happens when opportunity meets preparation.

If you had any advice to give an actor before coming to New York, what would be it?

TN: If you're going to move to New York City to pursue acting, I would highly recommend visiting for at least a week and attending auditions, seeing Broadway and Off-Broadway theater, and getting a feel for the Big Apple. It's important to explore and see if the fast-paced lifestyle here is a match. A trip like N.Y. Connection that my business provides is a great way to do much of this all in one week and not break the bank. I would also recommend saving enough money to not only make the big move, but also to live on while getting settled (to pay rent deposits, living expenses, etc.). If you do move, I would recommend getting a headshot done by a New York photographer. You want to make sure that your business tools look their very best, so make sure you've got a top-notch headshot and résumé It's also important to know that you're entering into a highly competitive market, so be prepared for the highs and lows of show business. It's all about persistence, and if you really want it and have the talent, you will have an acting career.

PM: Know the industry. Know its people, from producers to casting directors to managers and agents to actors. Know your type, your range, and your ability to fight hard to be seen and heard. Know that you have a headshot that accurately represents who you are and what's going on behind your set of unique eyes.

TE: Make sure you're ready. Be prepared. Stay in your own regional market to gain all the experience and knowledge you can before you come to the big city. From a practical point of view, come with some money in your pocket so you don't have to work your life away to pay for your New York apartment, leaving no time to do what you came here for. Have New York quality headshots with proper résumé format. Try your best to become Union in a regional market because it's harder to gain union status in a national market and can take years and years. Come with a sense of realism, knowing that this business is a process; expect to take many years to hone your craft. Learn to market yourself properly and have moderate expectations. Finally, have a foundation. Have some friends you can rely on to talk to.

MI: The decision to be an actor is a major commitment, which needs a lot of focus and dedication to achieve success. Don't take this step lightly. Where there is a will there is a way, but you need faith, commitment, and perseverance.

Interview with Bob Ost, Theater Resources Unlimited (TRU)

What is TRU?

BO: TRU is a service organization dedicated to helping people navigate the business of theater. We focus on the needs of producers and theater companies, but include among "producers" the forgotten masses of self-producing artists who go out there and create opportunities for themselves to be seen and heard. That includes a lot of actors—and it is especially important to remember that the entire concept of the "Equity Showcase" was originally to create a means for actors to "produce" themselves and be showcased, so they could be discovered by producers. Much has changed over the years.

One of our best-known programs is our TRU Voices Play and Musical Reading Series, which differs from most other readings series in that we encourage producers to submit works they want to try out; we also invite writers to submit, and if they pass into finals we actually hunt around for a producer for them. I have come to refer to TRU as "a dating service for producers, and we pay for the first date." The metaphor has become even truer these days because we have also initiated a Writer-Producer Speed Date that has become enormously popular.

How, when, and why did you create TRU?

BO: I created TRU back in the early 90s, along with three other writer friends of mine: Gary Hughes, Cheryl Davis, and Allison Brewster. Originally I thought that if I networked with producers and theater companies, I would get produced more as a writer. Ha! I learned how hard it is to produce.

I had this theory that perhaps one person had a piece of the puzzle that another was missing, and if I got people together, they might be able to complete the picture. So I invited three producers to my apartment to meet and talk about what they were doing. Thirty people showed up in my living room (good thing I have a large living room), and from that point on, I realized that there was a need for people who make theater to get together and feel like they were part of a community, that they weren't all going through this alone. From there I decided to offer informational speakers at my monthly networking meetings. And TRU grew and grew.

What resources does TRU offer actors?

    BO: Actors have always been welcome at TRU, originally because I knew that so many of them would find themselves producing one day. Then we got the notion that our company members might benefit from us arranging a weekend of open auditions, so they could all build their headshot files, or perhaps even cast specific shows. That's how the TRU audition event was born. Our spring reading series is cast from the audition event, and every actor who auditions goes into our headshot books, which we make available for our member companies to cast their shows. So suddenly we were a presence in the acting community, and more and more actors were joining as members. In order to serve that segment of my membership, we created special monthly programs for actors: an actor resource night and "Speed Date." We gather two or three casting people, plus coaches, photographers, and other resources we think might be of interest, and every actor gets three minutes to meet and talk one-on-one with each resource before we blow a whistle and they have to move to the next resource. We have also started a series of free monthly workshops for our actor members. Now we have added a monthly series of informal table readings to our programming, and everyone who brings a play to us is required to go through our casting books and at least consider using TRU actors.

Any advice that you have for actors coming to New York to pursue a career in New York?

    BO: Be prepared for some fierce competition. But also understand that every time you go into an audition, you are there to solve someone's casting problem. You may not be the solution every time, but come from a place of confidence, and value yourself and know what you have to offer. And please, although they call it "drama," you do not need to be dramatic. No divas allowed. Most of us feel that no matter how talented someone might be, we would generally rather work with nice people. I personally believe that it's not what we do that defines us as successful, but rather the quality of the relationships that we create when doing it.

Here are some books I recommend to learn more about the business aspect of acting:

Alterman, Glenn. *Promoting Your Acting Career: A Step-by-Step Guide To Opening The Right Doors.* New York: Allworth Press, 2004.

O'Neil, Brian. *Acting as a Business: Strategies for Success* Portsmouth, New Hampshire: Heinemann, 1999.

Henry, Mari Lyn and Lynne Roger. *How to Be a Working Actor.* New York: BackStage Books, 2000.

WHAT YOU NEED TO KNOW ABOUT THE INTERNET AND ONLINE CASTING SITES

I believe you'll find the insights of the following Web site designers, Doug Barron and Kristine Kulage, to be of immense help answering many of your questions about the Internet and Web sites.

Actors and the Internet

The Internet is here to stay. Use of the Internet as a tool is growing exponentially every minute, in all parts of our lives, whether we like it or not. Growth of the Internet as a casting tool has started from the bottom up. It is just plain easier and less expensive to put out a call for actors, view résumé photos, schedule auditions, etc., via e-mail and the Internet This is creeping more and more up the chain of the industry. Now agents trying to introduce new talent will refer the casting director to a performer's Web site, that is, if the agent feels the actor's Web site is a business tool, not a site for friends and family.

Talk to fellow actors to find out what sites they use, where they search and find good casting listings, good classes, video services, etc. The Internet changes faster than any previous business or device known to man. So talk to colleagues, and use search engines Google. Everyone must start somewhere, and the information and opportunities you will find on the Internet will help you to gain experience and find your way into this business.

Sites Helpful to the Actor

Below are just a few of the hundreds of sites that can be helpful to the budding actor, so check them out.

Internet Movie Database: *www.imdb.com*
Actors Access: *www.actorsaccess.com*
Breakdown Services: *www.breakdownservices.com*
Playbill Online: *www.playbill.com*
Showfax: *www.showfax.com*

Mandy.com: *www.mandy.com/1/cast.cfm?jt=usa*
Craigslist: *http://newyork.craigslist.org/tlg*
Casting Networks: *www.nycasting.com*
Casting New York: *www.castingnewyork.com*
NY Castings.com *www.nycastings.com*
Actors First NY: *www.actorsfirstny.com* (sign up for free e-mail casting notices)
Backstage.com: *www.backstage.com*
Variety.com: *www.variety.com*
The Village Voice: *www.villagevoice.com*
The Drama Book Shop: *www.dramabookshop.com*
Actors' Equity Association (AEA): *www.actorsequity.org*
American Federation of Television and Radio Artists (AFTRA): *www.aftra.com*
Screen Actors Guild (SAG): *www.sag.com*
Playbill: *www.playbill.com*
Playbill Online's Theatre Central: *www.playbill.com/cgi-bin/plb/central?cmd=start*
The American Theatre Wing's Tony Awards: *www.tonys.org*
The Academy of Motion Pictures Arts & Sciences: *www.oscars.org*
Academy of Television Arts and Sciences: *www.emmys.tv*

INTERNET: The Actor and the Internet
Doug Barron, owner of Plaza Desktop Publishing

Do I need to be online?
Yes. It is that simple. Casting calls, especially those seeking younger, less experienced performers, are opportunities to gain experience and build your résumé; these are all online. Print versions are too slow for the current speed of life. Yes, the "big" jobs, Broadway, Hollywood, etc., do still work in the more traditional fashion, through casting directors and agents. But you have to start somewhere. Obviously, when you peruse the casting calls online, you must use a bit of common sense as to what to apply for. There are many more repetitive listings online than there ever were in the print listings. Many online listings do not charge for casting listing, so anyone will put anything up. Craigslist is good in that there is a lot of material there, but there is also a lot more sleaze. Common sense should be your guide. If it sounds too good to be true, it probably is.

Is it necessary to use sites that have paid memberships for casting?
I recommend you listen to the buzz and check with colleagues. Sites are always appearing and vanishing. Only pay for the most reputable sites, one that have been around for some time. The advantages of many paid sites are that they tend to be more organized attract more professional listings and better opportunities. In addition, many of the paid sites contain a good database of performers

signed up for their services. Occasionally, casting directors, directors, etc., will search these databases for performers who meet their requirements or needs.

Do I need to pay for more than one membership site?
Generally, no. Just pick the one that is the best for you. Many of the sites out there are listing the same casting calls. Why pay for more than is necessary? Again, check with colleagues. Everything about the Internet is always changing.

WEB SITE
Do I really need a Web site for myself?
If you are coming to New York having already starred in a major Hollywood film, or a network or cable television show, with a hotshot agent, to do a Broadway show, then perhaps not. Then again, you may then need it to reach out to your fan base. This is perhaps your least expensive tool, and it can be updated easily. You can have pictures, a résumé, video, voice demos and more readily available. Anything someone may need to get a handle on your talents.

What about sites such as Facebook or MySpace? Can I use them instead as they're free?
Facebook and MySpace were developed and designed to be places to stay in touch and contact with friends and family. They are not nor are they meant to be a professional way to access the elements your Web site should contain. They can be an additional tool, but not a replacement. How serious are you about your career?

Is it really necessary for an actor to hire a professional web designer?
No. That is, if you know how to do a Web site and have good taste. You only have one shot at making a first impression. Make sure your Web site makes the impression you want and need. That does not mean the site has to be complicated. On the contrary, it should be easy to find what the viewer is looking for and convey a bit of your style and personality. There are many technical things to know in order to build a successful site, and graphic design talent is needed to accomplish this goal. When you do a play, do you consider a set designer necessary? A lighting designer? A director? In a way, your Web site is much the same. Except you are the play or the product.

What needs to be on my Web site?
Here is the hard part. If you are new and just starting out, you may not actually have much to actually put on the site. But you do have the minimum. At minimum, a site should contain:
- A menu. A clear and easy to find menu, so a casting person with twenty more sites to check out can get what they want and get out. If they want more, they will look for it. But make it easy for them. Help them help you.

- Contact information. Agent(s) and manager if you have them. A contact for yourself. I recommend, especially for women, using an e-mail contact separate from your personal e-mail address.
- Headshot(s) and the ability to easily download them or to save to the viewer's computer.
- Résumé. It must be easy to read, easy to print, and easy to update. Currently, I recommend printing your résumé to an Acrobat PDF file and putting this online. It may look somewhat different than the other web pages, but you can make a change to your résumé print to PDF, and update online in less than a minute; it will look exactly like what you hand them in person at an audition. It is important to keep it current, down to one page, and printable. In addition, your résumé should contain your e-mail and Web site addresses. Even better, make them links. That way, if someone has a digital version of your résumé and returns to it at a later time, they can click on your résumé and see your site or e-mail you. If you use a PDF résumé, name it with your name. Can you imagine a casting assistant downloading thirty-five résumés all named résumé.pdf? Call it "MyName.pdf."
- Good meta data. Hidden in your Web site are keywords and a description to help search engines like Google find what the viewer is searching for. You want casting directors, directors, producers, etc. to find you. Most important, of course, is your name, then people or theaters you have worked with, etc.
- A reel. For film and television this is really a must. You can actually have more extended video on your Web site than you might have on your DVD reel. Plus, in most cases, it is easier and quicker to update video on your Web site than your DVD reel. When editing and putting together your DVD reel, have the video file(s) saved as a video file, such as QuickTime.
- Photographs from productions you have done. Good ones, not every one. The other ones can go on your Facebook page.
- Voice-over demos, book narration, etc.
- A short bio. A good idea on the home page or elsewhere. Does not have to be a complete relisting of your entire résumé. Show some personality.
- A current news or projects section. I tend to think this is a good idea—that is, if you keep it updated. Otherwise, it only highlights the fact that you haven't worked since your last listing.
- Pull quotes from reviews. The quality of the review will help you determine how prominently to feature it on your site. You can have a pull-out version of the review on the home page, and then a longer version on a press or reviews page.

The Web site should convey who you are as a performer, your range. This will evolve as you evolve. It should look inviting. The Web site should not be the star; you are the star. You should be the most interesting part of your Web site. If you are fortunate enough to have a good range of photos from professional-looking productions that show a range, you are halfway there.

You do not have to feature your headshot. Everyone in the business has seen a million of them. Don't get me wrong, your headshot is maybe your most important tool, and should be extremely easy to view, print, and download. But a Web site affords you more opportunities for range. If your headshot is the best photograph you have, then feature it.

How does a Web site benefit an actor?

So much of the industry on the ground floor is based on the Internet, because it is easier, cheaper, and quicker. Off-Off-Broadway, independent films, student films—all of these now operate via the Internet or e-mail. I myself actually got a film from a director viewing my video selections on my Web site without ever auditioning. An actor's Web site is like a beginning agent, or if it's a good site, a valuable tool for your agent. In the past, if you were working out of town and an audition came up, you missed it. But now with the Internet you can video your audition yourself and put that online. It will decrease your chances, but it is better than nothing, and may actually get you the job. In addition, your Web site can begin to help you build and contact any fans. If you happen to become a "known" performer, this can be an invaluable tool. It can contain blogs, fan materials, links, etc. If done thoughtfully and with care, a Web site can only help you.

Kristine Kulage, Web Site Designer

Why does an actor need a Web site?

More and more, casting is being done online, and those actors who can forward a casting director to an official Web site containing a résumé, photos, and possibly video clips have a great advantage over those actors who do not have this Internet resource at their disposal. An official Web site is an incredibly important asset for an actor professionally, as well as a way of gaining more public attention.

Is it really necessary for an actor to hire a professional webmaster?

Web sites must be both functional and visually compelling, serving as an extension of the actor's body of work. A site for an artist, in this case an actor, absolutely needs to be a work of art in itself, from personalized seamless background patterns to eye-catching logos. A good Web site designer tailors graphics to an actor's personality, connecting them to a theme or recurring image. A good Web site designer simultaneously acts in the role of promoter or agent. They promote the actor's visibility through Internet advertising—an electronic version of word of mouth. On a technical level, this means submitting links to pertinent Web sites and Internet search engines. But on a personal level, this means conducting interviews and compiling or writing reviews to post on the site, and even building Internet fan bases to help make the actor more marketable to potential employers.

How does a Web site benefit an actor's career?

The benefits of a Web site to an actor are innumerable. Because the Internet has become a major force in communication, advertising, and business, a presence on the Internet is no longer a luxury, but a must-have for actors. Some benefits of a Web site are

- an easily accessible online résumé

an official Web site serves as an online résumé that is easily accessible from any computer anywhere in the world. There, prospective hiring directors and agents can view an actor's résumé, headshots, and career highlights, as well as a bit of their personality represented on the site. An actor's chances of being cast for the part are increased, even if they are unable to make it to a certain city for the audition, thanks to the online résumé, headshots, and even audio or video clips.

- A Web site serves as a second "agent" for actors

This visible Internet presence makes the actor a more recognizable and marketable commodity, and thus more likely to be hired for a role. This Web site "agent" promotes an actor twenty-four hours a day, seven days a week, around the world. This increased visibility helps to sell the actor to potential hiring "buyers" and can literally sell the actor's various contributions (books, DVDs, shows) to the industry.

- membership in the Web world

The Internet is filled with theater- and entertainment-based Web sites, which are industry resources for actors and hiring agencies. When an actor has an official Web site, he is immediately part of that world. Many of the sites, such as BackStage.com and Playbill.com, offer databases of performers. In addition, an actor's site should be registered with all of the major Internet search engines, so that by typing in "Actor's Name" in an Internet search, their official Web site will be one of the first to appear. Again, this helps increase overall exposure and visibility for the performer and with both large and small casting companies that also have Web sites.

- a readily accessible source of information for fans and potential employers

When someone in the audience sees an actor on stage that they have never seen or heard of before, and they are amazed at their talent, the first thing they want to do is go home and learn more about them. And the first place they go to is the Internet. They will probably type in a search for "www.actorsname.com" to see if the actor has an official Web site. Usually, they are interested in other shows the actor has performed in, if they have any recordings, and if they possibly did see them in another show, but may not have known it. All of these can be found on the actor's official Web site.

How involved with the site does the actor want to be?
The answer to this question usually dictates the general direction the site is headed. An actor can be involved as much or as little as he or she wants with a Web site. It can be very informal—an online résumé for prospective jobs—or it can be very personal, offering visitors an opportunity to e-mail the actor directly through the Web site.

What aspects should be covered in the Web site?
I usually recommend a typical actor Web site to at least have
- a main or introduction page that lists a table of contents for the site;
- a résumé or biography page and various pages focusing on major roles they have had;
- a "welcome" letter to visitors;
- a guest book for visitors to sign;
- a "critics" page listing reviews they have garnered for past roles;
- a "photo gallery" featuring headshots and photos of them in various roles;
- some sites may also include audio clips from recordings and video clips from performances;
- a "questions and answers" page;
- a page of links to other pertinent Web sites;
- pages covering other aspects of their careers, such as directing, coaching, modeling, etc.

What raw materials does the actor have to work with?
Résumés, bios, headshots both old and new, photos from shows, DVDs featuring the actor for audio clips, review clippings—the more material from the actor's career there is to work with, the more complete the Web site will be.

Online Casting Service Interviews

Thom Goff, Breakdown Services (Actors Access) (TG)

Breakdown Services, Ltd., is the parent company of Actors Access, which was started in Los Angeles in 1971 by Gary Marsh. Breakdown Services was the first company to provide standard character breakdowns for film and television and theater projects to franchised agents and established managers. The New York office was opened in the late 1970s, and Breakdown Services now has a regional office in Chicago and a Canadian office in Vancouver. We are affiliated with Spotlight in London, England; Showcast in Australia; and Converse-Smith in Toronto, Canada. As technology has advanced, Breakdown Services continues to provides online content through Actors Access, Casting About, and Virtual Channel Network. Our goal is to provide actors and their representatives the information they need in order to work and create.

Alexandra Parker (with Beau Bonneau) Casting Networks (AP)

Casting Networks is an online casting service for casting directors, agents, industry professionals, and talent. Created by casting director Beau Bonneau in 2001, we were the first to revolutionize online casting. We offer software solutions for all players in the casting world that are efficient and innovative, encompassing the entire casting process from the talent search to the booking. Since 2001, we've had 95 percent of commercial casting directors using our software to book their jobs.

What do actors need to know before signing up for your service?

TG: Actors Access is a free service. You can place two pictures, a résumé, and profile information online; use the e-mail feature and create a custom URL that goes directly to your information without ever being charged a cent. Your Actors Access account is connected to your representative accounts, so the items above are updated for your representatives once you update your Actors Access account. Video and additional photos may be added for a one-time charge, and they will also connect to your representative accounts. Submitting electronically on released breakdowns is also a charged service. We will never ask for any billing information unless you are adding a pay service.

AP: If you already have an agent then you are probably already online! Casting Networks is the most widely used Web site by agents. If your agent uses Casting Networks, you can sign up for free. If you are not represented, go to *www.nycasting.com* to sign up.

Specifically, what services do you offer actors?

TG: Marketing: we offer actors the ability to create an online marketing area that benefits an actor as well as their representatives. For small additional one-time fees, they can add video and additional photos to their free account that can be attached to their representative account for use during the submission process. This allows actors to create one area that contains all the tools they need in order to be competitive in today's marketplace. Submissions: actors can submit themselves on any breakdowns that are released directly to them by casting directors. This can be done online or through our mobile app. Video submissions: our Eco-Cast service allows actors to receive a request from casting directors for a pre-read or video audition that can then be uploaded directly to the casting director. Sides: our Showfax service allows you to sign on and download sides for your audition without leaving your home or office. Information: through our Casting About service, actors can discover which projects are currently casting and find out how to submit to them directly if there isn't a current breakdown released.

AP: Create a multimedia résumé, build a Web site, host your demo reel, upload your headshots, and submit to projects. Instantly send your pictures, video, audio, and résumé to anyone from anywhere. Be seen! More roles are cast through Casting Networks than any other online site. With Direct Cast™, you can submit yourself to projects posted by professional casting directors and independent filmmakers. With Talent Scout™, you can be scouted by top agents; and with Multi-Media Résumé™, you can add your video and/or audio reel to your résumé

Can your services be of value to actors of all levels of experience?

TG: It is always good for actors of every level to have an area that holds all of the marketing tools they need to advance their career. Actors Access allows this to happen by also connecting to the information your representatives are using to promote you. Actors Access gives you control in what is being used to market you online. Showfax allows any actor to get their sides, and Casting About allows you to gather information about current projects. This information is valuable for every actor.

AP: The acting business is a very tough one to break into. Direct Cast™ allows talent to find and submit to thousands of film, television, and commercial roles online. We make getting in the door that much easier. Casting Networks also has the Talent Scout™ program to make it even more rewarding to be a member. Agents can search for exactly what they want and contact our Talent Scout™ members directly and schedule an interview. Also, any talent who is auditioned by casting directors using our service will have their résumé and photos available to the producers and ad agencies who are viewing the auditions online. The process goes full circle using our software!

Are there any misconceptions about online casting services that you feel need to be clarified?

TG: While many online services have breakdown listings, not all of them connect with casting directors. The listings on Actors Access are specifically there because a casting director told Breakdown Services to release the information to actors. When you submit through Actors Access you know someone is looking at the submissions on the casting side.

AP: The main misconception about online casting services is that they are not saving the actor money. On the contrary, before there were services like Casting Networks, talent had to spend hundreds of dollars a year on printing headshots, sending out mailings, etc. Now the fees they pay go towards making their online profile a one-stop look for casting directors and agents. Also, they now have more access than ever to jobs that they can submit to as well as a multimedia enabled résumé that includes customizable submissions for photos and video.

What can an actor using your services expect from membership?

TG: Actors Access is free. You can expect to put up two photos, a résumé, and profile information; e-mail out your information; and create a custom URL for free. You can look at current breakdowns for free. A yearly membership with Showfax will allow you submit electronically on breakdowns and download sides for your audition.

AP: We work hard to provide the talent and their agents with the tools necessary to get their most relevant image in front of casting directors. Committed to helping to create professional-looking profiles with photos, sound, and video, we are also attentive to the needs of the casting director so that they can make the best casting choices. The actor can expect that when a casting director is viewing their résumé, the photos and video are high quality, giving them the opportunity to put their best foot forward every time!

PART III

Your Business Collaborators and Advocates

NETWORKING: THE BASIC CONCEPTS

Many actors don't fully realize the importance of networking in an acting career. They may think it's "what those actors do at parties in Hollywood." They believe that networking is just "shmoozing." As in many other businesses, networking can play an instrumental and vital part in the success of an actor's career.

The word "network" is defined as "a group you know or can get to know for the purpose of sharing information." It is basically a social activity. In a business where the more people you know, the better your opportunities can be, networking plays a major role. The actor who is totally reliant on the trade papers or an agent for auditions, whether he is aware of it or not, is more than likely missing out on many potential opportunities.

The point of networking is to develop relationships with people or groups of people with whom information can be exchanged that may lead to further employment. Generally, the most effective contacts are made in person, but in a city like New York, a great deal is done on the phone, by e-mail, and through the mails. By meeting people, exchanging phone numbers, e-mail addresses, and home addresses, a new contact can quickly be created that can last for an entire career. The more contacts you have, the bigger your network.

Business cards, particularly photo business cards for actors, have become an important networking tool. You can hand them to anyone you meet during your day. That casting director or agent that you meet at the theater who wants to know how to contact you—just hand him your card with your contact information. You can have these cards made when you have your headshots done.

I receive e-mail invitations every day from actors, directors, and playwrights about projects that they are involved in. It's the quickest, most inexpensive way to let people know about upcoming work.

Many actors mistakenly feel that networking is just "using" people. That's an incorrect idea. If done correctly, it is a very fair sharing of information about all aspects of the business, but most importantly, about potential job opportunities. If an actor merely collects information from others and doesn't return information to those who have given it, then indeed, that is acting selfishly and is not, in the truest sense of the word, networking. Networking is "sharing," not just taking. If you know of an audition that actor A might be right for, and that actor is someone you've been in touch with on a regular basis, it is your obligation to notify him immediately and let him know about it.

Who and Where to Network

Actors mistakenly think that they can only find out about casting information from other actors; not true. The hairdresser on the commercial you just worked on may know of a shoot coming up where they're looking for actors in your age range and type. That stylist on the set may know of a commercial shoot coming up next week that will need fifty union extras. These crew members may even know who's casting it. In addition to other actors in your acting class (and at auditions, at the theater, on a movie set, at theater-based parties, and in actor support groups), producers, directors, playwrights, makeup people, stage managers, receptionists in talents agents' offices and casting directors' offices may all be information resources. The list goes on and on.

The Rules of the Game: How to Network Effectively

First of all, you must know what you want. Your career goals should be precise and clear. We've discussed goal-setting previously. Review that information. The clearer you are about where you want to go in your career, the more effective the communication will be with the people in your network.

Commit yourself to this for the long term. So often, you come across actors who are burning with passion to succeed in the business, but after a few rejections or bad auditions, they give up, even become bitter, negative. You want to develop a passion for acting that continually flows like water, not a passion like fire that burns out quickly. To network effectively, relationships have to be developed over a period of time. You must put some energy into maintaining these relationships. Communication must be ongoing and consistent.

Be supportive of those with whom you network. Everyone needs a hand now and then; everyone screws up an audition. It's important that you be there for the people in your network. When you're down and out, when you're having a bad stretch, you might need their support.

Share the wealth. You must be willing to share information with others. You can't be a secretive person, withholding valuable information from others, and network effectively. When you are networking, it's important that you maintain a positive energy. Sure, it's easy to moan and groan about how unfair this business can be, but people don't like to network with complainers. Try to get yourself in the right frame of mind before you pick up that phone.

The way that you communicate is very important. Be a good listener and observer. Many actors are too self-absorbed and don't always hear what others are saying to them. Respond appropriately when someone is talking to you. Give the person you're listening to appropriate feedback. A nod, a smile, a question responding to what they've just said. Make sure that the communication is open.

Always make sure that the information that you share is correct. Giving out misinformation is a waste of everyone's time and energy and can cost you. All information must answer these basic questions:

- What?
- When?
- Who?
- Where?

Be willing to share your successes. I know that sometimes in this business, there is a fear about sharing your triumphs with others. But you should realize that your shared triumphs can be a source of hope for your network. Naturally, you must be sensitive to how you share your success. If you are with someone who is suffering about their career, you don't want to boast. Try to use your good news as a source of encouragement for the person. Let her know that if it can happen to you, it can happen to her. So very much of this business is based on luck, being in the right time at the right place. We all need to be reminded that that next phone call can be the one you've been waiting for.

You must be dependable. It's very important, when you network, that you always keep your word. If you've offered to call your agent on another actor's behalf, you must be certain to do it. If you tell someone that you'll call them next week, make sure you do. How reliable you are is an important factor in successful networking.

Networking Socially

Some of the main places where you'll be able to make and develop contacts are social gatherings. But you must be well prepared and organized.

Know as much as you can about the event that you are going to; for instance, what is the purpose of the event? Who will be there? When it comes to knowing who will be there, it's not appropriate to ask your host that question straight out; actually, that's rude. If you can find out if this social gathering will include people that you might want to network with, fine. If not, just go, and enjoy yourself anyway.

Before you leave for the event, be certain that you have a pen and a good supply of your photo business cards.

When you arrive at the event, it's always good to take a moment when entering the space to stand in the doorway and see who's there. See if there is anyone you know or want to know. It's also a good time to get yourself together, to be certain that you are composed. Even though it's a social event, you are there to make contacts.

One thing that I feel I need to mention: be very careful about any overindulgence of any kind. Always have your wits about you.

Size up the situation. See what's going on in the room. Is it bustling with energy or very quiet? Are people moving around, mingling, or standing alone or in small groups? You can make these assessments very quickly and act appropriately once you've entered the room. By and large, power groups, those in power, for some reason generally hang out in the corners of the room. You'd think that those in power would want to be the center of attention. But generally speaking, this is not the case.

After you've sized up the situation, it's now time to move into the room. Circulate! Decide which people you want to make contact with, and then take the bull by the horns; go to them. If you don't know anyone, there are two areas you can go to: the bar area or the food area. Generally, there will be someone else at those places with whom you can start a light conversation. Making contact, especially if it's someone that you don't know, can sometimes be a bit uncomfortable. It's just something that you have to do, so get used to it. The more you do it, the less painful it'll be. Three basic things you'll need to do: First, make eye contact. Second, smile. Third, introduce yourself. And a fourth, if it feels appropriate: shake the hand of the person that you just met. Watch for his or her response. Try not to be too aggressive, too pushy. That can be a real turnoff. That first impression that you make can be very important. Also, you may notice some people prefer not to shake hands. I've noticed a lot of germaphobes in the last few years who prefer not to shake anyone's hands. Don't be thrown if someone refuses to shake your hand. Just move on with the conversation and make nothing of it.

The question asked so often is, "What do I talk about?" Talk about the event itself, the room, the food, the person whose party it might be, etc. If the person that you're talking to is a casting director for whom you've auditioned, it's all right to remind her that you've met previously in a business situation. Don't get into complaining that you never heard from her since then, or anything like that. If it's someone whose work you're familiar with (actors, directors), that you've enjoyed, feel free to be complimentary.

Try to keep all conversations light. Ask questions that are not too personal. Listen to what other people have to say. Be aware of how others are responding to you. If you notice that they seem uncomfortable, gracefully tell them that it was great meeting them and that you're going to circulate.

At any social event, you don't want to spend all your time with just one or two people. It's important that you meet different people, make several contacts. And always, if it feels appropriate, give people your card. If it's someone that you'd like to maintain contact with, make certain that he gets it before you say goodbye. Hopefully, he'll give you his card, too. If he doesn't—and this is a delicate area—you can ask for his card. If he seems at all reluctant about giving it to you, make nothing of it, just graciously move on.

We all meet people at social events with whom, for whatever reason, we'd prefer not to spend much time. You must always act in a gracious, polite, and businesslike manner. If you've been approached and decide that you'd rather not spend any more time with the person, give him a minute or two and excuse yourself with something like, "It was great meeting you, hope to see you again," or "There's so many people I promised to say hello to here." Smile, excuse yourself, and quickly find someone you'd like to talk to. If the person you're parting with wants to give you their card, be gracious and accept it.

When it comes to meeting casting directors, talent agents, directors, and the like, you want to be cordial, businesslike, and succinct. If it's someone you've wanted to meet, don't shy away. Introduce yourself, and see if she is open to a small chat with you. If you feel that she's not, just say, "It was great meeting you," and move on. If she is, stay awhile, keep the conversation light. Do not, and I repeat, *do not* recite your résumé. If she asks you about your career, it's okay to mention some highlights or a project that you've recently been involved with, but remember, keep it positive and short. If it's a casting director, and you've just seen a film that she's cast and you enjoyed the film, feel free to compliment her work. This is not the time to do extensive self-promotion or to talk negatively about anyone or anything. Be sensitive and aware of how she is responding to you.

Do not outstay your welcome. One thing you don't want to feel is that you are monopolizing someone's time. There are probably other people that you should be meeting anyway.

Maintaining Contacts

If the contact that you made at the party was another actor or a director, be sure that you keep in touch. If you've exchanged cards and have the person's contact information, give him a call or send him an e-mail. Remind him of who you are, where you met, and let him know that you enjoyed meeting. This is the point where, hopefully, you'll seriously begin the networking relationship. See if he's interested in meeting for coffee, lunch, or joining you to go to the movies or the theater. Make it clear to the person that you are just being friendly, would like to keep in touch, and that you're not "hitting on him." If he starts to offer a lot of excuses or seems reluctant about any future meetings, be gracious and tell him that when his schedule opens up, please give you a call.

Another way to maintain contact with people that you meet socially is to support their work. If you find out that they are appearing in a play or directing one, try to stop by and see it. Let them know that you were there. Try to be complimentary about their work.

As far as casting directors or agents that you may have met socially, the rules are different. It is not appropriate, unless they specifically requested it, that you contact them at their office. A picture and résumé, along with a note reminding them of your meeting, is the best thing to do. Of course, in your note, be certain to remind them where you met and how much you enjoyed meeting them. Make the note friendly, but businesslike and short. These contacts should become part of your database, and you should let them know of anything significant that occurs in your career.

For the most part, how you maintain your networking contacts is up to you. The most important thing is that you keep the relationships ongoing. The easiest way to do that is by sending them e-mails with any pertinent information. Try to contact them with blind copies rather than large group mailings; it seems more personal. As far as sending those cutesy poetry, positive story e-mails, I personally hate them and find them a waste of time and energy. I know, however, that many people love to send (and receive) them. Let that be your call.

And finally, one last way to maintain your contacts is by throwing parties and inviting contacts to your soirées. Social gatherings—be it a lunch, a dinner party, whatever—are a great way to maintain networking contacts. If you invite people out socially, then perhaps they will be reciprocal.

THE UNIONS

There are three unions that actors may belong to: Actors' Equity Association (AEA), the American Federation of Television and Radio Artists (AFTRA), and the Screen Actors Guild (SAG). Each of these unions covers different media in which performers work (AFTRA's and SAG's jurisdictions are obvious from their titles; Equity covers stage performance), and basically, the unions are there to protect the actor.

Equity offers its members guaranteed minimum salaries, pension and health benefits, and guaranteed safe and sanitary working conditions.

By being a member of these unions, actors have some protection against being exploited unfairly by producers. Through collective bargaining with producers, the unions provide standard contracts and safety rules for the workplace. Each union has a pension fund for the actors' retirement.

There are many nonunion opportunities where actors can receive "on-the-job training" prior to joining the union. Some actors prefer to remain nonunion because of the additional job opportunities offered to them around the country, and also perhaps because of a personal mistrust of unions in general. Of the three show business unions, only the Screen Actors Guild requires that an advertising agency or a producer must get permission before hiring a nonunion actor.

Actors' Equity

Actors' Equity is the oldest of the three major actors' unions. It was founded in 1913. Equity is a national organization that is governed and supported by its own membership (presently, more than forty thousand members). Democratically elected members serve on Regional Boards, Council, and many different committees.

Actors' Equity is located at 146 West 46th Street, New York, NY 10036. The membership office is located on the fourteenth floor, and the telephone number is (212) 869-8530.

Eligibility

There are three eligibility requirements that must be met before you can become a member.

Equity Standard Contract

If you're lucky enough to be offered an Equity standard contract, you can join the union right after you've signed it. Standard contracts include all Production, LORT, dinner theater, and stock contracts. Equity contracts such as TYA (Theater for Young Audiences), SPT (Small Professional Theater), LOA (Letter of Agreement), and the MINI contract include tiers that have wage-earning minimums and length-of-employment requirements that can also get you into Equity. For more information about Equity standard contract eligibility, check with the business representatives at Actors' Equity.

The Membership Candidate Program

This program allows nonunion actors to get credit from their work towards membership into Equity. There are many Equity theaters around the country that offer this incentive to nonunion actors. Along with a $100 registration fee, you must fill out a registration form and submit it to Actors' Equity. This initial fee is deducted from your total membership fee when you officially become a member.

There are two stipulations to this way of entering the union. The first is that you work for fifty weeks at an accredited theater (or theaters). Please note that this does not have to be consecutive weeks. Another way is to work for forty weeks at an accredited theater (or theaters) and then take a written exam. If you pass the exam, you're in. Visit the Membership Candidate Department at Equity for more specific information about this program.

Eligible Performers or Open Door Admissions Program

If you've been a member in good standing in one of the Equity sister unions, such as SAG or AFTRA, for at least one year, you can qualify to join Equity. Here again, there are certain stipulations. There is a "weeks worked" and/or a "minimum salary earned" requirement. Check with Actors' Equity as to specific details.

Basic Dues and Working Dues

Dues are $118 per year, billed at $59 semiannually each May and November. For more information about dues, visit the Membership Department's Billing Center at the Actors Equity Office.

Actors (and stage managers) also give 2 percent of their weekly earnings as working dues. This money is generally withheld from your paycheck and given to Equity by your employer. The maximum Equity earnings that can be subject to the two percent working dues is $150,000 a year.

Screen Actors Guild

The Screen Actors Guild was founded in 1933. Presently, there are more than ninety thousand members around the country, who work in film (including TV, theatrical, industrial, experimental, and educational). Over the last few years, there has also been a dramatic increase in music videos under SAG's jurisdiction. The main goal of the union is to provide competitive wages and safe working conditions for its members. The Screen Actors Guild doesn't provide employment. Like many of the acting unions, many of the members are without work. In 1998, a little more than a quarter of the members of the Screen Actors Guild did not earn any money under SAG's contracts.

The New York office of the Screen Actors Guild is located at 360 Madison Avenue, 12th Floor, New York, NY 10017. You can call them at (212) 944-1030.

Eligibility
Principal Performer Employment

If you've been a member of AFTRA or Equity for at least one year and have had a principal role, you may apply to SAG. If you've been offered a principal role in a SAG film, TV show, commercial, or videotape and have proof of employment (a SAG contract), you can join SAG. SAG requires a payroll check, a signed contract, a letter from the company, or a check stub as proof of employment. Obviously, this proof must include your name, the name of the project, your social security number, how much you earned, and the date of your employment.

According to the Taft-Hartley law, a non-SAG actor may be cast and permitted to work for a SAG signatory, with a contract, for thirty days. After that, he must join SAG if he wants to do any additional work in the union.

Extra Work on a SAG Project

If you've been cast and worked as an extra for three days on a SAG signatory-produced project and were paid full SAG rates, you're eligible to join SAG. Here again, the proof required is basically the same as for principal performer employment.

SAG Dues

To join SAG, a performer must pay an initiation fee of $2,277, plus the first semiannual basic dues. You may pay by money order or cashier's check (and in some cases, with a credit card).

The American Federation of Television and Radio Artists

The American Federation of Television and Radio Artists, or AFTRA, is an open union. That is, any actor, after paying the $1,600 membership fee, can fill out a membership form and officially become a member. This union represents actors and broadcasters in radio, sound recordings, television, and in the areas of interactive programming and DVD-ROMs.

AFTRA Dues

Dues are paid semiannually on a sliding scale, based on the previous year's income earned in the union. As a new member of the union, you'll pay $63.90 (the lowest amount) semiannually. AFTRA dues are assessed on May 1 and November 1 each year and consist of a minimum amount (base dues) plus a percentage of your AFTRA earnings during the previous year (work dues). Work dues are calculated on the first $100,000 at 0.743 percent and at 0.137 percent on earnings above $100,000. Dues are not calculated on earnings over $250,000; members earning more than that amount pay the maximum dues. Members who earn less than $2,000 pay only the base dues amount of $63.90, you may pay by cashier's check or a money order. Some locals accept a credit card. As in SAG, the Taft-Hartley Act applies. That is, you may do one job in AFTRA and then work in radio or TV for up to thirty days before you'll be forced to join.

Aftra is located at 260 Madison Avenue, New York, NY 10016. You can reach them by phone at (212) 532-0800 or online at *www.aftra.org*.

TALENT AGENTS

The job of the talent agent is to set up interviews and auditions for his client, and then, if the client books a job, to negotiate the contact. On the most clinical level, the talent agent is the seller, the casting director (along with the director and producer) is the buyer, and the actor is the product.

Different states have different rules of how talent agents may operate. Agents submit your photo and résumés to casting directors and try to get you in the door. To some degree, the talent agent offers career advice to his client and collaborates with him to (hopefully) make the smartest and most effective career moves.

Most talent agents are franchised, which mean that they are licensed by the state and are officially approved by any of the talent unions, which include the Screen Actors Guild, the American Federation of Television and Radio Artists, and Actors' Equity. To get a franchise, an agent must have previous experience in the business and an untarnished reputation. Each union has its own standards as to acceptability of agents. The union keeps a check on agents by periodically inspecting their offices. I advise that you only seek out agents that are franchised by these unions. By their union franchising, the agent must adhere to a strict code of ethical behavior. Even if you yourself are not a member of any of the unions, you can still work with franchised agents.

Agents receive a 10 percent commission for jobs that you have secured through their assistance. *Never* pay any agent a commission until after you have been paid for a job that they've negotiated for you.

There are two ways that an actor can work with an agent in New York: freelance or signed (exclusive). By freelancing with an agent, you have the right to work with other agents. A "signed client agreement" occurs when an agent and an actor have decided to work exclusively with each other. This may happen in one particular area, say in commercials, or "across the board," in all fields. Different agencies have different policies on freelance versus exclusive relations with actors. Some work only with signed clients, others will freelance with many actors. And some talent agencies have a signed client list, but will freelance with a limited number of actors.

How a Role for a Play Is Cast

I think one way to understand the role of the agent is to understand the way that a play is cast and the role that the agent has in the process.

- A play has been written and then optioned by a producer. The producer decides to produce the play. He hires a production team that includes a director and, in many cases, a casting director. The casting director's job is to help the producer and director find the right actors for the roles in the play.

- The casting director notifies talent agents that he is casting specific roles for this play. One of the main ways that he does this is though a company called Breakdown Services, Ltd. This organization sends out information describing both the play and the actor types that will be needed to fill the roles.

- Agents who subscribe to the breakdown service will then read the character descriptions and try to match what they are looking for with actors that the agent works with. An agent will usually submit any number of actors for a specific role, unless they are informed that they may only submit a limited number.

- The casting director then goes through the agent submissions and selects those actors that he feels are most right for the roles, contacting the agents, and setting up audition times. One of the things that I learned in many of the interviews that follow is that quite often, the casting directors have their own list of the actors they wish to see for a role. Many casting directors begin their casting search by contacting the agents of the actors on their original list. If the actor doesn't have an agent, the casting director will contact the actor directly.

- While setting up the audition times with the casting director, the agent will also offer suggestions of other actors he works with to the casting director. It's a way to give more of his clients a chance at the audition, improving the odds for the agency's success. To some degree, the agent's reputation is always on the line with every suggestion he makes.

- If the casting director trusts the agent's judgment and they've had a good working relationship, he quite often will accept the agent's suggestions and add them to the audition list, even if the actor is not known personally to the casting director.

- The talent agent then calls the actors that have been accepted by the casting director for the auditions.

- The agent will give the actor as much information as he can about the play, the character the actor will be auditioning for, the style of the play, where it'll be performed, where and when the audition will take place, where the actor can get a copy of the script (or sides), and anything else pertinent to this particular casting.
- The next step, of course, is for the actor to go to the audition, and hopefully book the job.
- If the actor books the job, the agent will negotiate what the actor's salary will be.
- In some cases, the salaries for the entire cast are preset and the same for all.
- For his work on behalf of the now employed actor, the agent receives a 10 percent commission.

What Talent Agents Look For

According to Jonn Wasser of Atlas Talent Agency, Inc., "Agents are looking for actors who aren't looking for agents. Agents are looking for actors who are going places."

Some actors mistakenly believe that if they only had an agent that all their career frustrations would magically disappear. Desperation sometimes sets in to "get an agent, no matter what!" That desperation can be a real turnoff for the agent looking for new talent to represent. Aside from talent, most agents are looking for actors who have a pleasant and engaging personality, who are open and eager to succeed.

An actor's passion can be very contagious; an actor's anxiety and neediness is not. There is a clear distinction between the actor who is confident and the actor who is arrogant. Actors who are overambitious, selfish, and insensitive will have a tougher road trying to secure an agent to represent them. Agents want to work with actors who are genuinely self-assured. As one agent recently put it, "We've seen every trick in the book. If they'd only just be themselves. Why can't they put things in perspective? The world is not going to end if they don't book that job! My biggest advice to most actors: get a life!"

So what are agents looking for? Talent aside, they're looking for actors who are professional, open, friendly, and "who play well with others."

How to Get an Agent
Introductions by Casting Directors

Actually, there are many ways to get an agent. Perhaps the best way is through a recommendation by a casting director who knows your work. One thing you'll discover about show business is that it's a business of contacts. Who you know in the business can be very helpful. Casting directors are in daily contact with agents. Agents want to keep solid relationships with the casting directors they work with. They trust casting directors' referrals, and if you can get one, you should easily be able to get an interview with the agent. Obviously, you should know the casting director well enough to ask for this favor. Hopefully, you've booked a job through her agency, or at least had some callbacks. When asking for the casting director's help, be professional, courteous, but above all, try not to seem too desperate. Their name and reputation go along with every referral.

Actor Referrals

Actors you've worked with in shows or in classes can easily introduce you to their agents. Asking them for their help can be a bit touchy. Make sure that the actor whose agent you'd like to meet believes in you. Perhaps he's complimented your work in the past. It helps if the actor and you are friends, or at least friendly. I realize that it may feel a bit awkward to ask for his help, but unless you at least ask, you'll never know. Find a moment when you feel comfortable and ask him if he wouldn't mind mentioning you to his agent. If he says yes, ask what he feels would be the best way for you to make contact with the agent. Would he feel comfortable calling his agent on your behalf? Or should you call his agent and use his name? Or (least preferable) should you send a picture and résumé and include his name in your cover letter? If, for whatever reason, he seems uncomfortable doing this for you and refuses, don't make a big deal about it. And don't let it ruin the relationship that you presently have with the actor. It may have something to do with his own insecurities and nothing to do with his assessment of your talent. Just let it go, and try to get an agent another way.

Networking Facilities—Paying to Meet Agents

Networking facilities offer agent/actor introductions and auditions for a small fee. You are not guaranteed anything from this arrangement other than the opportunity to meet with the agent.

Mass and Targeted Mailings

Sending out pictures and résumés unsolicited to agents is one way to get their attention. They may see something in your photo that interests them and call you in for a general interview. As I mentioned earlier, mass mailings are very expensive and largely a waste of time. With the cost of photographs, envelopes, and postage, this is a very expensive proposition. Agents and casting directors receive huge piles of photos on a daily basis. But there is always a chance that they'll see something in your photo. A targeted mailing to a select group of people is less expensive and may do the trick.

Making the Rounds

Years ago, actors could make the rounds of agents' offices and leave their photos and résumés with the receptionists. Many offices today have security intercoms; you won't get in unless you are buzzed in. Actors are asked to either leave their photos in a basket outside the door or slip them under the door. There are, however, still some agents whose offices are accessible. Quite a few agents leave baskets outside their door for actors to leave headshots. There certainly is no harm in dropping your headshot in as you pass by.

Interviews with Talent Agents

Clifford **Stevens (CS)** (Paradigm) began agenting in 1963. In 1977, he started the STE agency. In 1992, that agency merged with a few other offices and became Paradigm.

Mary Harden (MH) (Harden-Curtis Associates) has been an agent for thirty years. Harden-Curtis has been in existence for five years.

How, when, and where do you find actors that you work with?

CS: It varies. Sometimes, an actor is referred to me; sometimes, I'll see an actor in an Off-Broadway or Broadway play. Another way is, I'll meet an actor who is looking to change agency representation. I wish I had more time to work with beginners. I did a lot of that during the earlier part of my career; someone like Glenn Close. But those days are kind of gone now.

MH: Primarily from seeing their work. When I see a client's work, I, of course, see everybody else who's in the show. Also, from recommendations from actors who are already signed to us, as well as from artistic directors, directors, and casting directors.

If there is an actor that you're considering working with, that you see some potential in, how important is previous training and experience?

CS: I know actors who are trained within an inch of their life, and it doesn't happen for them. Some people don't have or need that much training; they have that gift. I don't think that you can look at someone, and just because they have extensive training, you're going to be enthusiastic about them. I'm not trying to diminish the attraction of a very well-trained actor, but there are many well-trained actors whom I don't find very interesting. Getting out there and doing it is very important as well.

MH: For me, it's very important. We work in the theater a lot, and so it's very important that we have actors who have received formal training.

What kind of things do you look for on an actor's headshot? Résumé? On their reel?

CS: I look for the headshot not to be touched up. I'm a very bad judge of headshots. Every time clients come in and ask me to look at their headshots, I say, "Don't ask me."

I review the résumé to see who they've worked with, the venues where they've worked. There are gradations in the theaters. If an actor has spent a couple of extensive years at one theater or another, that may make a difference in the way I look at it. I also look at the kind of parts actors have played and their training. I never make a decision whether I want to get behind, or have my office get behind someone, unless we've actually seen him perform. I always tell actors, never sign with anyone unless an agent has seen your work.

As for the reel, you never know what it is that'll get your eye. It's that unexplainable thing that gets to you. Acting is all in the eye of the beholder. Two people can have very different reactions to the same actor.

MH: If someone is absolutely beautiful, it helps to have a headshot that indicates that. But again, I turn it over and look at the résumé for theaters that I know, for teachers that I'm familiar with, signs that an actor has worked.

As for the reels, I look for a sampling, a wide range of their work.

When an actor comes in for a general interview, what kinds of things are you looking for?

CS: I ask them where they'd like to see themselves five years hence. What they'd like to do, what they wouldn't like to do. I really try to find out where their ambitions lie. I want to see if their ambitions are in some place where I can be of some help, to which I can be sympathetic.

MH: I look for someone who's professional, warm, and pleasant. I look for someone who has an understanding of the business and where he fits in. We tend to like clients who are very proactive, who are more interested in their career than we are. They should be the most interested person in their careers. I like actors who know that it is their job to stay busy, to do work on their own. They should become involved in readings, workshops. They should be building their own professional network, which should include directors, writers, and other actors. If they are not busy doing anything else, they should be working in an Off-Off-Broadway theater.

Do you audition actors, and if so, what kinds of things are you looking for in the audition?

CS: I don't audition actors. Some of the other agents here do. I don't find that's very helpful to me. Some actors are terrible at auditioning, and yet are wonderful actors.

MH: We do not audition actors here in the office. But we will, on occasion, rent audition space. Actors we see at those auditions do monologues or bring musical material to perform. We hold these auditions only for people that we are interested in.

What determines why you'll work with one actor over another?

CS: I couldn't tell you, it's instinct. And sometimes, the instinct is right, and sometimes the instinct is wrong.

MH: Totally personal response and taste. You feel that you can work with someone.

What kinds of things do you look for and encourage in your working relationship with your clients? What are the factors that go into terminating a working relationship with an actor?

CS: I think you have to have a resiliency. There are the natural things like always be on time, pick up the script, go and prepare. The actors that I work with, I look for the ability to say, "no," to walk away from something that they don't want to do. Colleen Dewhurst once said to me, "If you're really not committed to the material, you really shouldn't do it." Unless you're committed, you're not going to do very good work.

As far as terminating, I've only terminated with two actors in my life. That had to do with behavioral problems; they were behaving badly. And that's two in over forty years. There are actors who we've had to sit down with and just come to the conclusion that we're not very lucky with them. At that time, we may suggest that they may be luckier with another group of people, different agents. Sometimes, that's an easier way to let people down. Luck in this business is almost 60 or 70 percent of the game.

MH: I encourage an actor who will encourage me. I think the relationship that works best is the one where the actor is aware of the fact that part of his responsibility is to cheerlead any team that he's on, whether he's doing a film, a play, or a TV series, whether he's working with an agent or a publicity person. His communications skills should be such that people will want to do things for and with him. If I don't want to take someone's phone call, why in the world would I expect that a casting director or director would want to work with him?

Any actor pet peeves?

CS: In the last twenty-five years or so, there's been an increase in agents who are out there trying to lure successful actors from their agent affiliation. In many cases, the actors will go with the new agent, even though the actor's initial agent had helped bring about success for that actor. The actor will then go with the new agent, and really doesn't have a very valid reason for leaving. The actor is making the decision to go. I don't have a problem with the agent; that's what they're doing these days. I have a problem with the actor; the actor makes the decision to change. That's not true of every actor, but a lot of them.

MH: Sometimes, the communication is not right. The agent and the actor have very different ideas of what a working relationship is and how it should be. We're a business; I have to make money. No one in this office gets paid unless we make money. When someone says to me, "Well, you know, I just want to do independent film," it gets to me. That kind of statement is so unrealistic. What is an independent film? What do they mean by independent film? They can't answer you; they don't know what they mean. They don't know who's doing it. It's a buzzword that some actors have picked up. What that says to me is that it is someone who doesn't understand that most SAG experimental films don't pay enough for anyone to live on.

Eventually, actors can facilitate their own careers and their own communications to be specific and to recognize the fact that they are in a business and, therefore, have to be educated in that business.

A lot of times, young actors will say, "I want to be on Broadway," or on *Law & Order*. And I'll turn around and say, "Okay, who casts that?" They don't know. They live under the myth that if you get an agent, your problems are solved.

If you had one piece of advice to offer an actor who is thinking of pursuing a career in New York, what would it be?

CS: You've got to want to do it more than anything else in the world—more than anything.

MH: (laughing) Act good.

Take care of your craft. Learn your craft; it is the basis of your career. You ultimately are hired because of your talent and craft. Ultimately, if you deliver the goods, you'll work.

Make any situation that you're in as human as possible. Never forget that the people you're working with, auditioning for, or meeting with are also human beings. You may look at them as opportunities, but they're human; they have good days and bad days.

PERSONAL MANAGERS

In her book, *Henderson's Personal Managers Directory*, Sue Henderson defines a personal manager as "one who manages others' career-building affairs in a continuously dedicated, knowledgeable, and personal manner. He or she does what is required by the continuous advancement of one or more clients' interests and does what can't be done by anyone but a personal manager. When a professional aspires to a goal or goals that can't be attained without certain informed, prestigious, and wholly dedicated help, a personal manager is what's needed."

Ms. Henderson quotes Clinton Ford Billups, Jr., the former Eastern Executive director of the National Conference of Personal Managers (NCOPM): "First, let's explain what a personal manger is not. A personal manager is not an agent (whose role is to obtain employment). A personal manager is not a publicist (whose role is to generate publicity). Nor is a personal manager an attorney (whose role is to provide legal counsel). And a personal manager is not a business manager (whose role is to provide accounting, investment, and other financial services).

"A personal manager advises and counsels talent and personalities in the entertainment industry. Personal managers have the expertise to find and develop new talent and create opportunities for those artists that they represent. Personal managers act as a liaison between their clients and both the public and the theatrical agents, publicists, attorneys, business managers, and other entertainment industry professionals which provide services to the personal manager's clients.

"Picture a wagon wheel. At the very center is the axle. The axle is the performing artist around which everything revolves. The hub—that is, the personal manager—protects and supports the axle. The rim of the wheel is the artist's career that travels on what can be a long, bumpy, winding road. Connecting the hub with the rim are many spokes, which give the wheel support in different directions. These are the agents, publicists, attorneys, business managers, and other industry professionals who support an artist on the road to success. When the wheel is well constructed, the artist's journey can be smooth, speedy, and successful."

According to the latest accounts, there are well over a thousand personal managers on record in the United States. This figure doesn't include the perhaps thousands more who call themselves personal managers. Like the talent agent, the personal manager is a seller in the show business equation. Because the personal manager is not franchised by AFTRA, SAG, or Equity, he needs to work with franchised agents to complete union deals. The personal manager generally gets between 10 and 15 percent commission from an actor, but the percentage can be much higher. If a deal is negotiated with a talent agent, you must also add on an additional 10 percent. That's at least 20 to 25 percent out of the actor's pocket.

Gerard W. Purcell of the Conference of Personal Managers, an organization that overlooks the standards of its members, has said, "It's the manager's belief in the young actor that quite often enables him or her to live up to his or her potential. Many managers put up their own money to develop actors who they believe strongly in. They act as mentors, coaches. Managers have a more personalized relationship with their clients. They are more instrumental in career decision-making policies than agents are. They offer legal as well as financial advice to their clients, introduce them to talent agents, casting directors, publicists, anyone who can be of help in moving the actor's career along. They arrange for auditions for their clients, either from the daily breakdowns, through agents, or with specific casting directors. Generally, managers work with only five to twenty-five clients. They are not looking for the immediate commission. What they are interested in is, 'What will be the impact if this artist succeeds?'"

Personal managers have also been known to coach their clients for upcoming auditions, suggest wardrobe and grooming ideas, help them find strong audition material, and coach them in how the business works.

If you sign with a manager, you can expect your contract to be for two to three years, as opposed to the usual one-year contract with talent agents.

What to Look for When Seeking a Personal Manager

First and foremost, make sure that this is a person to whom you are willing to commit your career. You must feel comfortable with the person and trust his perceptions about both you and the industry.

Ask the personal manager what his immediate plans for your career are. By immediate, I mean within a month or so after you sign your contract with him. And, by the way, always have an attorney look over your contract with a personal manager.

Have the manager spell out as clearly as possible what his long-terms plans are for your career. Ask him which agents he plans on introducing you to. Find out how many talent agents he's connected to.

You'll want a well-connected manager. Make sure that he knows a substantial amount of people who can be of use to you in your career. Always ask the manager for his client list in advance. Find out if the manager subscribes to Breakdown Services, Ltd.

Because they are not franchised, personal managers can also be producers. See if producing is part of your manager's game plan. If so, are there any projects that he is developing that you might be included in?

Never pay any personal manager any money in advance. Generally, you'll agree to a 10 to 15 percent commission that is to be paid *after* a job is done and the money is received. Beware of personal managers who constantly avoid answering questions you have regarding the business and, particularly, your career.

Members of the National Conference of Personal Managers abide by a Code of Ethics, which includes

- having personal management as their personal occupation;
- dealing honestly and fairly with their clients;
- not deriving personal gains at the expense of their clients;
- treating client relationships in a confidential manner;
- not encouraging artists to breach existing personal management contracts;
- being proud of the personal management profession;
- exchanging information with other NCOPM members in the best interest of their clients;
- most importantly: NCOPM members never accept a fee from a client on the promise of attempting to obtain engagements for their client.

Interviews with Personal Managers

Nick Frenkel (NF) (Three Arts Entertainment) has been a personal manager since he got out of school about fifteen and a half years ago.

Rosella Olson (RO) (Rosella Olson Management) has been a manager for twenty-five years. Prior to that, she was an agent at Frontier Booking for five years.

What do you do as a personal manager?

NF: I oversee basically all aspects of an actor's career. I coordinate the professional people in an actor's life. That includes his agent, attorney, publicists, those kinds of people. You might say that I'm the head of the corporation, overseeing all of it to make sure that it's running well. If it's not, if there's some slack somewhere, it's up to me to pick it up.

RO: A good deal of the day I work on the breakdowns. I subscribe to Breakdown Services. I work with them in the same way I did when I was an agent at Frontier Booking. I got to know all the casting directors when I was an agent. I speak to my clients regularly. Sometimes, I coach them if they get an audition if either one of us feels that they need it. I like to keep a tab on what they're doing before they go into the audition, to make sure that they know what they're doing. I presently have fifteen signed clients. Fifteen clients is the most that a manager can work with. More than that number is against the labor code in the City of New York. That is one of the differences between an agent and a manager. Agents can freelance with as many clients as they want; a manager has to work exclusively with signed clients. One of the problems for an actor working with an agent is that there can be many actors in the agency that are similar to the actor; therefore, the actor is competing with actors within his own agency.

What would you say are the main differences between being a personal manager and an agent?

NF: The first really big difference is that an agent can handle forty or fifty clients, whereas I handle about eight. In general, a manager will handle up to fifteen clients. The big difference is that you have more time to handle each actor you represent and handle his career in a very specific manner. We are not just concerned with what auditions we can get for clients. We are much more devoted to the individual's career goals. That's not to say that a manager and an agent's jobs don't overlap; they do. Like an agent, I definitely look for jobs for my clients. It's my job to know what's out there.

There tends to be a perception that there is a conflict between agents and managers, because there is an overlap. All of my clients, except for two, have agents. The ones that don't have attorneys negotiate deals for them. It's a partnership. The partnership is made up of the agent, the client, and myself. The feeling is, whoever knows about a project, whoever has the connection, whether it's to a studio executive, a casting director, it's up to that person to make the call. The ultimate goal is to get the client in the room. I choose to make sure that the relationships that I have with the agents are very friendly. I speak with some of them three or four times a day, either by phone, e-mail, or whatever. It's a collaborative effort. Submissions, for the most part, I leave to the agents. But what we do is talk about individual projects. We see who should make the call to the casting person. Whereas an agent is pitching many clients at one time, I'm only pitching one. It's a little more focused. That's the advantage to having a manager on your side.

RO: If I have an actor who doesn't have an agent, I try to get him one through my connections. You can't always get an agent for an actor; sometimes, it's very hard. One of the main differences between an agent and a manager is that the manager's focus is on developing the actor's career. The agent just tries to get him a job. Basically, I'll pitch an actor to an agent.

As I said, I know all of the casting directors. Much of what I do as a manager is what I did as an agent. You make a submission to the casting director and hope that she'll want your client to come in for an audition. When casting directors call to set up appointments for my clients, I'll try to see if I can get some of my other clients in to see them for different roles. Many times, the casting director will call me directly requesting one of my clients, especially during pilot season. If the casting directors are very busy and don't have time to meet new people, they'll call and request specific clients. It's really during the slow times that they are most available to meeting new people.

How do you work with agents? With casting directors?

NF: Casting directors definitely go to the agencies first. What they do is ask for a submission of all their clients that might be right for a project. The agent will submit, let's say, twenty or thirty people. I usually get a call from a casting director when she specifically wants to see one of my clients who has not been submitted. Or I may get a call from a casting director if she's having trouble finding the right actor for a role and is interested in my suggestions. She'll ask me if there is somebody that she doesn't know about that might be right for the role.

A lot of times, after my client has had the audition, I call to get feedback on how it went. It's important sometimes for the clients to know how they did, good or bad.

Where do you find the actors that you work with?

NF: A combination of referrals from agents and out of the schools. The majority come from the schools. I currently handle two graduates from Juilliard and some people from NYU. In the case of Juilliard, I go to every play during the year to see actors. The competition is stiff. If I go there earlier than just at the end of the year, I'm better off. When I'm there during the year, they generally aren't aware that I'm there. At the showcase at the end of the year, they're very aware that there are people scouting actors in the audience.

RO: Usually, it's through referrals. It's been very rare that I've actually met an actor through a picture—although I must tell you how important the pictures are. The casting directors won't even turn the picture over if it doesn't grab them in the first place. With the headshots, I like my clients to have two or three variations. When I'm doing the breakdowns, I know what the casting director is looking for. Based on what I believe, I need the correct picture from my client to send to them. One picture doesn't usually cover it all.

Another place that I find actors is through recommendations from acting teachers. Other sources are casting directors, agents, and even other actors. The reason that an agent will send me one of his actors is the belief that through our combined efforts, we can get that actor much more work.

What do you look for when interviewing and auditioning actors?

NF: I have a very hard time answering that question, but I'll tell you, you know it when you see it. I look for someone who is a good actor, who has a grasp on a role that intrigues me. I look to see if they are commercially viable. Also, I look for someone who is not only a good actor, but is also somebody that I can pitch for a lot of products, that they're going to be a hot commodity in the market. They might be a phenomenal actor, but if I don't see them as someone who is commercially viable, then I won't sign them. I don't audition actors.

At the interview, I ask the person about their past, what they've done. I want to see if they are interesting. Sometimes, people get shy in interviews. But if I've seen their work and I was impressed, I'll take that into consideration when deciding if I want to work with them. I have to stick to my gut on the decisions that I make.

RO: I look for professionalism, charisma, and courtesy. In their monologues, I want to see their talent. All of those things combined. Then I look to see how viable they are for me to sell. There are certain age ranges and types that are easier to sell than others. I also have to make certain that they don't compete with someone that I have already.

But when I see their work, there has to be some real honest acting going on. Many actors just act on top of the lines. They are not acting from inside.

What do you expect from actors who work with you? What do you feel actors can do to help themselves in their careers?

NF: I expect them to put as much work into it as I do. I don't do well with actors who come up with excuses on a regular basis, who can't make auditions, for instance. My career is really important to me, and I expect the same from them. Perhaps I expect a little more than I should from actors. I expect them to be completely and utterly focused. They need to learn how to go into a casting room and start getting comfortable with whoever they meet. There isn't a lot of preparation that I ask them to do in that situation. I'll give them advice about going in there, but they have to learn to get comfortable once in that room.

RO: A lot of things. First of all, we go over the pictures. If the pictures aren't good enough, they must get new ones. Actors must be punctual about everything. If I call them, they must call me back the same day. If they don't have a cell phone, they must have a pager. When I ask for more pictures, I need them right away. They need to be in acting classes. There are a lot of good professional classes in the city. They should do some student films to get experience if they've never done a film before.

What factors go into making the decision to terminate your relationship with an actor?

NF: I'm extremely understanding of the fact that a career can take a while to go. I also know that some people drop clients because it's just not happening fast enough. When I first start working with a new client, I put a schedule in my head of where I think they should go in, say, two years or so. I don't necessarily stick with it, but it's a way to start out, to plan a career. I may start to see, after some period of time, that my relationship with the client is not working. That's not to say that they're not talented. It's just that maybe I'm not the best person to represent them.

RO: I know that a lot of people will terminate an actor if he doesn't bring in money. I don't do that, because I know how difficult it is. If I see progress, if the actor is getting callbacks, then I want to keep working with him. Once in a while, you come across a difficult person. On very few occasions, I've come across a person who was very scary. Fortunately, that's very rare. In those cases, you try to let the person know that the relationship is not working, and you let him go his own way.

Any actor pet peeves?

NF: I wish that the actors that I find out of the schools were better trained for auditions. Most are also not well trained for the business. I tell my clients, when you walk in the door, you are the business actor, you're putting on the business face. Charm the people, and convince them that you are the person for the role. And then your training kicks in; start auditioning.

RO: I don't like to be called on weekends or after hours unless it's an emergency. But certainly not just to check in or ask why I haven't been sending them out lately. I need actors to return my calls promptly. I really don't like actor jealousy. It's a very bad emotion. I really feel that everyone is unique, and you can't really compete with anyone else.

Any advice for actors who are thinking of looking for a personal manager?

NF: I tell people who are just starting out, set your team early. Select the team that's going to represent you—the agent, the manager, whoever it is. The reason that I suggest this is that when you start doing well, when you're successful, you won't know who you can trust. The person who pursued you at the beginning, because he really appreciated your acting and your skills, is the one that you're really going to trust in the end.

Judge the person who represents you by his company, based on what he can do for you, and most of all, whether you feel that you can talk to him and whether or not he understands where you want to go in your career.

RO: I really feel that finding a manager is the way to go these days. Usually, it's so hard to find an agent, and the manager can open doors for actors looking for agents. It's particularly difficult for actors looking for agents if they don't have many credits on their résumé.

Anybody can say that they're a personal manager. Actors need to ask around, find out who is legit. I'm on the board of directors of the Conference of Personal Managers. It's very hard to get into our association. We screen the people we allow in. If an actor has a complaint about a manager, he can bring it to the organization and have an arbitration. You just don't know who you're signing with if you sign with a manager that you know nothing about. Be careful about managers that ask for money up front and tell you that they're going to get you pictures and put you in their book.

Any advice for actors thinking of coming to New York?

NF: The best thing that I can say is, put yourself in a high-track area. Join a theater company or whatever you need to connect with others. Look through *Back Stage*, which is extremely useful. Get yourself into a show, and make sure to get people to see your work.

RO: It's almost impossible to find an apartment; make sure that you start your search well in advance.

CASTING DIRECTORS

Casting directors are the "sellers" in the show business audition–casting relationship. Many casting directors belong to the CSA (Casting Society of America). The casting director sets up the auditions, where the client (producers, directors) can determine which actors will best fit the roles for the project that they are involved in. The producers and directors depend on the casting director for their contacts.

There are several types of casting directors. First, there are the independent casting directors, who are hired for a particular project by theater, television, film, or commercial producers. Most of these independent casting directors have offices, but some move around, depending on the project they are involved with. Next, there are the casting directors who work for advertising agencies. It's their job to find actors for television commercials, radio spots, voice-overs, and print. And lastly, there are the in-house casting directors, such as daytime serial casting directors, who specifically work for the studios and networks.

There are generally three ways that casting directors find their talent for a specific audition:

- They go through their files and select talent from actors whose work they are familiar with.
- They contact talent agents and request submissions for the project.
- They release a cast breakdown on a breakdown service.

Some casting directors will hold preliminary auditions. During these auditions, they eliminate those actors whom they feel are not right for this particular project. During this early stage, actors will be "typed out" or lose out due to a poor audition. When they've narrowed down the playing field to the most likely candidates, the casting director will then invite the producers, directors, and playwrights to the auditions where the decisions as to who will actually be cast in the roles is made.

How to Meet Casting Directors
Casting directors go to showcases, Broadway, and Off-Broadway plays; watch movies and television shows; and look at actors' reels to become familiar with

actors in the available talent pool. Aside from an agent's submissions, you can meet casting directors through referrals by another actor, through mail submissions, or by paying for introductions or auditions at places such as Actors Connection and TVI (networking facilities). Another way is to make rounds, stopping by the casting directors' offices and dropping off a picture and résumé—the least successful way, usually frowned upon, but every once in a while, it does pay off.

What Casting Directors Look For in Auditions

According to Risa Bramon Garcia, independent casting director, "I want to see someone who's focused on the work and has a real sense of himself. It's amazing how people sabotage themselves. They say things like, 'I got this yesterday and didn't have a chance to look at it.' Or 'What are you guys looking for?'"

Lori Openden, executive vice president of Talent and Casting at the CW, says, "Actors should make strong, definite choices and go with them. And at the same time, they should be accessible to directions if they're given an adjustment. I look for actors who add something to a scene that others didn't."

Bernard Telsey, of Bernard Telsey Casting, says, "You look to see if they're prepared, if they have a sense of the project they're auditioning for. The actor who takes that audition scene and can make it as colorful as the whole two-hour play or movie is a real find."

Observes Peter Golden, vice president of Talent and Casting at CBS in Los Angeles, "I look for actors who are listening to their auditioning partners or to the reader. A big 'don't' for me is to have the words so memorized that it's all mechanical. It's all too rehearsed, too planned, not spontaneous or in the moment."

Interviews with Casting Directors

Among the many films cast by **Juliet Taylor (JT)** are *You Will Meet A Tall, Dark Stranger, Whatever Works, Vicky Cristina Barcelona, Cassandra's Dream, Scoop, Match Point, The Interpreter, Melinda and Melinda, "Angels in America"* (2003) TV miniseries *Interview with the Vampire, Schindler's List, Sleepless in Seattle, Hannah and Her Sisters, The Grifters, Postcards from the Edge, Working Girl, Heartburn, Terms of Endearment, Arthur, Bullets over Broadway, Wit, Big, Manhattan, The Birdcage, Small Time Crooks, The Exorcist, Annie Hall, Julia, An Unmarried Woman, Curse of the Jade Scorpion, Everyone Says I Love You, Close Encounters of the Third Kind, Angela's Ashes, People I Know, Purple Rose of Cairo, The Mission, Blind Assassin, Meet Joe Black, Sweet and Lowdown,* and *Crimes and Misdemeanors.*

Avy Kaufman (AK) has cast a number of films, including *The Beaver, Salt, An Invisible Sign of My Own, Rubicon (TV series), Just Wright, Jack Goes Boating, Welcome to the Rileys, Brothers, Amelia, Public Enemies, Land of the Lost, Taking Woodstock, Baby Mama, What Happens in Vegas, Sunshine Cleaning, Lions for Lambs, American Gangster, The Sixth Sense, Blow, A.I. (Artificial Intelligence), Ice Storm, Ride with the Devil, Lone Star, The Hulk, Searching for Bobby Fisher, A Civil Action, Home for the Holidays, Little Man Tate, Divine Secrets of the Ya-Ya Sisterhood,* and *Dancer in the Dark*.

Some of the films Ellen Lewis (EL) has cast include Morning Glory, Letters To Juliet, *Shutter Island, Mamma Mia, Revolutionary Road, Before The Devil Knows You're Dead, Charlie Wilson's War, The Departed, The Devil Wears Prada, Gangs of New York, What Lies Beneath, Company Man, What Planet Are You From?, Wit, Titus, Bringing Out the Dead, Ghost Dog: The Way of the Samurai, Stepmom, Meet Joe Black, Pleasantville, Primary Colors, Casino, Forrest Gump, Age of Innocence, A League of Their Own, Scent of a Woman, Goodfellas,* and many others.

Jay Binder (JBi) has cast many plays for Broadway, including *Looped,* the recent revivals of *The Miracle Worker* and *Broadway Bound,* the recent revival of *Finian's Rainbow, Passing Strange, The Lion King, The Iceman Cometh* (recent revival), *The 39 Steps* and *Last Night at Ballyhoo*.

Stephanie Klapper (SK) has worked on and Off-Broadway: recently, Horton Foote's *Dividing The Estate* (with Elizabeth Ashley), *Bells Are Ringing* (Broadway) and the Off-Broadway production of the Pulitzer Prize–winning play, *Dinner With Friends* (plus several regional productions). She has cast for Primary Stages theater company for the last ten years. Other companies she has cast for include New York Classical Theatre, Adirondack Theatre Festival, Capital Repertory Theatre, Cincinnati Playhouse, Hangar Theatre, Delaware Theatre Company, Vermont Stage Company, and the Pittsburgh Playhouse.

Jerry Beaver (JB) has cast many TV commercials. He is also focusing much of his energy these days casting plays for theater. He has cast for the Signature Theatre in New York, the O'Neill National Playwrights Conference, Hartford Stage, Hartford Theater Works, the Wilma Theater, the Alley Theater, and the Working Theater, among others. Last year, he cast *Tabletop* for Off-Broadway.

Some of the films and TV series Louis DiGiamo (LD) has cast include For Love Alone, *Baby on Board, Made In Brooklyn, Hannibal, 100 Centre Street, Gladiator, G.I. Jane, Donnie Brasco, Sleepers, Homicide: Life on the Streets, Thelma and Louise, Rain Man, The Godfather,* and *Good Morning, Vietnam*.

What do you look for on an actor's picture? Résumé?

JT: When I get a picture and résumé, I am looking for a combination of things. Let me start with the résumé first. If someone has a very interesting résumé, if she's worked in interesting theaters, or if she's studied at an interesting place, I really register that. Then if she's interesting-looking in one way or another, that's a good combination. There are some people who have a very unremarkable résumé, but might have a great or unusual, either real or humorous face. And I put that aside into sort of a "good face" pile. Let's say for Woody Allen, that pile might be very helpful. I think actors should always send out pictures that look like them, are real. Try not to do photos that are very arty and overlit. I tend to get exasperated with those. Sometimes, I won't even bother with them, because my suspicion is that that person's picture is not accurate.

AK: It all depends. If I'm on a particular project and I have a particular character that I'm looking for, and that actor has the right something for the role—whatever I feel from reading about the character—and then I see something in an actor's picture, then I might call him in. A lot of times, actors will send in pictures that really don't represent who they are, but who they feel people want. So it's really about a feeling you get about a character that you're working on, and then finding the best actor for that role. I see what they've done, who they've studied with, where they've gone to school. Every little thing adds up.

EL: What I look for in the picture depends on the movie that I'm working on. It's really hard to put into words what really grabs you in a picture; it's just something there. I read the résumé to see what kind of theater experience and training they've had. I don't just look to see where they've worked, but to see if they've done any regional theater.

JBi: The picture should look like something that I think the part looks like. I like a picture that looks like a person who has a degree of openness. Even the ugliest character in a play, someone who's a crone, has to have an appeal about them. With a young actor who doesn't have a lot of experience, I look for training. I look for the kind of parts they've played, so that I get a sense of what their range can be. But mostly with a young actor, I look for training. And just because you went to Yale, that doesn't mean that you're a good actor, but it lets me know that you've had training. For TV or film, actual formal training is not as necessary as it is to work in the theater. For the more experienced actor, most often, I know the résumé.

SK: I look for life and personality. So many pictures have expression-less faces, and I really like personality. On the résumé, I find it very important that the credits be legitimate. I find it useful to know what the roles are that the actor played, where they did it, and who the director was.

JBe: The picture, to me, is just a calling card. Many of the actors I already know; I've either seen them audition for a play, a musical, or a commercial. The picture is just a reminder. I look for sincerity, intelligence, a sparkle in the eye, charisma. On the résumé, I look for the truth. What is the actor's most recent credit, what sort of role does he get cast as. I sometimes see if there is a something that I can open up, so that the actor can explore a side of their acting technique that he might not have explored so far.

LD: To be honest with you, pictures don't really grab me unless there was something that I was specifically looking for. Now if there are two openings for a day, and I don't know an actor, but his picture looks in the ballpark of what I'm looking for, I might call that person in. But a lot of actors don't look like the pictures that they send in. Basically, where they studied. If someone studied for ten years, it doesn't mean that they're great actors. It's just a place to start from.

Do you have general interviews with actors? If you do, what do you look for in the interview?

JT: I do. It's basically an intuition about the kind of impact that the person may have. There are some people that are highly castable. You can imagine them bringing a nice kind of reality of their own into a movie. There's the old hackneyed phrase, "a good type." That comes from the fact that certain people replicate real life in some way.

In the general interview, I'm always interested in the kind of work that someone's doing. I want to get a sense of the kind of place that I might be able to use them. And of course, it's always a pleasure to talk to new people; it's fun. I think part of our job as casting people is intuitive. I follow the actor. If he's shy, I don't make it uncomfortable for him.

EL: Sometimes. I've always found that it's best to meet people within the context of casting on a particular project. I may feel that they're not right for the particular project that I'm working on, but there may be something coming up that they're right for. Sometimes, there's something about an actor that sticks with you, and you remember them for other projects. Hopefully, I make it a friendly environment for the actor, and they feel comfortable in the interview.

JBi: I look for intelligence, and I don't mean intellect. I mean intelligence of focus, of how they see themselves, where their reality is, whether they're living in a dream world, how dedicated and serious they are. And also for me, on a scale of one to ten, what is their sense of humor about life and themselves. I try to determine what people's interest is outside the theater. I feel that your interests outside the theater inform you, and you can be a better actor. You have a point of view of the world, and a point of view about what you think, other than just being in the theater.

SK: On occasion, but not often, because I don't find them that effective. I look for the actors to be articulate, have personality, speak well in a comfortable and intelligent manner.

JBe: All the time. When I meet someone and our eyes connect, I formulate an immediate opinion about him. I can see if he is in a good place in his life, if he's feeling good about himself, or does he have to pump himself up to impress me. I like people who are intelligent, who can carry on a conversation that is meaningful. I look for a sense of humor and charisma.

LD: Generally not.

What kinds of things do you look for at the audition?

JT: Someone who can make a part sound real.

AK: I think it's very, very specific. In certain movies, I've cast children. And the director is telling me what she's looking for. I look for that. If I'm reading a script, I get a feeling about the characters. The reason that people hire us is, we follow the script, and we try to find who the characters are and match that with the right actors. There are times when someone comes in that isn't what we thought the character would look like, but the actor makes the role his own. I did that with Haley Joel Osment for *The Sixth Sense.* Sometimes, you'll say to a director, "I know that this isn't what you're looking for, but look what he did." Those kinds of surprises can be really great, as they can when an actor who hasn't done much acting comes in, auditions, does a good job, and ends up getting a break.

You must realize that we don't make the final decision. When we bring an actor in to meet the producer or director and say we really believe in this person, there is always some risk. But in the end it, isn't our decision as to whether the actor gets the role or not. The producer and director hopefully trust you, but they, in the end, make the decision.

EL: There isn't a specific thing for someone to do. And I think that's one of the difficulties. Hopefully, the actors will be somewhat familiar with the scenes they've been given. They don't have to memorize it. There is never a problem with an actor having the sides in her hands. She just shouldn't have her nose in it.

JBi: I look for sheer ability to act, and also somebody who knows how to bring her own personality into a room and into her work. Auditions are a very strange thing. What I hope for all the time is that the actor walking in the door is the perfect person for the role. Many years ago, when I first started working with Neil Simon, he told me that he had invited Marsha Mason to auditions one day. And at the end of the day, he said that he liked the same people that Marsha liked. And then Marsha said, "Now I understand. The actors pick you, you don't pick the actors." Sometimes, an actor comes in, and that particular magic happens; they "own the part." When Kate Burton auditioned for *Jake's Women*, she opened her mouth, and the part came out. Neil was very enthusiastic, and we just asked her to keep reading well past what she had prepared. And the part just came out. Casting is subjective. We were casting *The Music Man*, and it was a great challenge, because every star was afraid to step into Robert Preston's shoes. And yet when Craig Bierko walked into the room, it was clear instantly that he had the understanding, the sensibility, and the presence. And even though he had never played a major role on stage since college, he became the role (and got the part).

SK: Proper preparation, and there should be a certain comfort that they have with the role that they're auditioning for. It's very chemical. There's intuition involved. When someone walks into the room and auditions, we're, of course, looking for the actor to solve our problems and land the audition. What that means is that she has a real handle on the role and a true understanding of what she's coming in for. She should read the project in its entirety and understand it. If there is an entire copy of the script available, she should read it first or come early to the audition to read it.

JBe: Intelligence and understanding of the play. It always helps to understand what you're auditioning for. Ask yourself, "What is this play about? Who is the character?" Actors come in and they have the sides, and they are not given any direction. It's the actor's interpretation of what this character should be. You must do your homework, be prepared. When auditioning for a play, you have to spend a lot more time thinking about the character and the totality of the project; you can't fake it.

LD: That really becomes a gut feeling. It depends on what other actors have been cast surrounding the actor I'm auditioning. The actor's look is an important factor. I just need to believe the actor in the part, the character that he's reading for. It doesn't have to be the overall best reading, as long as the actor hits certain notes and I can believe him in the role of that character. If I've seen an actor in a play or a movie, and I believe in him, and for some reason, he gives a not so great audition, generally, I'll have him back again.

Aside from agent submissions, what are the best ways that an actor can make themselves known to you?

JT: By appearing in workshops, Off-Off-Broadway plays, and smaller theater companies. Sending in a picture and a résumé is always a good thing. But sending in the pictures is a catch-as-catch-can thing for actor submissions. It really depends on how diligent the office is at looking at the actors' pictures.

AK: Pictures and résumés. It's a tough road. I can't really say how I get to know different actors. If we're looking for an odd type, we go to different places to find those types. If you're looking for someone really different, you have to find the source.

EL: I really do look at pictures. I realize that it can be hard for actors to find me, since I don't have a permanent office space. I try to go to theater, films, and watch TV. Living in New York, I try to watch *Law & Order* all the time. It's really a great resource. Suzanne Ryan does a great job casting on that show.

JBi: Write to me. Send me a flyer or postcard telling me if you are in something. If you have an agent, it's the agent's job to try to get me to come to see your work. It all depends on who represents you and how strongly they feel about getting someone to see you.

SK: Through postcards and sending me notices about projects that they're involved in. No phone calls.

JBe: Let me know when you're in a play; send me a flyer. Either I or someone who works for me will try to go down and see it. A referral from another actor or agent always helps.

LD: By working in plays, sometimes a photo submission. A lot of actors don't have agents, and a lot of times, a photo will come in, unsolicited, by an actor, and it's right for the role. In this business it's timing and luck. You have to do everything you can.

Any actor pet peeves you'd like to mention?

JT: When an actor comes in to audition for a job, when I prescreen them and they do a really good job and I call them back to see the director, sometimes, they come in totally different. They decide that they'll dress as though they were the character. That really makes me crazy. Out of anxiety, they usually go too far, wanting to please.

Sometimes, certain younger actors think that it's going to make them appealing to be kind of unprofessional in a funky kind of way. They'll come in, and they're just too cool for school. They have a little bit of an attitude, have uncombed hair. Their behavior indicates, "I really don't want this job." It's so boring and annoying.

AK: Yes, but I can't say. People misinterpret me all the time. I think that actors sometimes feel that they have to protect themselves. And sometimes, they say things, and it comes out wrong. I've had actors come in and say the oddest things. They'll say things to impress you, to make you feel bad, everything. Actors aren't always aware that they're doing it. One thing I don't like is when actors cancel. There, I'll have a director flying in from somewhere, and the actor isn't there, he's cancelled that morning or the night before, and I can't fill that slot. They're taking a job away from another actor.

EL: Be as comfortable as they can. I know that it's difficult. But hopefully, the casting office will help that. It's hard for me to find a particular pet peeve. I just hope that I can put actors at ease and they can do the best job that they can.

JBi: Being late, being unprepared. Something that really gets me going is when an actor walks in and asks, "What are you looking for?"

I would actually like to give a class teaching directors how to audition. Many directors really don't know how to audition actors. They don't realize that when actors come in and give you a good reading, and it's clear that they're good actors, their readings sometimes just need direction. Few directors will actually do anything in the audition room. Someone like Jerry Zaks really knows what he's doing. When Jerry sees a spark of any talent in anybody, he'll get up on his feet and work with him. I love working with British directors, because they don't know anybody. They have no preconceived notion when someone comes in. In *The Iceman Cometh,* Howard Davis gave everyone twenty minutes of real, genuine work, so he could tell at the end of twenty minutes if they could act or not.

SK: Some actors don't realize that we get into a pacing, and they don't realize that when they come in, they should be prepared for us. They should be ready to go. That means that they should have all their materials prepared: their picture and résumé, the sides they're reading from, and if they're singing for us, the music should be right there, they shouldn't have to start looking for it. I really like when actors' pictures and résumés are stapled together properly. I don't like when actors have their résumé printed on the back of the headshot. Sometimes, we have to fax it to a client, and it's always easier if the résumé is separate and stapled on.

JBe: Actors shouldn't sell themselves. It really gets hard listening to actors who just talk about themselves and all the stuff they've been doing, when their conversation becomes about me, me, me! Talk to me about something more interesting, something in the news perhaps, an art gallery and an artist. Talk to me about a new group, a jazz artist that you just discovered. Be on time.

LD: I think everyone's pet peeve is when actors come in, they've had sufficient time, and they say that they're not prepared. Another pet peeve is getting tapes from actors, and they're not clear; it's a bad copy.

If you had any advice to offer an actor who's thinking of coming to New York, what would it be?

JT: The best thing to do is to come to New York and study. Try to keep yourself working in workshops, in smaller theater groups. Concentrate on the work more than on the process of getting work. Don't use up all your time in getting the perfect pictures and résumés. They really don't mean all that much in the end. Whether you're good is what means anything in the end. If you fight really hard to get an audition, and you don't know what to do once you get there, it's not going to do you any good. Going back to the first things I said, there really aren't that many people who are that special. People in my end of the business are always looking for them. If you're that good, and even if you're working in small venues, people will find and notice you. We're always looking.

AK: In New York, there is so much to see. And I don't mean just theater. Of course, there's great theater, but I mean this city has everything. I believe New York is a truly fascinating place to be if you're an actor. Actors become so many people in all the roles that they play. In New York, you just have to look around, just listen and look. It's a great place to learn about people.

Know who you want to study with. Also, do your homework before you come.

EL: One thing I must say is that I don't think that New York and Los Angeles are the be-all and end-all. I think that there are different communities that have strong acting and theater. I think that Chicago, San Francisco, Seattle, and Boston are great places to go to work. I just don't think that actors need to feel that they have to be in New York, or that they have to be in Los Angeles.

I really feel that actors must make peace with the audition process. I know that it's really difficult. They should know that their goal is to go on as many job interviews in a day as possible, whereas the rest of us would want to go on as few as possible in our lives.

JBi: Get some sort of job where you are awake during the day. You must get out there every day and try and be an actor. Find groups that read plays, and offer your services for free. See plays. You can see any Off-Broadway play by volunteering to be an usher. See plays and actors. Develop an objective opinion about why you think an actor is good. Understand what is going on in the business. Try and identify who people are, so you're not just a fish swimming upstream.

SK: Research theater companies. If you're interested in film, check out the film publications. Create opportunities for yourself before you get here, so you have opportunities once you arrive. Don't come here blindly. Become familiar with the periodicals that tell you in advance what's coming up. Make sure you have a place to live.

JBe: Do your work wherever you are. Wherever you are in the country, do good work. Learn something about the business end of acting. Learn to audition. Some actors need to develop a better acting technique before they come to New York to find work.

LD: (laughing) Stay home. You have to try to continue in your craft. Always be aware that a career involves a lot of luck and timing. Even if an actor is not so great, but he keeps trying, with a little luck and timing, things can happen. I've seen actors who are not so great get nice recurring roles on TV series. Once again, it's luck and timing.

PART IV

The Work Scene

BEYOND THE GREAT WHITE WAY

Many actors come to New York because they dream of performing on Broadway. But even those lucky few who get that opportunity will not necessarily do all, or even their most satisfying, stage work on Broadway.

Let's face it, New York is primarily the town for actors who want to perform on stage. People who are most interested in film may gravitate towards Hollywood, but those who crave live performance favor New York. And what a plethora of opportunities there are! There are literally hundreds of Off- and Off-Off-Broadway theaters. What follows is just a small sampling some of those theaters.

Off-Broadway Theater Companies
New York Shakespeare Festival
Under Joseph Papp's leadership, a group of actors got together to perform scenes from Shakespeare's plays for the public, free of charge. The group was originally based in the Emmanuel Church on the Lower East Side. In 1957, Mr. Papp began presenting Shakespeare in Central Park using a mobile theater. In 1962, this group was named the New York Shakespeare Festival. The Delacorte Theater in Central Park was erected as the festival's permanent summer home, with productions in June, July, and August. That institution of free Shakespeare in Central Park continues today and is one of New York's favorite summertime pleasures.

In 1967, the former Astor Library on Lafayette Street became the permanent home of the Festival. It was called the Public Theater. The first production was the world premiere of the musical, *Hair*. Some other noteworthy New York Shakespeare Festival productions include: *Take Me Out, No Place to Be Somebody, The Basic Training of Pavlo Hummel, That Championship Season, Short Eyes, A Chorus Line, For Colored Girls . . . , Threepenny Opera, The Pirates of Penzance, The Normal Heart, The Mystery of Edwin Drood, and Caroline, or Change.* Following Joseph Papp's death in 1991, the Astor Library building was rededicated as the Joseph Papp Public Theater.

This theater nurtures new and exciting voices in the theater, as well as focusing on classical productions. The Public Theater is well known for its policy of nontraditional casting for all its productions. The theater is always open to meeting, auditioning, and working with new talent.

Contact:
Casting
The Public Theater
425 Lafayette Street
New York, NY10003

Ensemble Studio Theatre Company (EST)

The Ensemble Studio Theatre was created in 1972 with two primary goals: to nurture individual theater artists and to develop new American plays.

Under the late artistic director Curt Dempster's guidance, the theater's membership grew from twenty theater artists to more than 450. Among them are winners of the Pulitzer Prize, Oscar, Tony, Emmy, and Obie. A lifelong artistic home is provided for member playwrights, directors, actors, designers, technical personnel, and administrators.

Each year, EST produces more than three hundred projects, including readings, staged readings, and fully produced mainstage full-lengths. The company has developed more than three thousand full-length plays, which have been produced at more than 360 theaters across the United States.

For those interested in becoming part of this company, there is an internship program at the theater.

Contact:
Ensemble Studio Theatre
549 West 52nd Street
New York, NY 10019

Playwrights Horizons

Playwrights Horizons was founded in 1971 at the Clark Center YMCA by Robert Moss. From its very beginning, this theater was known as a writers' theater. Playwrights Horizons is dedicated to the creation and production of new American plays and musicals. Under Mr. Moss's direction, the group eventually moved to Theater Row on West 42nd Street.

In its thirty-seven years, Playwrights has presented the works of over three hundred playwrights. Some of the theater's award-winning productions include: Lobby Hero, Sister Mary Ignatius Explains It All for You, Marvin's Room, The Heidi Chronicles, Driving Miss Daisy, Falsettos, Sunday in the Park with George, Floyd Collins, and the musical version of James Joyce's The Dead.

Contact:
James Calleri, Casting Director or
Alaine Alldaffer, Casting Associate
Playwrights Horizons
630 9th Avenue, Suite 708
New York, NY, 10036

Manhattan Theatre Club

Manhattan Theatre Club (MTC) produces plays by established and new voices in the theater. The theater was founded in 1970 and presently has a subscriber base of more than twenty thousand. Under the leadership of artistic director Lynne Meadow and executive producer Barry Grove, Manhattan Theatre Club has grown in three decades from a prolific Off-Off-Broadway showcase into one of the country's most acclaimed theater organizations.

MTC has two performance spaces within the City Center complex on West 55th Street. Stage 1 has 299 seats, and Stage 2 has 150 seats. Many of the company's plays have moved to Off-Broadway and Broadway for extended runs.

Some of the award-winning plays produced by MTC include *Ruined* (Pulitzer Prize); *The Rabbit Hole* (Pulitzer Prize); *Proof; The Tale of the Allergist's Wife; Love! Valor! Compassion!; Lips Together, Teeth Apart; A Small Family Business; Sight Unseen; Collected Stories; Putting It Together; Sylvia; Ain't Misbehavin'; Crimes of the Heart; The Piano Lesson;* and *Seven Guitars.*

Manhattan Theatre Club's productions and performers have won many Tony Awards, three Pulitzer Prizes, and more than forty Obies, as well as Drama Desk, Drama Critics Circle, Outer Critics Circle and Theatre World Awards. MTC has won the Lucille Lortel Award for Outstanding Achievement, a Drama Desk for Outstanding Excellence, and a Theatre World Award for Outstanding Achievement.

Actors such as Sarah Jessica Parker, Linda Lavin, Nathan Lane, Christine Baranski, Bernadette Peters, Tony Roberts, Charlayne Woodard, Alison Janney, and James Naughton have made Manhattan Theatre Club their home. The theater has produced new plays by Terrence McNally, August Wilson, A. R. Gurney, Athol Fugard, and Donald Margulies, to name a few.

Contact:
Administrative Offices
Casting Department
Manhattan Theatre Club
311 West 43rd Street, 8th Floor
New York, NY 10036
Phone: (212) 399-3000

Atlantic Theater Company

The Atlantic Theater Company was founded by the playwright David Mamet and the actor William H. Macy when they both taught an intensive workshop at New York University. In 1985, after completing their studies with Mamet and Macy, their class of twenty actors began producing plays. The group was inspired by Anton Checkhov's exhortation to the Moscow Art Theater to "create the theater that exists in your heart."

The Atlantic Theater Company has presented over eighty plays in New York, Chicago, and Vermont. Some of the most noteworthy productions include: *Spring Awakening*, (eight Tony Awards, eleven nominations) *The Beauty Queen of Leenane* (four Tony Awards, six Tony nominations), *Mojo, Edmond* (by David Mamet), *Dangerous Corner* (by J. B. Priestley, adapted and directed by David Mamet), *Boys' Life, The Lights* (presented at Lincoln Center Theater, winner of two Obie Awards and ten Drama Desk Award nominations), *Distant Fires* (winner of an Obie Award and a Drama Desk Award nomination), *The Joy of Going Somewhere Definite, Shaker Heights, Minutes from the Blue Route, Trafficking in Broken Hearts,* and *Missing Persons* (by Craig Lucas).

In 1991, the company moved to its present theater. Shows produced by the Atlantic Theater Company have garnered two Lucille Lortel Awards, five Obie Awards, an Outer Critics Circle Award, seven Outer Critics Circle Award nominations, fourteen Drama Desk Award nominations, and four Tony Awards.

Theater Location:
The Atlantic Theater Company
336 West 20th Street
New York, NY 10011
(212) 645-8015

Contact:
Administrative Offices
The Atlantic Theater Company
453 West 16th Street
New York, NY 10011
(212) 691-5919

The Wooster Group

The Wooster Group is a company of artists who develop and produce innovative theater and media pieces. Started in the 1970s, the group is well known for its experimental use of sound, film, and video in productions.

The Wooster Group's members include Jim Clayburgh, Willem Dafoe, the late Spalding Gray, Elizabeth LeCompte, Peyton Smith, and Kate Valk. It is under the direction of Ms. LeCompte that the group creates and performs all of its theater pieces at their home, the Performing Garage. The company has toured widely in the United States and Europe, as well as to Asia, Australia, Canada, and South America.

The Wooster Group has won National Endowment for the Arts, State Arts Council, and the City Department of Cultural Affairs grants, and a Village Voice Obie, recognizing fifteen years of sustained excellence. Director Elizabeth LeCompte received an NEA Distinguished Artists Fellowship for Lifetime Achievement in American Theater.

The Performing Garage accepts volunteer interns on an ongoing basis throughout the year. Interns do filing, typing, and help with promotional mailings, etc. Some interns who are technically skilled assist the technical director in the theater. Interns sometimes get to observe Wooster Group rehearsals and have access to the extensive video archive of the Performing Garage.

The internship program allows the interns to become familiar with the administration and creative process of the Wooster Group. Interns are encouraged to make time to observe rehearsals outside of their scheduled time at the Garage. Becoming an intern is an excellent way to develop an ongoing relationship with the company.

Contact:
The Wooster Group
Internship Coordinator
Post Office Box 654
New York, NY 10013
(212) 966-9796
Fax: (212) 226-6576

The Pearl Theatre Company

The Pearl Theatre Company's mission is to set an American standard for the production of classical theater. They primarily look for actors with "the technical abilities and the artistic inclination to create a character rather than to recreate a type, and to approach each play on the playwright's terms, so that style is a vehicle, rather than a substitute for honesty," according to their website.

The company maintains a core company of fourteen actors, ranging from twenty-seven to eighty-two years of age, who work together season after season, continuing to expand and deepen their craft. Only by being "in shape" can an actor step from Coward's comedy to Shakespearean tragedy to French plays performed in rotating repertory.

The Pearl is a resident Equity company. Non-Equity actors are used for all understudy assignments. Understudies are given Equity points for the weeks they work and a small stipend. They also work with an Equity stage manager and have access to the experience and knowledge of the company members. The Pearl holds one session of non-Equity auditions each spring to see all of the actors who have sent in their headshots and résumés throughout the year.

To be considered for an audition, you *must* send in your picture and résumé prior to the actual auditions. They prefer no calls.

Contact:

The Pearl Theatre Company
307 West 38th Street #1805
New York, NY 10018
(212) 598-9802

Interviews with Actors Who Started Their Own Theater Companies

In this chapter I included two theater companies that I interviewed in the first edition and two new ones for this edition. You'll notice that some of the interview questions for this edition vary slightly from the ones in the first edition.

Robert LuPone (RL) founded MCC Theater with co-artistic director Bernard Telsey in 1986, with a simple mission: to present new theatrical voices to New York audiences. MCC was founded in 1986 as Manhattan Class Company, then a collective of young actors, writers, and directors eager to take a leadership role in their own artistic development. Initial peer-based "classes" led to showcases and eventually to the kinds of full-scale productions that have made MCC Theater one of New York's leading Off-Broadway theater companies. Past and present members of their playwright coalition include Stephen Belber, Adam Bock, Stephen Adly Guirgis, and Lucy Thurber.

Seth Barrish (SB) is the co-artistic director of the Barrow Group, a company of actors, directors, playwrights, and designers. The company was founded in 1986. Originally founded and operated out of a railroad flat on Barrow Street, TBG has grown into a midsize theater organization providing inspiration and resources to the entire arts community of New York City. With the TBG Arts Center and the Barrow Group School, they serve as an artistic home for some of New York's finest actors, directors, playwrights, filmmakers, designers, and visual artists.

TBG received a 2005 Drama Desk Nomination for Best Play for Tony Award–winning David Edgar's *Pentecost*. TBG developed Mike Birbiglia's *Sleepwalk with Me* (winner of the 2009 Nightlife Award for Outstanding Comedian in a Major Engagement and Lucille Lortel Award Nominee for Best Solo Show) and Martin Moran's *The Tricky Part* in 2004 (Drama Desk nominations for Best Play and Best Solo Show and an OBIE Award). In 1995, The Barrow Group received a Drama Desk Award for Off-Off-Broadway Excellence.

Whose idea was it to start this company? What were the reasons behind starting a new theater company? What were your goals?

RL: I was teaching acting to eight students and we all got bored after two years. We liked each other and wanted to stay together, so the next logical step was to form a theater company. The tradition was the Shakespearean actor-manager idea where we'd read plays every week together and then try to formulate a theater. I was trying to find some theater roots for myself after working in this town for a number of years. I, personally, was in some ways confused. I followed along with Bernie's (Telsey) idea of starting a theater company, which was something he'd always wanted to do. Bernie, aside from being a theater major at NYU, was also a theater administration major. From 1983 to 1986, we tried a for-profit company. We were going to work on new plays and then sell them at backers' auditions to producers. Then we'd go back to the studio and work on new plays. We did eventually get options for two Broadway plays. But the money wasn't enough to keep us afloat. Bernie convinced us that the best way to go on was to go nonprofit. For a while we were at the Nat Horne Theater on Theater Row doing our one-acts, and then eventually we got our own space.

SB: It was my and Nate Harvery's idea. It was a combination of factors. We were a group of actors looking for a place to be able to play and work in a way that was fun for us. We were young, just going out in the real world to work in various places. A lot of times it was frustrating for different reasons. We had complaints about the directors we'd work with, the plays, whatever. We had become fascinated with an acting style that was particularly "documentary-esque," ultra real. We didn't feel that we were expert at it, but it did interest us. Our main goal in acting was that the audience lose sight of the fact that they were watching an actor and feel like they were in a room with a real person. We didn't plan on producing originally, it just worked out that way.

What problems did you face originally? How did you eventually overcome them (if you did)?

RL: Clarity, about what an artistic mission is, funding, overcoming ignorance—both artistically and financially—and working out the dynamic of relationships. An organization has many growth processes. You start off with enthusiasm and innocence, and then you work toward survival, and then as you become more professional, volunteers fall by the wayside so you have to hire a staff. It's all an evolution. Bottom line: long hours, grit, and determination! How do you overcome the problems? With passion and belief in the theater. Always keeping in mind the importance and nobility of it.

SB: Raising money was the first major hurdle we came to. We were artists and we had to learn about the business side of the business. We hooked up with people who were adept at doing this type of work. A lot of it we just learned while doing, making horrible mistakes along the way, but always learning and getting better at it.

What was your first public production? How did it go? What lessons did you learn from doing that production?

RL: It was the *Class One-Acts*, in 1986. We really didn't know what we were doing back then. One thing we learned was the amount of work it takes to put on a production. Also, the fragility of corralling all the creative talents along with your own ignorance toward a united vision.

SB: The first thing we did was a one-night event at the Perry Street Theater. We raised $7,000 that night. We did the public premiere of some of Joe Pintauro's plays. In some ways it went very well; in others, not. We put a ton of attention into the artistic side. We invited prospective board members. The evening was successful in that we got an instant board of directors. We were thrilled that we were able to pull it off. We learned about the process of working with each other and designers in a production mode. The main thing we learned was that it was possible to do.

What are the advantages of being part of an artist-created theater company? Any disadvantages?

RL: Shorthand and communication are a couple of the advantages. Working with other like minds toward a common vision is very rewarding, very satisfying. Some of the disadvantages are the difficulties you encounter in fundraising, professional management of an office, marketing, getting an audience, advertising. The list goes on.

SB: The advantages are you quickly learn there are no excuses. You get a constant reality litmus test about how you're doing. It's easy to blame the world and not really grow. Also, you develop a working shorthand with people so that certain kinds of things can happen quickly. There's a possibility for a kind of aesthetic that everybody shares. The disadvantages are you attach yourself to a family that's bound to be dysfunctional. As people grow, their agendas change, and you sometimes have to compromise or separate.

What advice do you have for other actors wanting to start their own company?

RL: If you want to start a theater company so you can act, don't do it. If you want to start a theater company so you can say something about the world we live in, that's a good reason. Involving myself with this theater has taught me a lot about interpersonal relationships, and that has impacted on me as an actor. I've had to talk with press people, public relations people, even with fellow employees. By and large it's been immensely rewarding.

SB: Terence McNally's advice to me about creating my own theater company was, "Be patient. It's a long haul." Someone really has to be in charge. It makes things much easier. Originally, we started off as a democracy, but we learned that a group functions best with a leader.

John Gould Rubin (JGR): Actor, director, co-artistic director/executive director, board member of the LAByrinth Theater Company

LAByrinth Theater Company is a multicultural collective that produces new plays reflecting the many voices in the New York City community. They are fully committed to maintaining an ensemble that combines emerging artists with seasoned professionals. It is their goal, as an ensemble, to take on all the roles involved in the collaborative process of creating new theater. Through these works, their members are given the opportunity to write, act, direct, design and produce. They support multidisciplinary growth as well as discovery and exploration. They give artists from diverse backgrounds the opportunity to work.

LAByrinth Theater Company was founded in 1992 when thirteen actors joined forces to form a place to work. The idea was to create a home where the group, for three hours each week, could engage in a variety of theatrical exercises designed to push each others' limits and bind together into a tightly knit, uninhibited and impassioned ensemble—one in which each member is given the opportunity and support not only to act, but to write, direct, produce, sweep, paint, hang lights, etc.

The fact that the company now consists of more than a hundred members from a wide array of cultural perspectives did not occur through some political design. It grew out of a shared artistic sensibility and a desire to create personal work that reflects the community in which the company lives: New York City.

Whose idea was it to start this company? What were the reasons behind starting a new theater company? What were your goals?

JGR: LAByrinth started in response to some press related to *Death and the Maiden* on Broadway in 1992. There was a protest through AEA about the fact that a show about Latin America had no Latin Americans in it, and in response to this, someone associated with the production stated that they had sought Latin American actors but couldn't find any. In response, a group of actors including Gary Perez, David Deblinger, Paul Calderon, and John Ortiz founded LAByrinth so that next time someone was looking for a Latin American actor, they would know where to look. LAB is actually an acronym for Latin Actors' Base.

What problems did you face originally? How did you eventually overcome them (if you did)?

JGR: How to produce, how to fund production, how to expand the company. They did auditions, brought in friends, began exercises at space loaned by INTAR. They held parties for slim entrance fees and produced shows for a few hundreds of dollars. They learned how to do all the other functions of theater, which indeed became part of the ethos of LAByrinth; that everyone should pursue various disciplines of the Theater.

What was your first public production? How did it go? What lessons did you learn from doing that production?

JGR: It was *Nobody's Home*, 1992, written and performed by David Deblinger, directed by John Ortiz, produced by Gary Perez: a kaleidoscope view of one boy's journey into manhood from Queens to Manhattan on the F train.

What are the advantages of being part of an artist-created theater company? Any disadvantages?

JGR: The advantages are that you get to participate in a more democratic ensemble and collaborate in the development of your aesthetic and goals. The disadvantage is that that very democracy is messy and means you have more issues to address than a led company has.

What advice do you have for other actors wanting to start their own company?

JGR: Do it. We are dedicated to the creation of companies by groups who want to determine the work they do. It is part of our master classes, and part of what we believe. The collaborative act of creating a theater company whose work is determined collaboratively by the group is, to us, the height of theater production.

David Pincus (DP), Managing Director of the WorkShop Theater Company, New York City

Briefly, how and why did your theater company get started?

DP: The WorkShop is dedicated to honing the creative skills of emerging playwrights and to assist them in reaching their next level of development. We have more than forty member playwrights who are actively working with us in the development of their individual projects. One NEA panelist recently noted that, although there is no lack of theatrical companies in New York City that dedicate time and resources to develop new works, the WorkShop Theater Company is unique in its commitment in offering early playwrights so much support, stating, "No other institution [in NYC] allows this much time to mainly unknown playwrights."

The company continually develops new theatrical works by supporting a structured creative process that takes scripts from their initial inspiration, through various sit-down and three-day staged readings to early runs of promising work. For the scripts the WorkShop believes demand critical reception and a wider audience, four-week showcase productions with significant design and technical support from the company are given.

In 1994, actor-teacher Sam Schacht started a collective of theater artists to meet informally and read new plays. Eventually, the group secured a fifth-floor walk-up on West 42nd Street. We held regular meetings and began to stage readings and modest productions of projects created by company artists and established writers.

In 1997, our board of directors was created (advised by Jerry Stiller, Anne Meara, Israel Horovitz and Joy Behar, to name a few) and the 42nd Street WorkShop, Inc. received nonprofit status. The WorkShop began creating the process through which we develop projects. We set aside Monday and Tuesday evenings for in-house readings to give writers feedback on new scripts. Company writers such as Murray Schisgal and Allan Knee created new work with working actors and directors from stage and film. We established a Sunday reading series, with a talk-back, to include our audience in the creative process. Outreach projects like "ACT-SO Evening of Theater," in affiliation with the NAACP, became a regular feature of our calendar.

By 2002, the company had so grown in size and scope that, as the redevelopment of Theater Row loomed, we needed a new home. Since we moved from 42nd Street, we changed our name. WorkShop Theater Company pioneered the new Off-Off-Broadway scene in the Garment District. We built our current home (in what is now known as "The Theater Building") on 36th Street. Our company artists constructed two brand new, air-conditioned, handicapped-accessible spaces: the Jewel Box, an intimate thirty-seat modular theater for developing new work, and the sixty-five-seat Main Stage.

When, why and how did you first get involved with the company?
DP: I am the managing director, and have been so since December 2006. Before that I served the WorkShop as a producing director from 2002 to 2006. I was first asked to join the company as an actor, after I successfully auditioned for a one-act that the WorkShop produced in 1999.

What type of plays do you produce? Is there a specific style?
DP: For the most part, we develop and produce original plays written by our company artists that go through our development process. Although there is no one particular writing style, the company is known for our interest in a strong narrative (not necessarily linear); and we do appreciate a well-constructed play.

Where do you find the actors for your productions?

DP: Because of our reputation as a theater company that supports and nurtures the creative process, the WorkShop Theater Company has an unusually high number of emerging artists who seek membership in our company. The WorkShop accepts unsolicited inquiries. This selection process is outlined on our Web site, *www.workshoptheater. org*. Current membership includes artists who have found us through word-of-mouth, our Web site or by participating in other aspects of our programming either as an actor, director, or audience member. In addition, the artistic staff regularly attends theatrical work created by other New York City companies, as we are committed to fostering creative relationships with emerging artists whose artistic potential we value. As a result, actors are often invited into the WorkShop after their work has been seen elsewhere.

What is the best way for an actor to contact your theater company?

DP: The best way for an actor to become associated with the WorkShop is to become familiar with the work we do by attending productions or availing himself of our free, open-to-the-public script development process, where the audience is regularly made a part of the dialogue between the playwright and the artistic staff. We want actors who want to be a part of our company for very specific reasons. Not just a place to hang their hat for a while, but a place they want to call their creative home.

A Sampling of Off-Off-Broadway Theater Companies

What follows is a very small sampling of the some of the new (and refurbished), up-and-coming Off-Off-Broadway theater companies that are open to meeting actors seeking acting work in New York. I selected these companies primarily because I personally have had some professional contact with them and know their work to be of high quality. Basic information about the companies is followed by interviews with some company members.

The Vital Theatre Company

Founded in March 1999 by Stephen Sunderlin, Michael Schloegl, Laura M. Stevens, and Scott C. Embler, the Vital Theatre Company exists to provide a permanent home where the creative impulses of theater artists can be nurtured and explored. Vital provides a thorough developmental process for emerging artists and builds a sense of community by offering affordable, educational entertainment for young audiences. The goals are really very simple: tell a great story, pay the bills, and provide a community. For this company, the answer lies in the playwrights' text.

After many regional and big-city gigs with little to no pay, Sunderlin, Schloegel, Stevens, and Embler realized that these experiences left them cold. Their answer was to start their own company where they could do honest theater work that would feed their souls (if not their pockets). They found a space on 42nd Street. This intimate theater allowed the group to do riskier theater pieces and establish a strong connection between the actors and their audiences.

Contact:
Vital Theatre Company
The McGinn/Cazale Theatre
2162 Broadway, 4th Floor
New York, NY 10024
(212)579-0528

Abingdon Theatre Company

In January of 1993, a group of professional theater artists eager for regular collaboration and greater control over their creative lives began to gather in a brownstone near New York City's Abingdon Square Park for biweekly readings of new plays. After a few months of informal meetings, enthusiasm grew, and the artists pooled their theatrical experience to establish an open-door home, where they could collaborate, invite their colleagues to join them, and develop new plays by American playwrights. Since then, Abingdon Theatre Company's (ATC) actors, directors, designers, producers, and dramaturgs have collaborated with nearly two hundred playwrights on developing original plays.

From the outset, ATC has espoused four values: a commitment to creating a community for professional theater artists, an interest in varied genres of theater, a dedication to quality in the performances and technical aspects of production, and a fiscally responsible approach to producing.

Under the advisement of artistic director Jan Buttram, ATC initiated a developmental process that has evolved into a comprehensive program. At every stage, ATC and its membership devote their collective passion and resources to helping emerging and established American playwrights realize the full potential of their plays.

ATC was founded on common goals by five artists, all of whom are still integral to the company. The group expanded over the next several years to a core group of twenty members, and today is supplemented by artistic associates (artists who work on a project-by-project basis with ATC).

ATC is proud to have extended three productions for Off-Broadway runs: *Dance with Me, Private Battles,* and *Zona (The Ghost of Greenbrier).* Several of ATC's other plays have been published, received readings at other New York theaters, and are presently under consideration by regional theaters for their 2002 seasons.

Contact:
Abingdon Theatre Company
312 West 36th Street,Sixth FloorNew York, NY 10018
(212)868-2055
E-mail: ATCNYC@aol.com
Web site: www.abingdon-nyc.org

I interviewed Stephen Sunderlin and Jan Buttram for information that will be of particular interest to actors regarding their theater companies.

Stephen Sunderlin (SS), The Vital Theatre Company
Jan Buttram (JB), Abingdon Theatre Company

Briefly, how and why did your theater company get started? What was (is) your involvement with the company?

SS: After a number of years freelance producing and directing theater projects, my own and for other companies, I became tired of the itinerant existence and had a strong desire to find an artistic home base from which to continue my work and to help facilitate the work of other theater artists. In 1998, I become aware of the availability of the space in which we are currently located. I approached my long-time collaborator, Michael Shloegl, a talented writer, director, and performer, and two other partners, and after six months of planning, we formed Vital Theatre Company. We moved March 1 of 1999 and opened our first show on March 15, and we have been off and running ever since.

JB: As the company's literature says, Abingdon Square Park started as biweekly readings of new plays. After a few months of informal meetings, the artists pooled their theatrical experience to establish Abingdon Square Theater Company. I am a founding member and (along with Pamela Paul) artistic director.

What type of plays do you produce? Is there a specific style?

SS: We primarily produce new work of established and emerging playwrights of any style. We look for plays that tell a compelling, *dramatic* story (you'd be surprised to see how many "playwrights" forget to include this element) with interesting characters. We have an in-house playwright's workshop, where we develop both short and full-length scripts of our member playwrights. We also have a very active submission process headed up by our literary manager. On occasion, we will present previously produced or published plays not yet presented in New York City.

JB: The company does not gravitate to any specific style of theater. That said, we look for works that both appeal to a broad audience and thematically celebrate the human experience. Full-lengths are preferable, requiring no more than nine actors.

Where do you find the actors for your productions?

SS: We cast primarily through Breakdown Services. However, we do post casting notices in *Back Stage.*

JB: Equity Principal Auditions, professional recommendation, agent submissions through Breakdown Services by individual project. We've worked with casting directors, most frequently, Cindy Rush, CSA.

What is the best way for an actor to contact your theater company?

SS: Send a picture and résumé with a Post-it note on the front saying they'd like an opportunity to audition for us. Nicely typed cover letters are great, but they usually get tossed after a quick reading. We are not evaluating your writing skills. I want to get to your picture, your credits, and your training. Several times throughout the year, will have open calls to meet new actors for upcoming projects.

JB: Abingdon has an "open door" policy at our regular in-house readings. Call (212) 736-6604 for the upcoming schedules, or check out our Web site at *www.abingdon-nyc.org.* Sending pictures and résumés is probably not the best use of your money.

Listings of Off-Off-Broadway Theaters

As I mentioned previously, there are hundreds of Off- and Off-Off-Broadway theater companies. What follows is a listing of some of the better-known theater companies in New York City. Some of the companies listed here could be defined as "artists' collectives," wherein most of the artistic work is attended to by core members; some could more properly be called "producing entities"; some are a hybrid form. Obviously, casting policies, contracts, performance venues, etc., vary greatly, so it will be up to you to check out the organizations. I've listed whatever information (address, e-mail, etc.) the company provided.

Classic Stage Company
136 East 13th Street
New York, NY 10003
E-mail: info@classicstage.org

Dixon Place
309 East 26th Street
New York, NY 10010
(212) 532-1546
Fax: (212) 532-1094
Web site: www.dixonplace.
   org

HERE
145 6th Avenue
New York, NY 10013
(212) 647-0202
E-mail: info@here.org
Web site: www.here.org

Irish Repertory Theater
New York, NY 10011
(212) 255-0270
Fax: (212) 255-0281
E-mail: irishrep@aol.com

LAByrinth Theater Company
16 West 32nd Street
New York, NY 10001
(212) 513-1123
Web site: www.labyrintheater.
com

LaMaMa Experimental Theatre
Club
74A East 4th Street
New York, NY 10003
(212) 475-7710
Web site: www.lamama.org

Mint Theater Company
311 West 43rd Street, 5th
Floor
New York, NY 10036
(212) 315-9434
Web site: www.minttheater.
org

New Georges
109 West 27th Street
New York, NY 10001
(646) 336-8077
E-mail: newgeorges@aol.
com

New Group Theater
154 Christopher Street,
#2A-A
New York, NY 10014
(212) 691-6730
Fax: (212) 691-6798
E-mail:newgroup1@
earthlink.net

Pan Asian Repertory Theatre
47 Great Jones Street
New York, NY 10012
Web site: www.
panasianrep.org

Rattlestick Theater
Company
224 Waverly Place
New York, NY 10014
(212) 627-2556
E-mail: info@rattlestick.org
Web site: www.rattlestick.
org

Repertorio Español
138 East 27th Street
New York, NY 10016
(212) 889-2850

Second Stage
307 West 43rd Street
New York, NY 10036
(212) 787-8302
Fax: (212) 397-7066

Signature Theatre Company
534 West 42nd Street
New York, NY 10036
(212) 967-1913
Fax: (212) 967-2957
Web site: www.signature-
theatre.org

Theatre for the New City
155 1st Avenue
New York, NY 10003
(212) 254-1109
Fax: (212) 979-6570
Web site: www. theaterforth-
enewcity.org

Vineyard Theatre
108 East 15th Street
New York, NY 10003
(212) 353-3366
Fax: (212) 353-3803
E-mail: Boxoffice@Vine-
yardTheatre.org

Periodicals Actors Should Be Familiar With

Back Stage is the definitive actor resource and destination for job opportunities, industry news and career advice. Since it's inception in 1960, *Back Stage* has been the bible for the acting community.

Back Stage provides hundreds of casting notices from across the nation, plus deep coverage of film, TV, commercial and theater. *BackStage.com* enhances the experience by providing more than a thousand casting notices, updated daily, and provides all of the tools an actor needs to succeed, including an online portfolio of headshots, résumés and demo reels. In addition, *BackStage.com* subscribers have access to the Call Sheet online database of casting agents and directors, where users can print out mailing labels of top industry contacts. (Online at *www.backstage.com*)

Show Business is a weekly trade paper for New York City's performing arts industry, providing up-to-date audition and casting notices as well as comprehensive trade resources to help guide actors, singers and dancers toward success in their careers. Additionally, *Show Business* provides the latest performing arts-related news and information along with in-depth reviews of theatrical performances from Broadway to Off-Off-Broadway.

Summer Theater Guide: This periodical is published once a year and lists employment for union as well as nonunion theaters. It can be purchased at *Amazon.com* as well as the Drama Book Store.

American Theater Magazine: This magazine, which comes out ten times a year, offers insightful interviews with directors, actors, and regional theater artistic directors, as well as a new play published every other issue. Their theater articles are informative and helpful, especially to the actor interested in working in regional theater.

Variety: This newspaper offers entertainment industry news, movie and theater reviews, as well as entertainment industry events. (On the web *www.variety.com*)

VOICE-OVER WORK

A voice-over is the audio portion of a radio or television commercial or promo. The term "voice-over" originally came into use when actors had to put their "voice over a motion picture." The job of the voice-over actor is quite simply to sell a product. What the voice-over actor is doing is creating a visual image with their voice.

According to David Zema, a voice-over specialist, "The voice-over performer must have the ability to read copy in a natural way, so as to make it sound as if it is being spoken spontaneously in a believable, sincere, and trusting manner by someone who is highly involved personally, understands the message, and can communicate it to a specific listener for a specific reason or reasons."

Voice "types" cast in voice-overs include the straight (or spokesman), the animation character, and the commercial character. Venues include educational, religious, and industrial areas (informationals); documentary narration; slide shows; telephone recording systems; talking books; and promos.

The voice-over actor who does television commercials wants to entertain the listener, to make sure that, through his voice, the listener will somehow remember the product that he is representing. The secret to this kind of work is to make it sound "as natural as possible." Certain types of voices are better suited to particular products. There are some actors who specialize in just animation, others who specialize in television commercials. This, of course, does not mean that you can't, or shouldn't, strive to find work in both fields.

Animation work (voices for cartoons) requires voices that are extremely colorful and uninhibited. Actors enjoy this kind of work because it calls for voices that are really out there, off the wall.

There's the commercial demo, the commercial character demo, CDs, narration in films, medical-technical and industrial demos, which include infomercials and training films, and cartoon demos.

Promo voice work can be very lucrative, as the spots are constantly changing. Promo casting directors are generally looking for actors with a very straight announcer's voice.

Another area in which voice-over artists can find work is the field of industrials (or industrial films). It's not unusual for the voice-over actor doing industrials to have up to twenty pages of very technical copy. Unlike television commercials, where you can have many takes to get it right, industrial producers try to get it "in the can" in relatively few. The voice-over actor must learn to totally act with his voice and his voice alone.

Nine Tips for Voice-Over Success

by David Zema

- On a daily basis, you should listen to professional voices and listen for their performance styles and qualities. Record these voices and try to emulate each style.
- Read aloud daily. Books, magazines, newspapers, and even ketchup bottles can be helpful.
- Work on a good tape recorder with a separate microphone.
- Find your own strengths, the copy styles and products your voice is most suited for.
- Project your entire personality into your voice.
- Work on your resonance and diction daily.
- After developing your strengths, work on opening your vocal and performing style range so that you will be more versatile.
- Work with a supportive, positive coach on a regular basis.
- Wait until you have mastered your skills and feel confident about what you have to do before making up a demo. Do not send a homemade demo to the top talent agencies.

Everything You Need to Know to Make Up a Good Voice-Over Tape

According to most of the voice-over agents that I spoke to, almost 90 percent of all voice-over tapes that they receive end up in the garbage. Why? "Because most of them are not very good, don't sound like they've been professionally made."

Every serious voice-over actor must have a demo tape. The demo tape is generally an audiocassette tape that includes short selections from the actor's previous work.

- If you do character work, make sure that each character is as brief as possible. Characters should only exist on the tape for as long as it takes to establish who they are, then on to the next one.
- Generally, you should use copy that was used for a real product rather than original material. But try not to use copy that has been used too often.
- Start the demo tape out in your own natural voice.

- Try to grab them in the first ten to twenty seconds of the tape.
- If you're including commercials that you've actually done, make sure that they don't indicate (in their content) that they were done a long time ago.
- Only include your best work on the tape. If you can only do two or three voices, well then, that's all you should include.
- If you can, try to vary the copy you select with things like pitch, pacing, and hard and soft sells.
- After you've selected the right copy for your demo and have decided in which order you want it to play, you'll need to find the best music and sound effects that will complement the copy. Start with music that you have at home, then ask around—sound studios, other actors, etc.
- Don't depend on loose pages of copy to make up your demo. If at all possible your copy should be bound. It's very helpful in the studio if you can give the engineer a copy of the exact script of the work you're planning on doing. All the material should be neatly typed in script format.
- Since this is a very competitive field, it is to your advantage to have an excellent, high-quality, professional demo tape. A good-quality demo tape will run you from about $500 to $1,200. It generally takes between two and three hours in the studio. The smart thing to do is shop around, find the best price. But don't sacrifice quality for saving a few bucks. Ask around for recommendations from actors, casting directors, and talent agents. Some actors gather together a group of performers who want to make up a demo tape and get a group rate from the studio.
- If you've been a voice-over student and don't have any professional selections, you must make sure that the copy that you use on your demo tape is top quality and shows you (your voice) in the best light. Never write your own copy for your demo tape. You can acquire copy from ad agencies.
- Be sure that the studio in which you make your demo reel is a full-service studio, not a studio that does just demo reels. Also, don't make your demo tape in a music studio or in a studio that primarily does industrials.
- Find a studio that does ad agency work. Star Tracks studio in Manhattan has been highly recommended. You must be well prepared before you go into the studio. Make sure that the reads are well rehearsed.
- You want the box that your demo tape is in to look professional. You'll want your name either typewritten or typeset on the box. You should have a one-word title for each selection and the running time of the selection.
- If you've been working with a voice-over teacher and the teacher does not provide these studio services to make a demo tape, you can check out publications, such as the "services" section of *Back Stage* or the yellow pages for the names of professional voice-over studios. Another good source for studios can be found in the *Directory for Commercial Production and*

Postproduction. This publication is published annually by *Shoot Magazine* (1515 Broadway, 12th Floor, New York, NY).

- One thing that you should remember: Your first demo tape is not your *only* demo. As you start to book jobs, you'll be updating your demo tape.

The Best Way to Go About Getting Voice-Over Work

A good place to start is by checking out such trade sources as *The Standard Directory of Advertising Agencies,* and David Zema's *Voice-over Marketing Guide of Advertising Agencies: The Motion Picture, TV, and Theater Directory* (Tarrytown, New York) comes out twice a year. Here is the best procedure for seeking voice-over work.

First, call and find out exactly who the casting directors are at an agency, and ask if it's okay for you to send them your demo reel. Aside from casting directors, you'll also want to target agents, producers, ad agencies, and even recording studios. More than likely, you won't get your demo tapes back. (Some big ad agencies actually do, however, take the time to return them, if you've included a SASE with adequate postage.) Follow up by calling all the places to which you've sent your demo tape. Be brief, professional, and polite on the phone.

One sending of a demo tape and follow-up phone call is not always enough. You may have to do another round. You may have to follow up with a postcard, a note, and two or three follow-up phone calls. Here, perseverance is quite often a necessity.

Another way to get people to become familiar with your voice-over ability is by making rounds. Go in person to the offices of casting directors, agents, and to studios. Just so that you know, studios are also in a position to recommend you for work.

The Voice-Over Résumé

Actors who are serious about voice-over work should specifically have a voice-over résumé. What follows are two examples of voice-over actors' résumés. The first is the résumé of a relative beginner, the second is for the more seasoned voice-over actor.

STEVE BEGINNER

Contact: (212) 877-3876

COMMERCIALS

Delboy's Pizza	(Cable TV)
Rienze Hairstylists	(Cable TV)
Stevie's Men's Clothing	(Cable TV)

EXPERIENCE

News Announcer	(Emerson College Radio)
Weekend Update Announcer	(Emerson College Radio)

TRAINING

David Zema's Voice-Over Success Workshop

Weist-Barron Voice-Over Classes

CHARACTERS

Surfer Dude

Cowboy

Young Boy (8–11 years old)

Corporate Boss

Yuppie

ACCENTS

Southern

Brooklyn

French

British

(Fluent in French and German)

JOHN EXPERIENCE
Contact: Abrams Artists
(646) 486-4600
SAG – AFTRA – AEA

COMMERCIALS AND PROMOTIONAL EXPERIENCE
The following list represents this year's credits:

- Siam Delight	(Local Radio)
- Blockbuster	(National Radio)
- Macy's	(Network Television)
- Alps Pharmacy	(Local Radio)
- Starry's	(Local Radio)

A complete list of this year's credits (as well as previous years' credits) are available upon request.

PRESENT ANIMATION EXPERIENCE

- The Booby-Doops	(Kelmons Cartoons)
- The Scary Night on Ring Mountain	(Fun Time Toons)
- Up the Hill to Barney	(Rory's Animax)

Past series credits are available upon request
Accents Include:

French	Brooklyn
Scottish	Bronx
German	South Dakota
Russian	

The Voice-Over Audition

You get a phone call from your agent that you have an audition for a voice-over. Generally, you won't be given too much information about the spot, perhaps just that it's a pizza spot. Be aware that more than likely, you'll arrive at the audition and barely have any time to read the copy.

Do some vocal warm-ups. Clothing, jewelry, and lots of loose change can make a lot of noise in the sound studio. Speaking of clothing, some actors feel that wearing wardrobe that makes them feel right for a role actually works for them. If you're auditioning for a pizza boy, wearing a suit may affect your mood. Before you leave your home, make sure to get yourself in a positive, relaxed mood. Make sure to bring extra demo tapes and headshots with you to the audition.

When you arrive, sign in, and get your copy. Go off in a corner, and do a few "speed-throughs" to loosen up your jaw and get very familiar with the copy. Mark the copy to assist you in any way you can, so that you'll give a good read. You will have a gut feeling of how the copy should be read; go with it. But also prepare a couple of "alternative ways" to do the read.

When you enter the studio, smile, and say hello to the casting director, making sure to introduce yourself. When you meet with the director, ask any questions you have regarding the copy or pronunciation of words. Place the copy on the stand, and wait for the engineer to adjust your mike. When you're asked for a "level," begin reading the copy just like you plan on reading it at the actual audition.

The engineer will slate your name, or you may be asked to slate your name (see chapter 21, "Why Do Commercials?", for a discussion of slating). Give yourself a moment, then just do the copy as best you can. Give it your best shot up front and then improve on it in each subsequent take. If you make a mistake with a word, it's always okay to start again. If the director gives you an adjustment to make, make sure you're clear what he wants, and make the adjustment as best you can. If you're not given any adjustments, there's no reason that you can't ask to try it another way.

After you've done the audition, thank everyone, and then leave the room in a relaxed, confident way.

Animation

For those actors interested in doing animation, the sky's the limit. Here, you can allow the child in you to really fly. Whereas commercials require actors to pretend to be a such-and-such character or type, animation is the area of almost unbridled creative freedom. The secret to this kind of work is not to work just by the voice alone. The work here begins with your imagination. As in commercials, you must first "see the character" in your mind's eye. It is through your imagination that you'll discover the sound of his voice. Many actors, unfortunately, go about this backwards and try to find the voice first. The more specifically you see the character that you want to create (age, height, personality, etc.), the more your voice will be able to follow.

For More Voice-Over Information

Susan Blu and Molly Ann Mullin's book, *Word of Mouth* (Pomegranate Press., Ltd, November 1992), is a book I highly recommend if you have any interest in voice-over work. I have found the information in this book to be of great value in my research for this book.

For further New York City voice-over instruction:

David Zema's Voice of Success Programs—(212) 643-6449
Weist-Barron—(212) 840-7075
Steve Harris—(212) 517-8616

THE LAST STANDING NEW YORK DAYTIME SERIAL

Work on a daytime serial can be very rewarding for an actor, both financially and professionally. Some of Hollywood's biggest stars started out working on the "soaps." Alec Baldwin, Meg Ryan, Kevin Bacon, Kevin Kline, and Kathleen Turner are just a handful of actors who benefited from the exposure that they received on a daytime serial. Because an entire one-hour show is shot in one day, the challenge for actors (as well as everyone else involved) can be quite intense. Yet, there are actors who not only work on a soap during the day, but also find the time (and energy) to work in the theater at night. In the last few years New York lost the following soaps: *Guiding Light*, *All My Children* (moved to Los Angeles), and *As the World Turns*. The sole survivor is *One Life to Live*. Because this show offers actors quite a few job opportunities on a weekly basis, I've decided to include daytime dramas in this book. Also, there is always a chance that you'll be cast here in New York (they put you on tape) for soaps in Los Angeles. For those that are right for this type of work, the pay and exposure can be quite lucrative.

There are different categories of acting jobs available for actors in daytime.

Extras

These are actors who do background work on the show. They do not have any lines. You'll mainly see extras in restaurant scenes, airport scenes, hospital scenes, funerals, and in busy office scenes. Every week, many actors are hired for extra work on the shows. When there are wedding scenes or courtroom scenes, the number can increase quite a bit. Extras should be seen and not heard, and they should be careful not to cross (unless directed by the stage manager) between the camera and the main actors in the scene.

Under-Fives

These actors literally have five lines or under. They are noncontract roles, such as deliverymen, waitresses, shopkeepers, police officers, and bank tellers. Some under-fives can recur (sometimes for years). What's difficult about under-five work is that you have to create a character with very little dialogue. The secret to these roles is to try not to make too much out of them. Just do what must be done, and be on your way. Don't try to milk the moment in any way.

Day Players

These one-day roles have over five lines and can be recurring. If they do recur, and become important enough in the story line of the show, the actor may be asked to sign a contract.

Contract Roles

As the name implies, these roles are played by the stars of the show and are continuous. For how long? It depends on the contract that the actor has been offered. Generally speaking, most new character contract roles tend to go to younger actors. These can be wonderful opportunities for actors new to the business. The new character roles created for older characters are usually given to actors who have substantial acting experience.

Many of the casting directors that I interviewed for this book recommended that actors who were seriously interested in work on daytime serials should try doing some extra work first. They felt that by doing extra work, the actor could get a sense of how the day was structured on soaps and what the studio was like. There are many actors who don't aspire to speaking parts on the soaps and are quite content to do extra work. Some of these actors are hired with regularity by the casting directors for scenes that recur—hospitals, offices, and police stations, for instance.

Interview with Daytime Serial Casting Director Rob Decina

Rob Decina (RD) is the owner of Rob Decina Casting and a casting director for Cinema 59 Productions and RPG Productions. He is a five-time Emmy-nominated and eight-time Artios Award–nominated casting director. He received those nominations during his ten years of work for the CBS Daytime drama *Guiding Light*. While at *Guiding Light*, he was the New York casting director for the feature films *The Scorpion King* and *National Lampoon's: Van Wilder*, the final season of *Dawson's Creek*, as well as some independent films. Prior to *Guiding Light*, he worked as an associate casting director for Warner Bros. Television in New York, where he worked on many television pilots, including *The West Wing* and *Third Watch*. Rob is also a college professor; he has been an adjunct in communications at Pace University for seven years, where he created and developed four classes, and has taught Auditioning at NYU's Tisch School of Drama. He is a published author. His book, *The Art of Auditioning: Techniques for Television*, is one of the more respected books on the subject.

How did you become involved in casting for daytime? What kind of work were you doing prior to this?

I was the associate casting director at Warner Bros.' television studios in New York. I was working on pilots and some episodic shows that shot in New York. Basically, one of the talent agents that I was friendly with knew that this position had opened up, and I interviewed for it.

What do you feel are the most important things an actor needs to know about work on daytime prior to making themselves known to you?

I think actors need to know that daytime serials are hard work. I think that an actor who thinks that a job on a daytime show would be a great backup plan for a career is misguided. An actor should feel very fortunate to land a job on a daytime television show. I come from a theater background. Before I was in prime time, I was directing. I've been around different venues, and the actors in daytime work harder than anyone else I've known. I'm not comparing the genres, but it's really hard work. Actors should be aware of that going into the audition.

Specifically, what things do you look for on the actor's headshot? The résumé?

I like simplicity. I should get a good grasp of who this person is. I'm not one who believes that you can tell one's personality through their picture. I want to know that if I bring actors in, that that is what they're going to look like.

In terms of the résumé, I look for two things. I look for television credits, and I look for training. However, it really all comes down to, "Are they talented enough"? If someone comes in and they have incredible potential, but have never booked anything, or they're in high school or college, then that's fine. As a casting director, you want to find very trained actors for the show, but in the same sense, you also like to "find" someone that may not have been on another show yet. With inexperienced actors, it can be risky. But sometimes, it's the actor with the least experience who gets the job.

How important is training to you?

I went to graduate school, so I like people who have MFAs, who have training. I look for people who come out of the reputable graduate theater schools, conservatory schools, or even theater schools and colleges that I'm not aware of. There are hundreds of New York acting studios, and they all have different degrees of merit. It's valuable to see that an actor is taking classes, studying his craft.

If an actor doesn't have an agent, aside from photos and résumés, what are the best ways they can make themselves known to you?

Well, it's hard. I think you need to let someone like me know that you're active in New York, that you're in a showcase, a play, a regional play. Even if someone in this office can't come to see you in the play, at least we know you're active. By showing us that you're active, you stay active in our minds. Another way is to get into the mix of a daytime casting office by doing background and under-five work. The majority of the people that I see are through agents. The majority of the people that the associate casting director sees do not have an agent. In a sense, there is a bit of a grooming process that goes on here. We don't work separately. Many times, when I'm working on a contract role, I'll ask her to make a list of people that have been working for her and are perhaps ready to go to the next level.

In terms of an actor doing extra work, many young actors who don't feel that they should do it at least once may be protecting a career that they might not have yet. They're waiting for a phone call that might not come. I'm not saying to make a career out of being a background actor, but in terms of daytime, you're talking about sets that are small, intimate. If you're smart, you'll get on the set and learn, absorb. I don't think you need to do it ten or twelve times (unless you feel comfortable doing it). I think you might do it a handful of times, and perhaps, you will get moved up to under-five or day player. I've never told anyone that they can't audition for me because they were a background actor. Last week, we had a couple of recent Juilliard graduates doing a day of background work.

Is there a difference in acting style between daytime serials and, say, film or stage?
I don't think so. Actors have come in here and said, "Should I do this more 'soapy'?" When we get to the pet peeve question, that's one of them. I don't know what that means. Now, there are certainly technical adjustments that one must make by playing the scene towards a single film camera or playing it for daytime with three cameras. When you're on a Broadway stage, your projection will obviously be different than if you're on an Off-Off-Broadway stage. There are technical adjustments that an actor must make. To me, acting is acting.

Do you look for specific types for daytime? If so, what are they?
No, I don't. If we're talking about a contract role, well, most of those roles are written for great-looking people. Yes, there are roles for very good-looking people, but they're also roles for "real"-looking people. On some shows, the people are so good-looking, you can't believe it. As far as character actors, there are lots of other roles that are being cast here all the time. There are recurring roles, day players, all kinds of opportunities for character actors. There are lawyers and doctors and students and teachers. There are great villain roles that we're always casting.

When an actor comes in to interview with you, what things are you looking for at the interview?
Charm and passion. You want to get a sense of this actor's personality. You want to feel that there is a charming person sitting there. Daytime, as well as

prime time television, wants charming people. The audience wants to watch charming people. You must feel their passion for what they're doing, their work, their craft, their career.

If an actor is offered a screen test for a role on your show, what's the best advice you can offer for preparing for the test?
Be as prepared as possible. Make specific choices as to what you want to do. But the key to the screen test is to be available to the other actor in the scene (and, of course, to the director). A lot of times in a screen test, it's about compatibility.

What do you feel an actor needs to know once he's booked acting work on your show?
When I first started working on *Guiding Light*, one of the directors told me to tell one of the actors I'd just booked that "it's going to be okay, that it'll take about six months to feel comfortable." When you start out here, there is a lot of learning on the job, day by day. Ask a lot of questions, like, "Who is my character?" "How is he (she) related to the people that I'm dealing with?" A lot of the time, it's knowing what you're playing in the moment, and not so much knowing where the character is going later on. For day players, it's very hard sometimes, because they're coming in midstory. Their character may be involved with some crucial plot elements that they're not aware of. You should also rely on the stage managers to guide you through. The stage manager is, in a sense, the mouthpiece of the director once the shooting begins. Also, just be nice, polite to everyone. Make friends, be honest on the set. You must realize that you are part of a very big puzzle. You must find out where you fit into this puzzle without making it hard on other people.

Any actor pet peeves you'd like to mention?
I love actors, and it's hard to make me mad, but it happens. Like I mentioned before, the actor who comes in and asks, "Should I make this a little 'soapier'?" It comes across as insulting to me. It's also a naïve statement to make. It comes across like, "I know how to act, but do you want me to act less, or more, for you?"

When an actor is working in the background and uses that as an opportunity to crash the casting director's office. You shouldn't use your being there as an opportunity to move yourself up the grooming process and the ladder. It's not a smart way to get yourself in good graces. We are very busy in the casting office, and it disrupts our day.

If you had one bit of advice to offer actors, specifically regarding work on daytime, what would it be?
You should watch the show that you're going to be auditioning for or working on. Pick up on the style and tempo of the show. Come in to the job as an

open sponge, and try to learn. If you have a role, make strong choices, choices that you can live with. You're not going to have time to start trying out new things on the show. Be as prepared as you can be.

Ellen Dolan, Daytime Actress

After finishing graduate school at the University of Iowa in 1980, I helped some friends move to New York. They just called one day and asked if I wanted to go with them. I was very lucky in that Shirley Rich was an alumna of U of I and would do workshops with us in Iowa. When I got to New York, she got me meetings with three agencies. When I finally settled here in '81, I had been here in New York for about a month when I got a call from Milwaukee Rep., asking if I would do Katrin in *Mother Courage*. They had seen me in the TCG national finals. They said they would pay me and I would get my Equity card. So I got my first professional job, my Equity membership, and three agencies to freelance with all within months. Then, I got a call that I had been cast as Maureen Reardon on *Guiding Light (GL)*.

Really, it had been my plan all along. I had gone to school in London (Weber Douglas Academy) and while there I met Kathleen Cullen (later to be Amanda on *GL*). I started watching *GL* because I went to school with her the summer before I came to New York. And, as intended with daytime, I got "hooked." I thought, if I ever go to New York, I should probably do a soap—good training—and if I do a soap, it should be *GL* (the only soap I knew) —and if I do *GL* I should be one of the Reardons—they were the Irish family. One year later, I had accomplished all this.

What I first learned was learn your lines! It's rude to not do the job you were hired to do. I still have problems with lines, but I work overtime to get them loaded in. It is a loading process. I tell people—because they always ask how we remember it all—it's like an answering machine: you load it in and dump it. Every day. A play is a whole different beast. With daytime, it's all just load and dump. Load and dump. Hmmm, sounds like another daily process. I've been in daytime for twenty-eight years, *Guiding Light* and now *As the World Turns*. To stay in daytime, you must learn to get up anywhere between 5:00 and 5:30 a.m. every day. This can be hard if you are doing a play at night. You have to be awake and be fast. These days, when money is the only factor, you get little rehearsal and usually just one take, unless you are awful or a diva. Your instincts must be sharp, and you need to make interesting choices. There is no other stage you can be on where you get this chance. Every day, a new day. The only thing I can compare it to is improv. The drawback is that you forget how to retain or explore further than your first choice. Never forget, it is just one stage of many you will be hired for. Don't forget how to act just because it's fast and fun.

Daytime won't be here for much longer, so do it while you can. If you're in New York, I hope you like *One Life to Live*, as that's it now.

Mary Sue Price, Daytime Scriptwriter, *General Hospital*

I've been writing daytime television for about fourteen years. I was a newspaper reporter for ten years before I started writing plays. My short play, *That Midnight Rodeo*, is published and frequently produced. Various other work has been produced throughout the United States. I have an MFA in dramatic writing from Tisch School of the Arts, New York University. Presently, I am a scriptwriter for the daytime serial *General Hospital*. This means I write at least one hour-long script per week. I sometimes write two. I've worked at *General Hospital* since 1997. I've won two Emmys as a member of the *General Hospital* writing team. Before *General Hospital*, I wrote scripts and the occasional breakdown (episode outline) for *Another World*. I also wrote scripts for *As the World Turns*.

As a scriptwriter, I am part of a writing team that consists of a head writer, an assistant head writer/editor, breakdown writers, and script writers. It is my job to transform a breakdown (outline) of an episode into a script. Basically, I turn a narrative into dramatic writing on deadline.

The main difference in writing scripts for daytime and writing plays is time. Daytime television has no reruns and no hiatus. That means we write at least five episodes per week, every week. The structure of daytime is very strict. At *General Hospital*, the episodes consist of six acts and a prologue of short teasers at the beginning of the show. There are approximately thirty to thirty-five scenes in each show.

I tend to put more actor-oriented stage directions into a soap script than I ever would a play. This, too, is related to time. There isn't much rehearsal time in daytime, so subtext and emotional moments which might be discovered in a long rehearsal process in theater are simply written into the script.

I have no interaction with any of the actors on *General Hospital*. It's made in Los Angeles, and I live in Vermont, although I lived in New York City for more than twenty years and began my soap career there. As a writer, I focus solely on the characters, not the individual actors. But I always appreciate actors who come from a real place. Even if it's a small role, the show is just better if the entire cast is grounded in emotional reality. Soap history is full of stories about actors who transformed a small part into years of work. Sometimes something just clicks. But it's much more likely to click if the actor is prepared, if he or she knows the lines and is able to make clear choices quickly.

Daytime requires a great deal of memorization and the ability to work quickly. It's very difficult, and I have undying respect for actors who can do great work, day in and day out, year in and year out.

Interviews with *One Life To Live* Stage Manager, Alan Needleman

Alan Needleman (**AN**) has been a stage manager at *One Life To Live* for more than nineteen years. He's been involved in the show in some shape or form since 1971.

What do you feel are the most important things an actor doing extra work on the show for the first time needs to know?

AN: They need to know that though they may not have any lines or specific business, they are just as important as the other actors on the show. They are brought in to make the scenes real, just as you might see in everyday life situations. They should motivate themselves as well as others. A lot of times, we'll tell them to bring a pad with them so that they can write down the blocking for their scenes. We may ask them to do specific things in the scenes. They should remember these things for later on, when we actually shoot the scenes. Quite often, we'll give them a cross that will lead us to another actor in the scene. It's very important that they remember exactly where and when that cross should occur. It's very important that they know that they are a very important part of the production; they are not the forgotten people. People who know me know that that's my credo; I treat everyone equally.

What do you feel are the most important things an actor doing an under-five or principal work on the show for the first time needs to know?

AN: They, too, must realize that they bring something to the table. They were hired for their specific skills, and they should come prepared and be ready to work. As far as acting, they should play the role the way that they've worked on it, but be open to any changes that the director might want. One thing: Let the cameras follow you, don't try to follow the camera. And of course, try not to be nervous. Try to relax yourself and be prepared to work. Play to your fellow actor, and the rest will take care of itself. With under-fives, you are generally there to interact with a principal. Keep your head and don't try to make too much of it. Don't be hammy about it.

With contract roles, I tell the actor that if there is anything I can do to make their time here a little bit more relaxed, just let me know. It's most important that they feel comfortable. There's a lot of extraneous people walking around, there's a lot of new people to get to know; it shouldn't distract you from the work that you were hired to do. You can't be intimidated by the personalities of some of the guys behind the cameras or the boom. It's your job, and you were hired because the powers that be felt that you could do it well. If an actor feels rushed or tense, it will come out in their performance. Even though we always have a tight time factor here, no one actor is more important than any other.

Can you describe the daily schedule on the show, things that actors need to know?

AN: When they walk in, they check into their dressing room for a few minutes. Dry rehearsal is first up, generally, about 7:00 a.m. What that is is a read-through, a walk-through in a rehearsal hall. There, the director will go over what he or she wants them specifically to do, scene by scene. We generally shoot the show by set. That means if an actor is in several scenes in a set, they have to stay around. But generally, the actors are in one set. After that set is rehearsed, the actor is free for a while. The next call is camera blocking on the set, about 10:00 a.m. We also do that in the same order that we're going to do the show. Again, it's scene by scene. After that, the actors are free for a while. "Free" meaning, they can go to makeup, hair, and wardrobe. Most of the times, they run lines with each other during that time. That prepares them even more for later on, to shoot. After a lunch break, we do a dress rehearsal of the scenes. The director will then give actor or camera notes, and then finally, we'll tape it.

Any actor pet peeves?
AN: Actors who are unprepared.

What is the best advice that you can give an actor who wants to work (in any acting capacity) in daytime?
AN: My best advice is that soaps are a fabulous vehicle. To name a few, Tommy Lee Jones, Dustin Hoffman, and Laurence Fishburne have all worked on soap operas and gone on to have terrific careers. You are being hired for your abilities. Don't get caught up in the technical stuff that's going on all around you. Just play the scene. You bring something to the table. Be yourself. You must be flexible, ready for change.

WHY DO COMMERCIALS?

Working in TV commercials can be a lucrative way to earn money in show business. They are also a great way to showcase your talent. There are many stories of actors whose careers were launched from the exposure that one TV commercial gave them—classic lines like, "Where's the beef?" and "I can't believe I ate the whole thing!" Those commercials not only identified a product, but gave the actor instant recognition. At one time, film and TV stars would never "stoop" to do a TV spot, but indeed, times have changed. Major stars such as Kevin Spacey, Donald Sutherland, Megan Mullallay, James Earl Jones, and Lauren Bacall can be seen or heard almost every day pitching one product or another.

Getting Commercial Agents

You'll need a commercial agent to get sent out for most TV commercials in New York. The agent receives the calls from the casting directors for the specific commercials and then calls actors that he represents to fill the audition slots.

There are several ways to get a commercial agent interested in you. A referral from a commercial casting director who knows you is probably the most effective way. If you know an actor that works with a commercial agent and is willing to put in a call for you, that's also helpful. Many of the one-on-one casting sessions, where you can pay to meet agents, have commercial agents working through them on a nightly basis. And of course, there are the targeted mailings. These aren't generally the best way to catch an agent's eye, but it's worth a try if the mailings are "very" targeted. Be sure when mailing to send the picture to each individual agent at the agency. Don't forget to follow your initial mailing with a postcard mailing and, if necessary, a phone call request to (hopefully) set up an interview.

Successful Commercial Agent Interviews

When meeting with commercial agents, here are a few things to keep in mind.

Dress appropriately for your type. It's okay to dress casually if that's called for, but don't dress *too* down. Remember, this is a business, and you are having a business meeting.

Try to project an air of confidence from the minute you enter until to the minute you leave. Remember, the interview begins the second you walk into their office. Try to be positive and upbeat. This is definitely not a time to be shy or withdrawn. Agents want to see you sparkle a bit. Just be friendly and accessible, the best "you" that you can be. And speaking of the image you are projecting, do your research, so that you come across as knowing something about the industry and, particularly, about the agent and agency that are interviewing you.

Let the agent lead the interview. It's one thing to be confident and self-assured; it's another to be pushy. Answer any questions asked with more than just one word; try to be open.

If you are asked to read copy for them, do the best you can, and don't apologize if you didn't read as well as you'd like. If you make several mistakes, if you really feel that you've started off on the wrong foot in the reading and didn't get into it, it's okay to say you'd like to start over again. If you do read it again, make sure that you do a better job the second time through. If the agent gives you any adjustments, try to the best of your ability to make them fully and with complete conviction.

Don't be discouraged if the interview is brief. Interviews with commercial agents are usually shorter than meetings with legit agents. Also, commercial agents aren't as concerned as legit agents if you haven't had extensive acting training.

When the interview is over, smile, say goodbye in a friendly and professional manner, and leave without dawdling. Make it a clean and confident exit.

In some commercial agencies, after the initial interview, you may be called back to meet some of the other agents in the office. Try to interview with all of the other agents in the same friendly, professional way as did in your initial interview.

Your TV Commercial Audition: What You Need to Know

If the interview has gone well and the agent starts to call you for auditions, always try to be upbeat, professional, and friendly on the phone. The agent may be calling a lot of actors for different audition slots, so time is of the essence. Don't waste valuable time on the phone chatting with him.

Be prepared to receive all the necessary information for the commercial audition. Have a pen and paper ready. The agent will give you the information quickly. Agents are bothered when they have to repeat the information more than once. Listen carefully. The agent may forget to give you valuable information. Don't hang up until you have all the necessary information. Calling them back and getting through to them may be difficult. Make sure you have

- the date,
- the time,
- the place where the audition will be held,
- when the commercial will be shooting,
- what the product is,
- who is doing the casting,
- what you should wear.

You must tell the agent at this time if you have any conflicts (similar products) with the product for which he is sending you out to audition. Also, find out how the commercial will run (i.e., "nationally," "regionally," "on cable only," etc.).

Dressing the Part

So you've gotten the call, and the day of the audition comes. First of all, try to dress for the part. If you're going up for a housewife, don't overdress or wear something too sexy. If you're a man who's going up for the CEO of a company, wear an upscale suit. As for colors, be careful with all white or black. Too much white reads as light and does funny things on camera. Black reads intensely on camera. Unless it's really appropriate for the character that you're playing, avoid too much of it. Things like bold prints and too much jewelry should be avoided, unless it's really specific to a character that you're auditioning for. These things tend to call attention to themselves, rather than where you want the focus to be—on you. Several commercial casting directors feel that clothing in soft pastels compliment most skin tones. Black or white or bold patterns should only be worn to specific commercial auditions where it's appropriate for the character.

Signing In

Before you leave your home, get yourself in a pleasant state of mind, relax, do some warm-ups, and don't forget to bring an extra picture and résumé (or two). Always show up early (at least twenty minutes before your actual call time) so that you can get familiar with the copy that you'll be auditioning from. One tip: don't sign in until you're ready to audition. Quite often, an actor will arrive, immediately sign in, and before he's had a chance to look at the copy or pull himself together, the agent, seeing his name on the call sheet will call them in to audition

The first thing you should do is analyze the copy, making the situation as real for yourself as possible. If there is a storyboard, study it carefully. The storyboard is a series of drawings depicting the "visuals" of the commercial; it's the map telling you the journey that the ad agency wants to take the audience on. By looking at the storyboard, you'll get a sense of what your part is in the journey and how to best go about it.

Once you've done all your preparation, sign in, have your photo taken (usually by a casting associate), fill out all pertinent information on the size card, sit and relax, and get yourself ready for your audition. Don't chat with the other actors in the waiting room. Don't waste valuable time sizing up your odds of getting the job. Quite often, even though they think they know what they want, they really don't. The right actor has to walk into the room and make it their own. I once went up for a MasterCard Platinum commercial and was told by everyone in town that they were probably looking for blond, blue-eyed types—something that I definitely am not. But I went in and did the best I could. Well, no one was more surprised than me when I booked the job and ended up going to India for a few weeks to shoot it.

There are times when they're behind schedule. Don't let that get you down; be patient. If you have a time conflict (another audition), let them know as soon as you can

When You're Called into the Audition Room

First, take a breath or two, stand up, and walk in with a confident and friendly smile on your face. Remember, as I've mentioned before, the audition actually begins the moment you enter the room. Once you've said hello to the casting director, take a look at the cue card. Try to get as familiar as possible with both the handwriting and where the words are on the card.

The casting director will give you a sense of what she's looking for. Be very attentive! If there is another actor (or actors) in the scene with you, there is no time to get comfortable with him. Smile, and immediately accept him as the character that he is playing in the script. This is not the time to evaluate or judge the other actor. Commercial audition slots are very short. You may only be in there for a few minutes, so you must be as prepared as possible. You must become the character that you're playing—instantly.

Generally, you'll be asked to do a rehearsal. Do it confidently, as if you were doing the actual taping. Based on what you do, the casting director may give you an adjustment. Once again, be attentive. Try to assimilate what she's said into your performance. If you are confused about any instruction that you receive, ask for clarification right then and there. Be clear about what she wants, and try to do it. You should always be prepared for any last-minute changes.

Next, you'll be asked to "slate your name." With your most genuinely warm smile, say your name. Try to even have a smile in your voice. Look right into the center of the camera lens. Make believe it's your friend, your best friend. When the casting director says "action," do the best you can with the copy. You must become the character; here is no wiggle room here. Trust yourself and all the choices you made. Relax, and go for it with complete conviction. Never let 'em see you sweat.

Some actors like to memorize the copy. I don't personally think this is advisable unless you have a photographic memory. First of all, the copy on the cue card may be slightly different, and secondly, this is an audition to see your acting, not to test how well you learn copy. You don't want to be concerned with "What's my next line?" If you go up on your lines, you may have to do another take. This is not desirable, but if you have to, just give it your best shot. Always try to talk to the camera as if it were a person—just one person, not a group (unless that's what's called for). Remember, this isn't theater; you don't have to speak loudly or project to the back row.

Exiting

After you're through auditioning, make sure that you leave with a smile on your face. Make your goodbyes quick and without fanfare. Even if you didn't think you did your best work, there's no reason to let them know that. Your opinion of your work isn't what counts here. Sometimes, casting directors see something in your look that is what they're looking for. Just say goodbye, thank you, and leave.

Callbacks

You may or may not get a callback for the commercial. Just because you don't get a callback doesn't always mean you didn't book it. I never had a callback for the MasterCard Platinum commercial. Also, there are times where you might get a call to go to the callbacks even though you didn't go to the original casting. I was called in during callbacks for a Wendy's spot even though I didn't attend the original casting—and I booked it!

Usually at the callbacks they'll have the casting director, the ad agency people there, the client, the director, and God knows who else. The room might be filled with unfamiliar faces watching your audition. Don't let that throw you! Don't try shaking everyone's hand or connecting with each person in the room. Stay focused on who is running the audition; usually it's the director.

If you do get a callback, here are some helpful things to know:

For the most part, it's always better to wear what you wore to the first audition to the callback. If, for whatever reason, you don't have the same outfit, try to wear something similar in color and style.

Sometimes at the callback, you'll be paired with a new partner for the spot. Although you'll want to keep your performance in the same mode as the original, you may have to make some adjustments to the new scene partner.

The other actor may give you something quite different than the person with whom you originally auditioned. You must make the adjustment in your performance. Be flexible and accessible.

Once again, try to be friendly, upbeat, and professional. Part of what is happening at the callback is the creative team is appraising what you're like personally as well as professionally, and, most importantly, how right you are for their commercial. They may talk with you for a moment or two. Be open, professional and not too chatty. Answer their questions as best you can, stay professional. Sometimes they'll ask you things as simple as "What are your hobbies? "Or, "What is you typical day like?" Don't try to second-guess what they're looking for. It's always best to remain upbeat and answer as honestly as you can. One word of warning, this is not a therapy session. I have heard of actors being too honest about private matters during this time. That's not appropriate. Just try to keep it light and real.

Part of what the director is doing is to see if he feels he can work with you. Naturally, you'll do everything in your power to follow his directions. You may not be able to do it exactly at that moment, but you must attempt to, even if you artistically disagree with what he's asking.

After the Callback

Anywhere from that same day to two weeks later, you may find out that you booked the job. Congratulations! You'll need to find out when (date and time) the commercial will be shot, where, and if possible, what wardrobe you should bring. Quite often, a stylist will be contacting you at a later time to discuss wardrobe.

The only thing I have to say about the actual shooting of the commercial is have a good time, be professional, and listen to any direction that you're given. Remember, you've now booked the commercial; you don't have to work too hard to prove anything. They—the creative team—obviously believe that you're the right actor for the job. They liked you, they really liked you!

INTERVIEWS WITH COMMERCIAL AGENTS AND CASTING DIRECTORS

Commercial Agents

David P. Cash (DC) formerly with CESD, and now with Henderson Hogan, began his career working as a production assistant for Music Fair Enterprises on the revival of *The King And I* (1976). Other theaters he worked with include the New York Shakespeare Festival, the Roundabout, and the Metropolitan Opera, where he worked for nine years. He worked as the company manager of *Without You I'm Nothing* with Sandra Bernhard, and then as an account executive at the Serino Coyne Advertising Agency. In 1991, he went to work as an assistant talent agent at the Harter Manning Woo Agency (HWA).

Tracy-Lynn Goldblum (TG) is starting her twenty-eighth year as an agent at the Abrams Artists Agency. Working at Abrams has been her entire experience in the commercial business. She is vice president in charge of the on-camera commercial division. She graduated from Wellesley and earned a degree in first amendment law from the University of Michigan. She also has a master's degree in journalism from Columbia and some art criticism experience.

What are the best ways an actor can prepare for a career in commercials?
> DC: Watch commercials, more to get a sense of what the marketplace is displaying. Be aware of the actors of your type. Actors should get into a good, solid acting class, plus a good, solid on-camera class.
>
> TG: Get good training and be the best actor that he or she can be. It also helps to take a commercial class to get some on-camera experience, just to see what kind of energy you should bring to the camera/audition. Comedy and improv technique are also valuable in commercial work.

What are the best ways actors can make themselves known to you?
> TG: I'm always anxious to work with people whose work I've seen and enjoyed. We go to a lot of Broadway theater, showcases, and comedy clubs. A recommendation is always valuable, too. The least information that I get about an actor is from a headshot.

What kind of things do you look for at that first meeting with an actor?

DC: Eighty percent of what I need is to get a sense of that person. I want them to be able to grab my attention for the duration of the interview. Even if an actor doesn't have much on his résumé, if I find him engaging and interesting, that's a real plus in my book, and I'll pass him on to my colleagues to get their sense of him as well. So much of the decision comes down to just your instinct, your belief about the actor.

TG: I look for some kind of personality. The personality has to pop. It doesn't necessarily have to be perky. It can be low-keyed, sharp-tongued, anything that pops out about that person. I want to make sure that when that actor is on camera for a commercial, you're going to get something. If you don't see that in a fifteen- or twenty-minute interview, then you're never going to see that. If I haven't seen the actor's work, the interview is all I have to go on. If I've seen his work and he's brilliant, and he doesn't come across in an interview, I have some other information, so I can make a different decision.

What kind of things do you look for in your working relationship with an actor?

DC: Trust on both parts. I want to feel that that actor will do everything possible to prepare for any job that I send him out on. I want the actor to feel free to tell us if he doesn't feel right for a job. We need to keep an open dialogue. Here, we have a very hands-on relationship with our clients.

TG: Sometimes, it takes a while for an actor to book, but in those cases, I depend on good feedback from casting directors to keep the relationship (with the actor) going.

How long will you continue working with an actor who hasn't booked?

DC: When an actor signs on with an agency, it's usually for a year. At the end of the year, there is the option to sign on for three more years. During that first year, if the actor hasn't booked anything, but the indications are there, such as lots and lots of first refusals, we'll re-sign the actor. If an actor has not done that well, but we believe in him, we'll have a meeting with the actor to see what the problem is. He may need a new look, to take a class, anything that can get him to the next level. If the actor has not done anything to improve his situation, has fought our suggestions, then we'll break off the relationship.

TG: I have absolutely no set time. I look for the feedback and professionalism, and I want to enjoy working with that person. I hear what people are like in their auditions. If they're prepared, professional, give a good audition, I'm satisfied. I want actors to be accessible, either with a beeper or a good answering service; that means something to me. Being ready to go is an important part of it. Casting directors really care about their sessions. They care about actors being on time, that they're in the right wardrobe. If you screw them up, I'm going to hear about it.

How should an actor keep in touch with you?

DC: Postcards are the best way. But generally, I'll let an actor know if I want him to keep in touch with me or not. There are some actors whose work I'm really interested in. I'll let them know they should contact me, even by phone, if they're doing something.

TG: Postcards are still the best way. The e-mails are getting too overwhelming these days.

Any actor pet peeves?

DC: My greatest pet peeve is actors who are really late for auditions and don't let us know. Also, actors who call four times a day to find out if we heard about the callback.

TG: There is no excuse for not acting like a professional. There is an art to this, but it's a business. You're dealing with huge corporations; everyone expects you to behave as a professional.

If you had one specific bit of advice to give a commercial actor, what would it be?

DC: Ask yourself, "Do you want this more than anything else in the world?" This is an extraordinarily tough business to crack. If you have decided that acting is something that you want more than anything else in the world, then don't let anything get in the way of it. That doesn't mean sacrifice your personal life; it means, don't let anyone tell you otherwise.

TG: The more interesting a person you are, the more interesting an actor (and commercial actor) you are. Have a life outside of acting and commercials. Hobbies, interests, get a life. Believe me, it shows in your eyes. Although this business is about training, as I've stressed, it's also about personality. The people that have a life are the people you want on camera.

Interviews with Commercial Casting Directors

Liz Lewis (LL) has cast the following commercials: Acura, Advil, American Express, Amtrak, AT&T, Blue Cross/Blue Shield, Bud Light, Citibank, Excedrin, Crest, Virgin Airlines, Sony, Reebok, Pepsi, Pizza Hut, Stouffers, Pepcid AC, Ocean Spray, Listerine, Levi's, Ford, Miller, Snapple, among many others. Films and TV include: *The Gypsy Years, The Daily Show, Saturday Night Live's Fuzzy Memories,* and *USA Live,* among others.

Donna Deseta (DD) began her career as a successful Broadway and television star. She has cast more than twenty theatrically released feature films starring, among others, Anthony Quinn, Gene Hackman, Christopher Walken, Jackie Chan, and Gerard Depardieu. Directors she's worked with include Ridley Scott, Herb Ritts, Joel and Ethan Cohen, Wes Anderson, Bryan Singer, and Josephine Abady. Theatrically, she cast the world premiere of *Whistle Down the Wind* by Andrew Lloyd Webber for director Harold Prince, as well as numerous productions for the New York Theater Workshop, Denver Theater Center, and others. Recent commercial castings include Target, Sterling Bank, Esprit, Gap, and Fidelity

How can an actor best prepare for a career in commercials?

LL: Take commercial classes to see how it all works and get practice before coming to an audition.

DD: First of all, they must be prepared as actors; that's the very first thing. Once they've honed their skills, they must become familiar with the business aspect of being an actor. Stuff like getting your pictures, doing mailings, getting into showcases, developing all the important business skills.

If an actor doesn't have an agent, what is the best way they can makes themselves known to you?

LL: Send me your picture. People have stopped by our office to drop off a picture, and we'll notice them and say, "Hey, wait, don't go anywhere." I advise that you shouldn't blindly send your pictures to everyone at an agency. Just pick one person at an agency. That way, you'll send out something like twelve pictures, not a hundred. Even though they say "don't call," I advise you to call. If no one ever calls to get an appointment, then no one would ever get an appointment. I don't have a problem with somebody calling me; I really don't. They may be pushy enough to get an appointment. My feeling is, you never know who's going to walk through the door or who you'll speak to on the phone.

DD: Postcards.

Specifically, what do you look for when an actor auditions for you? Any specific dos and don'ts?

LL: Do not come in unprepared. Come to the audition on time. Don't talk or socialize; get prepared. Sit and read your copy, and get to know it, so when you come in, you can have an exchange with the casting director and be free enough to be creative. I specifically look for the look, the way the actor carries himself. Sometimes, I don't know anything until the actor opens his mouth. I generally am looking for someone who is comfortable on camera, who knows what he's doing. The most important thing actors need to know is that the casting director needs them as much as they need the casting director.

You may be auditioning for a $100,000 commercial. Be as prepared as you can be, do your best at the audition, and then it's okay to go out and socialize with the other actors.

DD: Before you even walk in the room to audition, you should read the instructions that are posted. I can't tell you how many actors don't. Ask questions if you need to. To be ignorant is not smart. Like the old saying, the only stupid question is the one you didn't ask. But don't be annoying about it. If it's obvious, pay attention. If it's written there, if we've posted instructions, try to follow them. As far as while the actor is waiting in the waiting area, I like when actors enjoy my waiting area and are social. However, you shouldn't be too social, not at the expense of the audition. Look at the material, and know what you're going to do when you walk in the room. It makes me nuts when someone walks in the room and says, "Oh gee, I didn't have a chance to look at the material."

Specifically, I look for enthusiasm, someone who listens, who wants to be there, who is going to try to give me what I want, who will work hard for me. If I see they're working hard to give me what I want, I'll work real hard for them. They'll get the best out of me, what I have to offer.

Actors who don't listen to directions can be a problem. It's okay to not understand, but let me know that you don't, and I'll repeat it.

How should actors prepare for callbacks?

LL: Try to remember what you did at the original audition. Wear the same or similar clothing. Listen. Listen. Listen. The more you know the copy, the better. Know what the spot's about. Try to lose your nervousness. Listen to everything that's being given to you, and don't be afraid to take a chance.

DD: Wear the same clothes, and remember what you did to get the callback. Once you're there, there more than likely will be a director there. He may have some different ideas than I had at the original audition. Listen to him. Don't tell him, "She told me to do it a different way." Remember, the casting director is your ally. I'm on the same side; I want you to get the job. If the room is filled with a lot of people, like advertising agency people, the director, etc., don't get overwhelmed. Look to the casting director for your cue. Bottom line, you make me look good when you do well, and I appreciate that.

What are your main pet peeves about actors?

LL: The main thing is when an actor is unprepared. Being late and not calling bothers me a lot.

DD: I hate when an actor gives me a picture and résumé, and they're not connected. Also, when an actor doesn't keep appointments or is late and doesn't call ahead. There is a method to my madness. I have people grouped together, paired together. If an actor is late, it ruins the setup.

If you had one piece of advice to offer actors regarding a career in commercials, what would it be?

LL: We need you as much as you need us, and you shouldn't allow yourself to be treated poorly. You should always stand up for yourself. I know actors that won't go to certain casting directors, because they don't like how they're treated.

DD: Actors must learn that you can only be the best at being you. Don't try to change yourself to be what you think is the current "mold." Don't say to yourself the market is this, therefore, I'll adapt to that look, style, etc.

THE INS AND OUTS, UPS AND DOWNS
OF FILM EXTRA WORK

Doing extra work on films and episodic TV shows can be a very lucrative way either to supplement your acting career or, in many cases, to supply your total income.

If you work enough days (on union shoots), you can earn free health insurance for the next year. Also, working enough weeks can make you eligible for unemployment insurance, and the money you earn doing extra work adds up for your pension. Another positive feature is that there is always the chance of an upgrade to principal work on the film. If you're lucky, you sometimes get to shoot in some lovely locations outside the city or in some terrific restaurants and homes. Actors find it to be an excellent place to network. Because there is a lot of down time on the set, you can do some office work (mailings, letter writing, etc.). If there is a lot of down time, you can get to read that book you've wanted to read. Quite often, you get to work with top actors and directors. You can learn a great deal about working on films.

Like any other job, there are some unpleasant parts to film extra work. The days can be extremely long. The working conditions on film sets may be tough (bad weather, not always the best holding areas, etc.). Some film sets are pressure- and tension-filled. Working on sets with sometimes hundreds of other actors can have its drawbacks (personality clashes, bitter actors, etc.). The craft services (the food table) may not always stock the healthiest choices and may run out (rarely) early in the day. Also, you're never sure when you'll be working.

Interviews with Extra Casting Directors
Grant Wilfley (GW) (Grant Wilfley Casting): After an internship at the Stuart Howard office, Grant Wilfley did a summer internship with Joy Todd Casting. After that internship, he was hired by Joy Todd. Eventually, he began his own company.

Fleet Emerson (FE) (Sylvia Fay Casting): Prior to working with Ms. Fay, Fleet Emerson was an actor, and then began working in casting with Bernie Styles.

How do you prefer actors make themselves known to you?

GW: It's important to attend all of our open calls when we have them. We have a SAG registration in our office Mondays and Wednesdays between 10:00 a.m. and 12:00 p.m. The best way to let us know about you is by sending a picture and résumé, and then by sending picture postcards. We also have a database in our office. SAG members can come by and register.

FE: By postcard, that's the easiest way.

SF: By sending a headshot, and one that doesn't look any younger than the actor actually is. Many actors never change their headshots. They send us pictures that were taken years ago (laughing). We do get older and better.

What would you say are the main things an actor wanting to do background work needs to know?

GW: The main thing is that they should always be as professional as they can be. Follow all information, show up on time, bring the right wardrobe, and treat it as if it's a serious job. Extras are as important as one of the leads to us. Extras are a "stitch in the grand tapestry of filmmaking."

FE: Well, for one thing, they should be aware that it's the most boring part of the show. They should get the rulebook from SAG and know what the rules are on the set.

What should background actors be aware of once they've arrived at a location?

GW: Listen and pay attention. First thing, check in with the casting director (or someone from their office) who has hired you. Get your voucher from them. Don't forget to fill out the voucher, it's how you'll get paid. Then, go to the holding area, check in with the assistant director (AD) or the production assistant (PA) in charge. You'll be told what kind of behavior they want on the set, what kind of acting will be required for that day's scene.

FE: First, to check in with the AD or PA, or whoever is in charge. They should next have the wardrobe people check them out to see if they have the correct wardrobe. After they are checked out, then they can go for their coffee break. If they want to eat first, they should get there fifteen minutes ahead of time.

What are the most common mistakes background actors make?

GW: Wanting to be seen in front of the camera. If you do your job right, more than likely, you'll get to be seen. If the assistant director sees someone trying too hard to be seen in a shot, that's the first one that he'll move away from camera. It's important for actors to show their enthusiasm and their wanting to work without being abrasive. Actors shouldn't hide when they're on set. They should be in plain sight of the assistant director and available to work. It's important for extras to know, just because we're not on set, we still get reports of everyone's behavior. Some actors feel that as soon as the casting directors leave the set that they can do whatever they want to. It all gets back to us.

FE: They think that it's the end if they're doing background work. They don't feel they have much of a chance of being upgraded on the film. That's not true in New York. In Los Angeles, actors who do extra work just do extra or background work; not here. For instance, on *Law & Order*, every episode, at least five or six actors who do background work get parts on the show. They've been seen by the ADs, or the casting people who come on the set, and get upgraded. There are actors who, from being seen on the set, are called in for auditions. In every single episode, there are people who, from our file, get to do principal work.

FE: I would say that three out of four of the main actors on *Sopranos* have worked for us.

What do actors need to know about stand-in work?

GW: Stand-in work is a great way to learn the craft. You're actually watching your peer actors do their job. You can become familiar with blocking and camera angles, that kind of stuff. As a stand-in, you must be very sharp and pay strict attention. You'll want to mimic everything the principal actor is doing, so that they can set the lighting and other technical things. We select our stand-ins from actors who generally work for us on a regular basis as extras. We have determined that they are extremely reliable and professional, and we'll decide to give them the opportunity.

To be a stand-in, you have to be the same height, weight, and hair color as the principal actor. Ideally, you should look like the actor you're standing in for. As a stand-in, you can work on a very regular basis; we have between twenty and forty people who work in this capacity regularly.

FE: Patience is right. Being a stand-in, you are a member of the team. That means that you are part of the crew. You will learn about camera positions, what the director of photography is trying to do, you can learn a lot. Just by listening, if you're attentive, you can learn a lot about how the film is being shot. The stand-in is involved in the scene. You also learn where the key lighting is in the scene, many things. On *Law & Order*, the stand-ins do the scenes before the principals do the scenes. The stand-ins read the lines of the principal actors. Then when the principal actors step in, they tell them what happened, which way the angles will be, which way to move, and so forth.

What particular skills are necessary for doing background work?
GW: Actors should be able to pantomime in a scene. That is, they should give the impression that they are speaking, but they actually aren't. If there is a microphone near them, it will pick up their conversation along with the principles. They should be able to repeat an action from one take to another. They should be aware of where the camera is and make sure not to block the camera in a shot. They need to blend with the principal actors and make it look like you are part of, say, the office or a bar. You must feel comfortable acting out a role, even though you're not saying anything. When you approach a set, it's important that you determine who your character is in that environment and portray it.
FE: Again, patience is a must. Background actors don't speak, and it's tougher not to say something than it is to say something. It's difficult, say, when you're a waiter and the principal actor speaks to you, and you can't respond, because you're a background actor. In normal life, you would say something.

Does doing background work in any way diminish an actor's chance for principal work in film?
GW: Actors used to think that once you're a background performer, you're always a background performer. For some actors, doing background work is all they really want to do, and they make a decent living at it. But there are a lot of actors in New York who do it just to make extra money while pursuing much larger acting work.

How do you like actors to keep in touch with you?
GW: We like picture postcards. If actors haven't worked for us in a while, it's good to send us a postcard to remind us that you're available.
FE: Postcards, no phone calls.

Any pet peeves?
GW: I actually have a dos and don'ts list that I'd like you to put in the book.

The Don'ts
- Don't call the office every day, even if we have something you haven't worked on. Whether you realize it or not, calling in like that actually hurts you.
- Don't show up late for a job. Be there a half hour early.

- Don't chitchat with the casting people on set. We are busy trying to get our job done.
- Don't challenge us. If we say that we don't have anything for you, we mean just that. Accept it and move on.

The Dos

- It's a good idea to get yourself a pager. That way, you can get the call much faster, and it makes our job much easier.
- Send picture postcards frequently, and make sure that your phone number is on the card.
- Stop by our office during the open call registration hours to register.
- Always show up for a job on time.
- Always be professional and courteous.
- Use common sense.
- List all props, special wardrobe, and special skills on your résumé where it's easy to read.
- Maintain a positive attitude—very important. Some actors who do background work think, "Oh, I'm just a background performer." It goes along with a negative attitude that they have about the work, and believe me, it shows.

GW: Everyone starts somewhere. Doing background work is a great place to start, to learn. No one is born a movie star.

FE: We get a lot of no-shows and people canceling on us at the last minute. We have to try to replace them, and sometimes, they cancel late at night. Obviously, it's not easy to replace them the later it gets. Today, we worked on a movie with seven hundred extras. There were seventy-five no-shows. That's a lot of people.

Actors who want to leave early because they have made another engagement and didn't think the movie would be shooting so late. They want to leave the set. Actors double-book themselves. They think they'll be out, say, at three o'clock and book another job for after that hour. You can't do that. You never know when you'll be wrapped.

There are actors who hide from the camera when they are on set, rather than go towards the camera. Perhaps they don't want to be "established," in hopes of being upgraded. So even though they were instructed to walk towards the camera, they disobey the instructions.

Interview with Richard Rizzo (RR), an Actor Who Does Extra Work

What is your entertainment experience?

RR: I have always acted in theater, from elementary school all the way through community theater after college. I did showcases in New York City, industrial films, commercials, soap operas, print modeling, and films.

How did you first start doing extra work?

RR: I met some New York City actors when I was acting in an Ibsen play in Bloomfield, New Jersey. They helped me get a headshot, put together a résumé and told me about the casting directors in New York that hired actors for extra work.

How did you make the contacts to get the work?

RR: I mailed my headshot and résumé to the major extras casting people: Sylvia Fay, Joy Todd, Navarro-Bertoni, and Bernie Styles. In those days, you could also drop by the office to meet them.

Do you remember your first extra jobs? What were they like for you?

RR: My first extra job was through Joy Todd. She was looking for actors with cars for a night shot. I had a Mustang convertible and drove around the block for hours. It was very exciting to be on a movie film set, in New York City at 2:00 a.m. My first job with Sylvia Fay was the film *Somebody Killed Her Husband* starring Farrah Fawcett. I played a waiter and could actually see myself in the film when it came out. It was very exciting.

What does extra work actually entail? Talk about a typical day.

RR: The job entails being one of the people in a scene who fills the background of the scene while the stars of the film are talking or walking. It may mean being seated at a restaurant, walking on a city street around the stars of the film, being a waiter and bringing the stars food and drink or filling up a stadium—in other words, recreating a real life situation. A typical day may mean getting to the set (location) by 6:00 a.m. and being dressed in the clothes that the casting office has asked you to wear. Women should have all their makeup on and their hair styled. You may be sitting around for hours in a building (holding area) before you get called to set. Then a PA (Production Assistant) will place you in a certain spot within the scene and tell you what to do when the director calls for action. It may mean walking to another spot, turning around and walking back. The days can be exceptionally long: twelve hours or more.

What are the different types of extra work (film, TV, commercials) and how are they the same and/or different?

RR: Film and TV extra work are similar in that the actions and locations are often the same. Films have larger budgets and may use more people to recreate a scene. Sometimes films may be period pieces, which means that the production company gives you the clothes that it wants you to wear. This may mean going to a fitting before the day you actually shoot the scene. Sometimes a TV shoot can differ because it will be shooting several scenes the same day, in which case you may be asked to bring several changes of clothing. In a commercial shoot there may not be as many people in the shot, and the emphasis may be on the principal actors or the product they are promoting. The day can often be very long. In any case, your action is the same, whether it is film, TV or commercial: to move where you are directed to go.

What's expected of you on the job?

RR: The most important rule is to be on time. I have seen actors sent back home because they were late in arriving on location. You must also bring the clothing (wardrobe) you have been asked to bring. There is no talking on set unless you are asked to do so. Filming requires absolute silence when the starts of the project are being filmed. Men need to be clean-shaven, unless they are bearded, and women must have all their makeup applied and hair styled before arriving on set. You need to be alert for when you are called to set.

s are there to doing this type of work?

antage of doing this work is that you experience how a film, , or commercial is filmed. You get an understanding of the ice of lighting, sound, costume design, set design, props, and vork. You will then appreciate all the work and dedication nto filming a project. Another advantage is networking with :ors, who can give you information on where to find more sses, coaches, part-time jobs, and auditions. Of course there is the paycheck. Sometimes the money can be quite high. If you belong to one of the union: SAG or AFTRA, the pay can add up once you get into overtime. For non-union actors, the pay varies, from about $80 to $100 for the day (no matter how long that day turns out to be).

Things that you don't like (or difficulties) about this work?

RR: One drawback to doing this type of work is working outside in the extreme cold or heat. Women have it especially difficult because they may be asked to wear dresses and high heels in freezing weather. In most cases, actors are not allowed to wear hats or gloves in extreme cold weather scenes. In hot, humid weather actors may be dressed in business suits and standing outside for hours on end. The worst scenario is when a scene takes place in the summer but it is being filmed in March. You are asked to wear summer attire and the temperature is forty degrees or less. My first commercial extra job was a football stadium scene in which I wore a winter coat, scarf, hat and gloves. It was shot in August. Another drawback for some actors are the night shoots. They begin around sunset and don't end until 5:00 or 6:00 a.m. the next morning. If you are not used to being up all night long it can take a day or two for you to get back to your regular sleep/ wake cycle.

What advise do you have for actors thinking of pursuing extra work?

RR: If you plan to pursue extra work, make sure you have a wide selection of clothing: business suits and shirts/tee-shirts without logos on them. Certain props: briefcases, cars, bicycles, skateboards. It is also known that many agents and managers do not want their clients doing this type of work. They feel that if you are known as an actor who does a lot of extra work no one will want to consider you for principal work or will want to represent you. They caution you not to put extra work jobs on your résumé. This is true: do not pad your résumé with extra work jobs. I know many actors who make a good living doing extra work. They may never get the big speaking roles but have accepted that fact without regrets.

ALL ABOUT COMMERCIAL PRINT MODELING

Commercial print modeling is a very lucrative way to supplement your acting career. Unlike fashion models, who must be extremely attractive and be willing to spend a great deal of their day making rounds to photographers and ad agencies, the commercial print model has much more time available for auditions and classes.

Here are some benefits to pursuing this type of work:

- You don't have to be drop-dead gorgeous to be a commercial print model. There is work for everyone, from attractive "mom and dad" types to the person who looks like your everyday John and Jane.
- You can go on go-sees and accept jobs based on your availability.
- You get to use some of your acting skills in creating just the right mood needed for the ad.
- This work pays very well, an average of $250 an hour.
- The exposure in some ad campaigns can be very helpful to an actor's career.
- Some of the locations for a print shoot can be lush and beautiful.
- Most print agencies are very actor-friendly.

Some of the disadvantages of this type of work include:

- It's highly competitive. Especially for the big ad campaigns, they'll see hundreds of people for the same position.
- Cattle call go-sees can be time-consuming. You can get stuck at a big cattle call, sometimes for an hour or more.
- Like acting, there can be a lot of rejection.
- There is no union to protect you if any difficulties arise.
- There are some scam modeling agencies out there; you must research who you work with.
- There are some sleazy photographers who can try to take advantage of attractive young models.
- Generally, you have to wait a couple of months (or more) to receive your pay for any print job.
- There are start-up expenses, such as photography shoots, investing in a suitable wardrobe, composite cards, mailings, etc.

- You are hired as an independent employee (1099 tax form). No taxes are taken out, therefore, you cannot use this income for any pension or unemployment benefits.
- Trying to get copies of jobs that you did can be difficult. You must find out who to contact (the art director, the photographer, etc) and politely pursue them. This can be arduous at times or can be a matter of one phone call or e-mail; it depends.
- The commercial print agencies that I spoke with said they find their models through photo submissions and referrals. Some agencies go on model search competitions held around the country.
- Agents have said that they look for people with great energy in their face, good personality, a sparkle in their eyes, and good teeth and smile. Confidence is a big plus. Models must feel comfortable in front of a camera.
- The day rate is generally anywhere from $1,500 to $3,000 (or more). Editorial (magazines) can be $100 to $250 a day. You do editorial because you want the exposure or because it might be a photo you can use in your portfolio. A cover for *Newsweek* or *New York Magazine* can be very impressive, especially on a comp card.
- As for wardrobe: khakis, jeans, a suit, a tuxedo for men. Women need a variety of casual clothing, some business looks and some upscale outfits and dresses.
- Models need to have up-to-date pictures. If they change their hair color or style they should let their agent know.

Interviews with Two of the Top New York Commercial Print Agents

Stephanie Bellarosa (SB), CESD (Cunningham, Escott, Slevin & Doherty) a full service bi-coastal talent agency. Established in 1967, we represent actors and models for commercial print, on-camera and voice-over work. I am the director of the print department.

Ray Volant (RV), owner of Bella Agency in New York. We are a modeling agency representing models and actors of all ethnicities, age range from teens to adults. Our agency specializes in commercial print (product and advertising) catalog, editorial and showroom. With more than twenty years of experience in the modeling industry, Ray began as an agent at a small New York agency and went on to create successful divisions at Ford Models, including the first commercial print (lifestyle) division within a fashion agency. In 2004, Ray launched Bella Agency, which quickly became one of the leading boutique agencies specializing in talent for lifestyle and fashion print advertising.

The following year, to meet the increasing demand for more mature models, Bella launched a new division, forty-plus women, now one of the most sought-after for advertisers looking to target a specific demographic.

Today the Bella Agency specializes in lifestyle, fashion print, and catalog. Bella models have appeared in advertising for Neutrogena, Levi's, Target,

Colgate, MasterCard, Swiss Army, Delta Airlines, Polo Jeans, Uniqlo, and many other major brands.

What kind of people do you look for? How do you find most of your models?
> SB: We look for real everyday people. The great thing about the commercial print world is there isn't a height or weight requirement. Mostly we find our models through referrals, submissions, and seminars.
>
> RV: Our agency represents all ethnicities, so when we are meeting people, I think the number one quality—besides being photogenic—is personality. We find our talent though seminars, referrals from other models, or submissions directly to the agency.

Can anyone do commercial print modeling? What skills are necessary to be a model?
> SB: Yes, anyone can do commercial print. Knowledge of the business is extremely helpful. Also having a professional headshot or comp card is great for submitting to agencies for potential representation.
>
> RV: Commercial print modeling is not for everyone. Every agency has different criteria for what they are looking for. Some skills that I think are important are being comfortable in front of a camera, being able to convey different expressions, being photogenic, and having people skills; this is a relationship business.

Are many of your models actors? Do you think being an actor is a plus for this kind of work?
> SB: Each agency operates differently, but for CESD, most all of our models are actors as well. We think it's important to have some type of acting training for commercial print work.
>
> RV: Most of our models act. This is very important, as this helps the actor, when advertising a product, to convey different expressions or emotions the advertiser wants for that particular product.

What kind of money do print models make?
> SB: It depends on the product, rate, and usage. A model can make anywhere from a few hundred dollars to several thousand dollars per project.
>
> RV: There is a range in the amount of money a model can make. Some jobs are paid hourly, for example, $250 per hour; some pay a flat day rate, maybe $2,500. This all depends on the product and usage of the advertisement.

What basic wardrobe do print models need?
> SB: Basic business attire.

RV: Some basic wardrobe that models should have: something casual, businesslike, and evening. They should be neutral colors, and stay away from anything distracting or logos.

What's expected of models once they book a job?

SB: A model is expected to be at the job on time, to have all the necessary paperwork for the client to sign (voucher, model release), and most importantly, to be professional at all times.

RV: When a model books a job, it is very important to adhere to what we refer to as the three Ps: punctuality, preparedness, and professionalism.

How do you like models to keep in touch with you?

SB: We like e-mail and phone calls.

RV: Today's technology allows for more efficiency. E-mail is the most preferred and fastest way in keeping touch.

Any advice for people thinking of a career in modeling?

SB: Make sure this is something you really want to do. Always have a professional and positive attitude and trust your agent's judgment.

RV: I think if someone is starting out, you have to be persistent but professional. Make sure your pictures are current and then once you land an agent... listen to him!

Interviews with commercial print models: Roger Mazzeo (RM) and Nancy Ozell i (NO)

Photo of Roger Mazzeo (and young child model). By Michael Keudel, FOTODESIGN - GERMANY

Photo of Nancy Ozelli by Darryl Estrine

How long have you been a print model?

RM: I did my first print job when I was eleven years old for Smitty's Department Store in Phoenix, Arizona and, yes, I have the photo to prove it! Today, I am forty years young (y'all do the math!) and I am still having a great time in front of the camera.

NO: Since 2001.

What clients have you worked for?

RM: I have worked for clients literally all over the world, from Beirut to Capetown, Milan to New York, Beijing to Bombay, Istanbul to Lisbon, and everywhere in between! Here are a few clients that come to mind: Persol, Vodafone, Telecom, Magnum, Barilla, Greystone, Aprica, Ducati, Happydent, Dillards, Longhi, Vogue Mirto, Atkinsons, Clairol, Breil, Radiosa, *Entertainment* magazine, Schott, Honeywell.

NO: Tommy Hilfiger, Crystal Cruises, Avon Cosmetics, Reebok, Target, Vogue Knitwear, K-Mart, Sub-Zero Appliances, Sprint Communications, Merrill-Lynch, Smith Barney, Siemens A.G., Epson, Lexmark, Palm Pilot, various pharmaceuticals among others. Editorial: *Fast Company, Fortune, Golf for Women, Good Housekeeping, GQ, Harper's Bazaar, Vogue, Modern Bride, New York Times (Sunday Magazine), New York Magazine, Newsweek, O Magazine, Rolling Stone.*

What type of work you did prior to modeling (and if it's been of any value in this work)?

RM: Well, like many people in our business, I worked as a waiter. Being a waiter is a great way to meet and interact with people. In the print modeling business, even if you are not speaking words, you are selling a product. One of the "products" you're selling is you! Using what I like to refer to as "people skills," you can communicate effectively with agents, casting agents, photographers, clients, and all sorts of other people in the business.

NO: I was a high school Spanish and ESL teacher and teacher trainer. I also worked as a residential real estate broker.

What Drew You to Working in the Modeling Industry?

RM: Two things drew me to the modeling industry: the acting aspect and the financial rewards. I view modeling as performing and communicating an idea or an emotion! You are given the chance to play different roles and express the whole gamut of human emotions. This is appealing for any actor. As for the money aspect, what you earn doing a day of print modeling could be what you earn in a week or even a month doing some other type of work… and that is *not* hard to take!

NO: I began seriously thinking about it after several incidents of people misidentifying me as a model in restaurants, and the encouragement of friends in the industry.

How did you initially go about making connections with modeling agencies?

RM: My first contact with a modeling agency was through a photographer's recommendation. I was fortunate enough to have good friends who were also photographers and who were nice enough to lead me in the right direction.

Generally speaking, before any agency will agree to meet with you (unless you are scouted), you need to have good pictures in your book. Many modeling agencies have what are called "open calls." These are nothing more than one day of the week when they agree to see new faces and meet new people.

If, unlike my experience, you do not have any friends who are professional photographers, it may be a good idea to try and connect with other working models. See who they recommend, how they made their first contacts with agencies. It is entirely possible that they might even be willing to make a phone call on your behalf. Talk to as many people in the business as you can and ask their opinion.

The Internet is also a wonderful source of information. If you search for "modeling agencies in New York," you will be amazed what you come up with.

NO: I went to an agency with a handful of candid photos and was summarily rejected. A photographer friend, Nancy Ney, encouraged me to continue, took test shots, designed a comp card and set up interviews with six agencies. Five accepted me on the spot; the sixth, two days later. I have been freelancing ever since.

How did you prepare (pictures, portfolio, etc.) before you met with the agencies?

RM: I believe that good photos are fundamental in our business, so the first step I took was to try and get as many quality pictures as possible.

When agents look at your modeling book, they need to see how you photograph, so I would prepare as many looks and situations as possible, aiming for variety: a good headshot, couple shot, business shot, body shot, smiles, serious, etc.

I contacted good photographers who, because they were also friends or just starting out themselves, did not make me pay a great deal of money. With this said, you may have no choice but to invest some money in order to get good photos. It is, in my opinion, money well spent. If you do not have a lot of money to spend on photos, another great way to get them for your book (as well as practical experience in front of a camera) is to meet with stock photographers. Even if you are typically not paid for stock photos (with rare exceptions), you do get to keep the photos in exchange for your surrendering your rights to control the use of the photos.

Once you have the photos, you also need to make a composite card. Comp cards are really nothing more than a print model's business card. Just like a business card (and the impression you made during the meeting), it is what will remain after every interview, meeting, casting.

NO: I did not have a portfolio at the outset, but the comp card. I was advised to create a portfolio as soon as possible, so I collected Polaroids and tear sheets until I had enough to ask an agent to help me organize them.

What happens at interviews with print agencies?

RM: Generally speaking, agents want to see your modeling book/photos. If the agent likes what she sees, then she may want to get to know you a little better. She may ask questions designed to discover what type a person you are and what your personality is like. Are you a "serious" person? Are you responsible? Why do you want to be a model?

Depending upon how well things are going, you may be asked to fill out a form. The form usually asks questions about your personal and physical details (e.g., your measurements, age, sports, hobbies, interests etc.). You may also be asked if you have any objections to doing cigarette, liquor, and fur ads, or if you are comfortable doing underwear, topless or nude photos. Do you have piercings or tattoos? Some agents may also decide to take Polaroids.

NO: The model should bring a comp card and portfolio with tear sheets. There is very little time to make an impression because successful agents are under pressure during the day. Agents are also interested in how quickly a model can make a good impression because there is even less time to sell oneself during castings. Sometimes agents will take a Polaroid or digital photo. I guess that they are used as reminders but often wonder whether they are also taken for the unretouched image. If interested in representing the model exclusively, the agent will offer a contract. Most agents will ask for a written agreement even from freelancers. The terms vary, but at least give the agent the right to collect the model's fees and take their commission out of it.

What are the castings like? What must you do to prepare for them?

RM: My suggestion is that you should be ready for anything. Castings vary from what are known as "open calls" (where almost anyone can...and often does...show up) to scheduled appointments. Keep in mind, however, that even if you have a scheduled appointment, you may still have to wait an hour to get your foot through the door. Other times, you are in and out.

Sometimes a client will also be present at the casting. Whether or not this is the case, the person or people you meet with will look at your book and pictures. Other times you may see the agent and/or client just flipping through your book while simultaneously talking on the phone, nodding and pointing to the door. Good, bad or indifferent, these are the (sometimes harsh) realities of the business.

I always try to make a connection with the person doing the casting—a friendly "Hello" or "How are you?" Depending upon the response, you know how to proceed. Keep in mind that casting directors see hundreds, if not thousands of faces, and if you can do or say something that distinguishes you from the masses, it is a good thing. Whatever the case may be, remember to be yourself!

In terms of preparation, make sure you do your homework. Read the description of what the casting calls are for, or, in the event that this is communicated to you verbally (i.e., over the phone by your agent), try to conform to the image the client and/or casting director is looking for. Here, use common sense. If you are told (or understand) that they are looking for a typical businessman, wear a suit and tie and polish your shoes. If they are looking for a construction worker type, wear jeans and a T-shirt. During the casting itself, you may want to ask what it is that they are looking for. Do they want a serious look? Smiles? If they do decide to take a few pictures, I would suggest that this is the appropriate time to have an inner monologue (Yes, these are acting terms!). I ask myself: What character am I playing? What your lines would be. Doing this allows me to do more than just pose. It enables me to be the character and express what I am thinking.

NO: Gather as much information about the job as possible—the product or service or editorial setting and the "look" that is expected. Research the product to determine who the job will be marketing to and do your best to appeal to that market. Sometimes there is a prototype at the casting to help you with the look, and often the photographer will direct. The model should bring two comp cards with the name and contact info of the agent, and portfolio with tear sheets. The portfolio is usually looked at for fashion jobs (whether commercial or editorial), but rarely for other work. When you get to the casting, there is a sign-in sheet and a "size card" which is a form on which you provide your stats and other information. Unless it is a "request casting" with a specific time, there may be a long wait to be seen, and numbers are often assigned at sign-in. Sometimes the photographer is present, but not always. A digital photo will be taken. There is usually no conversation other than direction. The portfolio may be looked at by one person or several. Most of the time, many candidates for the job are seen, so the casting director can spend only a short amount of time with each.

What were your first print jobs like and what did you learn from those experiences?

RM: My first print jobs were not particularly easy for me because I was very shy and especially worried about what people were thinking about me. I had to learn to leave that insecurity at the door. One of the techniques I used to overcome this anxiety or discomfort was to remind myself that when I was in front of a camera, it was similar to being on stage—you are on! Today, on set, I make sure that I interact, move, gesture, think, laugh, and allow myself to display a funnel of emotions (that are appropriate). This makes the work more enjoyable and, ultimately, I have a great time. There is a fine line between playing and working, but it is important to remain relaxed.

NO: I learned that every job is different. Expect the unexpected. My first job was a fashion shoot for which I had to wade out to a large rock, climb it, and balance. That was followed by another fashion shoot for which I was balanced on a chair. I have had lots of fun working in unexpected environments, from deserted factories to magnificent estates. Sometimes models are asked on the job to sign releases that give rights that are broader or longer than the booking described. Ask your agent to clear any releases that the client wants with the agent and you beforehand. Each agent has a form of voucher that contains a model release with the agreed terms, and is countersigned by the client. Do not sign anything on the job other than the agent's voucher unless it is precleared.

Have you found that your acting background has been helpful with this type of work?

RM: My acting background distinguishes me from the vast majority of other models and, as such, has been helpful with print modeling.

When I do a casting, my first question is: what emotion are you looking for? What story do you want to tell with these photos? Many people have interesting faces, but in commercial print work, what more can you bring to the table other that your looks?

What is a typical print job booking like?

RM: My typical print job booking is making sure that I arrive on time and, in most cases, at least ten minutes early. I bring the following items with me: extra black socks, razor, trimmer, my own makeup, white underwear, extra comp cards, and my book. As soon as possible after I arrive, I start hair, makeup and wardrobe. Take a look at the layout of the job, and if you have any questions, make sure that you ask them as soon as possible. Even when I am fairly confident with what is expected of me, I still make it a point to chat with the photographer/client and ask them specifically what they need or want from me.

NO: The model is part of a team with hair, makeup, and wardrobe people, all working with the stylist and photographer toward the common goal of satisfying the client, who may or may not be there.

What's expected from print models by the photographer and client at a job?

RM: Again, common sense: you are expected to be on time and look like your picture or like you did when you had the casting. Extreme changes to your look should be avoided. Strange though it may seem, make sure you are bathed (it may seem obvious but you would be surprised), take direction, and finally, be comfortable with your friend, the camera.

NO: Follow preparation instructions: "clean clean" means "clean clean." Bring wardrobe choices if requested. Arrive on time. Follow direction by the photographer, producer, and client.

Any advice that you can offer to actors preparing to become print models?

RM: The advice I can and would like to offer to actors preparing to become print models is to make full use of your acting training, as it is one of the most valuable things in your bag of tricks. What makes you stand out from other models who do not have acting training is that you can give different emotions. This applies to all types of modeling, whether it is be commercial print, fashion, family, fitness, or or lifestyle.

NO: You will need standard-size comp cards with several photos and stats. Headshots are not sufficient.

SURVIVAL JOBS

Aside from film extra work and print modeling, there are many other ways that actors can earn additional income. Most actors have a "survival job" (or more than one). The secret is to find jobs that are not too time-consuming or physically taxing. You only have so much energy, and there are only so many hours in a day. Some places that you can begin your search for survival jobs are weekly ads in the show biz trade papers, as well as the *Village Voice* and the *New York Times* (especially on Sundays). Another place are bulletin boards in supermarkets and local shops.

The Actors' Work Program
The Actors' Work Program was created in 1986 for actors in response to an employment crisis among older actors. Actors were looking for supplementary work to help make ends meet. Eventually, the program became available to all actors of all ages.

The program offers retraining, counseling, and tuition to actors looking to expand their present skills and open up employment possibilities. Career counselors help actors define their present skills and create new ones. The Actors' Work Program offers seminars and workshops where actors can perfect such skills as job interviewing, résumé writing, and individualized career planning. Tuition assistance is also available for those actors who need specialized training.

The Actors' Work Program is located at Actors Equity, 165 West 46th Street. Aside from the different training programs that are offered, the Actors' Work Program has an excellent survival job bulletin board. Also, check out the job opportunity bulletin board at the Screen Actors Guild. You do not have to be a union member to look at their boards for potential work.

The Right Job for Your Needs
You'll need to find a job that'll allow you to take classes, go to auditions and interviews, make rounds, and appear in the occasional showcase. Such jobs,

complete with understanding employers that will allow time off for auditions, are not always easy to find. I felt that there was such a great need for this type of information that I wrote not only one, but two books on the subject: *The Job Book, 100 Acting Jobs for Actors* (Smith and Kraus) and *The Job Book 2, 100 Day Jobs for Actors* (Smith and Kraus).

There are the obvious jobs actors find, such as waiting tables, word processing, serving as a security guards, and substitute teaching. But with a little imagination and some perseverance, it's amazing what kind of job(s) you can find. Ask your fellow actors how they get by, and you'll find all kinds of ways to earn a living and keep the wolf from the door.

Be Your Own Business

One way to earn extra income, and be in charge of your time, is to capitalize on a skill that you may have. For instance, do you speak French, German, Spanish? All you need to do is let people know that you're available for either classes or coaching. The best (and least expensive) way to advertise is on local bulletin boards.

Are you adept at working with computers? There are two possible jobs here. First is helping those who are not computer literate by offering coaching or classes. The next is to set up a desktop publishing company, where you can create résumés or flyers for actors. You can branch off and expand these services by creating programs for theater companies, typing (and editing) scripts, etc. Other possibilities of self-employment include carpentry, teaching painting or other crafts, trainer, yoga instructor, or acting coach, to mention just a few.

PART V

Actors and Issues

SCAMS AND RIP OFFS

The actor arriving fresh to New York is vulnerable to the many rip-off artists trying to separate the actor from his money. Knowing that most newly arrived actors are eager and ambitious, scam artists work overtime to deceive the neophyte actor.

Casting Notices Too Good to Be True

In general, always have a healthy skepticism when reading casting notices that promise large sums of money to models or actor, even if they are inexperienced. The same holds true for casting notices offering "small roles" in movies, even if you have no experience. Quite often, many of these ads are to be found in reputable papers, like the *New York Times*, or in small suburban newspapers. Generally, what happens is you go in for an interview, and they compliment you endlessly and discuss all the potential that you have. But somewhere down the line, they'll discuss the classes that they want you to take (for a fee) or the headshots you "must" get from their photographers (for a fee).

Modeling Agency Scams

There are the model agency rip-offs. The ads say that they're looking for inexperienced models. You go in for the interview. Once again, you're told that you have a "great look." They tell you how well you're going to do as a model, but first, you must get a portfolio of pictures, and they know "just the right photographer." Believe me, there usually is a very strong tie-in between the photographer and the agency. That's not to say that the photographer may not be good, but you can bet your bottom dollar the photographer and the agency are working together. After you spent lord knows how much money on all these photographs and put together what they say is a great portfolio, you'll discover that you're never getting sent out by this agency, with excuses from "it's really slow" to "you're just not the type they're looking for now; we'll call you, don't call us."

Many years ago, when I moved to New York, I got a job at a well-known "modeling school." I taught acting at this school. I quickly became aware that anyone who was willing to pay the exorbitant fees for the school was told that they had "model potential." Some of these students that I worked with there were working two jobs just to be able to get by and pay for their classes. The bottom line was that many of them were just being ripped off. I quickly quit my job there.

The Internet Scam

The way that this one works is: Someone contacts you claiming to be an employer who has seen your picture or profile on an Internet Web site. They offer you some modeling or acting work through an employer that they represent. This person offers you an advanced payment (generally around fifteen or twenty percent) You're told you will be mailed a check for the amount. You're told you'll receive the balance of the money on the day you do the acting/modeling job. Of course they'll need your home address to mail their company check. When you do receive the check you'll notice it's for far more than just the advance amount (sometimes thousands of dollars). You'll receive an e-mail from the employer notifying you that the employer's "overpayment" is to pay for new headshots. Just deposit the check into your bank and keep your portion as your advance. They request that you send the remaining money to the photographer through Western Union. Hopefully by now a lot of red flags have alerted you that this is a big scam. When their check clears I'm sure you'll be notified by your bank that the check is a counterfeit. You've already sent the money to the photographer. Your bank will notify you that you are responsible for the lost funds. Whamo! Trying to contact the fictitious photographer will be a waste of time. And to add insult to injury you're told that you have to reimburse your bank for the entire amount of the check.

Rarely, if ever, is a an actor paid an advance. And bottom line, don't give or send money, or cash the check of anyone you don't know well. And one final thing, never use Western Union to pay an agent; always use your own check which you can hopefully stop before the fraud occurs.)

Agency Online Headsheet Scam
Being on the Online Headsheet (The Agency Web site Roster of Talent)

The online headsheet displays the photographs of the actors or models that the agency works with. For a fee (sometimes substantial), your photo(s) is included with all the other models or actors with the agency. Let me start off by saying that many legitimate agencies have online photos of their models to help clients book talent directly from the Web site. I've booked many jobs from agencies' online rosters of models and actors. This especially applies to the out-of-town agencies, where the actor/model can't go to a casting. In those cases, being on the online headsheet can be a smart move for the actor or model. The fees to be on the online headsheets vary dramatically. Ask if the agency would be willing to deduct the fee for the online headsheet from your first job. That way there is no out-of-pocket expense. I've made this arrangement with many agencies I work with and it's worked out very well. Not all agencies will agree to this, but it's certainly worth a try! The lesson is, be aware of who is representing you. Most of the "better," more established agencies have a legitimate online headsheets and being on one can work to your advantage.

The Guy Who Says He Can Make You a Star

When a man (or woman) approaches you in public, says that he's a talent agent, and that he sees "star potential" in you, be careful. You may be lucky—this can indeed happen—but quite often, the supposed talent agent or casting director may not be so legit and may have ulterior motives. There is no reason to give the "agent" your name, address, or phone number. Just ask for his card, and tell him that you'll call to further discuss this. Don't let him rush you by saying he must have your contact information immediately for a project. Tell him that you're uncomfortable doing that, but that you'll get back to him as soon as possible. There are several ways to check him out:

- Get a copy of the *Ross Reports*. The publication lists the names (and, in some cases, the phone numbers) of casting directors, talent agents, advertising agencies, producers, and packagers.
- You can call Actors Equity, the Screen Actors Guild, or the American Federation of Television and Radio Artists, and ask if the person you've met is "franchised" by them. You can also learn if the agent is in good standing with the union. On occasion, *Back Stage* publishes such lists.
- Call friends, casting directors, talent agents, or personal managers that you already know and ask if they've ever heard of this person, and if so, what do they know about him.
- You can see if the National Association of Talent Representatives knows anything about him.
- For information about casting directors, you can contact the Casting Society of America at (212) 333-4552.

It's more difficult to find out if a personal manager is legitimate, as he isn't franchised by any of the theater unions. You can, however, contact the National Conference of Personal Managers. The phone number is 1-866-91-NCOPM. To join this organization, managers must prove that they have been in business for at least a year or that they are knowledgeable about the entertainment industry.

In all fairness, just because someone has not joined any of these organizations doesn't necessarily mean that he is a crook. He may have not yet qualified or may have decided, for whatever reason, that the organization isn't for him. On the other hand, some very unscrupulous professionals have joined these organizations and have not yet been found out.

One last thing you can (and should) always do in these kinds of situations is to check with the Better Business Bureau to see if there have been any complaints made against the individual.

Acting Schools and Teachers

Unfortunately, New York State exempts acting schools from licensing. Therefore, anyone can claim to be a qualified teacher. Before you invest in any school or trust any coach or teacher, the best I can suggest is that you:

- see if you can find any former students, and see what they have to say.
- audit the classes. Trust your instincts as to whether the teacher is legitimate and knowledgeable.
- see if the teacher has written any books or articles.
- request a résumé or some biographical material stating where and how long the instructor has been teaching.
- trust your instincts. If you feel uncomfortable with this teacher or the class, pass on it.

Basic Protection

There are some basic things that you can do to protect yourself in any professional relationship.

- Whenever you enter into any professional relationship with someone, always get it in writing. A verbal agreement is not enough. A contract or written agreement is the ideal. Make sure that you receive receipts for any moneys that you have given them. If possible, it's always better to pay by credit card.
- There are no guarantees in this business, and anyone who "promises" you employment may be trying to deceive you. They may merely want you to sign some sort of exclusive contract with them or get you on their headsheet (for money).
- Needless to say, never put yourself in a position where you have to undress or feel uncomfortable in any way. If they ask you to remove your shirt or pants, leave immediately.
- It's true, sometimes film (and theater) producers hold interviews and auditions in their hotel rooms. But if the appointment is late at night, or if you feel the least bit uncomfortable about it, trust your instincts, and leave as soon as possible.
- If there is a hotel interview, the stage manager or assistant director should be there, too. The idea of you being alone with this stranger in his hotel room at night should make you feel suspicious.

- When it comes to upfront advance pay ments, be careful. Many acting schools ask for a partial payment up front; that's totally legitimate. Be very leery if a newly-met manager or talent agent asks for any money in advance. This is a sure sign that they are trouble. They may say it's for placement of your headshot on their headsheet, but I'd be very careful about that.

If You've Been Burned

Even the most seasoned actor gets burned on occasion. Scam artists are always perfecting their art. If money is due to you for some work you did through a talent agent or manager, and you haven't received it,

- you should continue to call the person, or go directly to his office.
- be sure to keep all copies of the letters. If you've been sending him letters requesting the money,
- threaten to, and then if necessary, report him to the Better Business Bureau.
- you might want to take the bum to small claims court. If the amount is small,
- report him immediately to both the Better Business Bureau and the New York City Division on Human Rights (as well as the police). If you have been sexually harassed or abused by this person,
- report all problems with agents, managers, or casting directors to SAG, AFTRA, or Equity. Hopefully, what happened to you won't happen to any other unsuspecting actor.

The Bottom Line

Actors sometimes, out of desperation, do reckless things, because they believe it will somehow help their careers. There are people out there just waiting for you to walk in the door. Be careful and cautious, and don't ever invalidate yourself or your personal ethics just to get ahead. There are nightmare stories that actors tell of mistakes in judgment that they made early in their careers. Don't be a casualty and do something rash just to get a job. In the end, I guarantee, it will haunt you forever.

ACTORS WITH DISABILITIES

Today, actors with disabilities have more opportunities for employment than ever before. That is not to say that a great deal still doesn't need to be done. With the passing of the Americans with Disabilities Act, there are now more jobs available in TV commercials, film, and theater. People with disabilities are now considered more a part of the fabric of this country. Roles in film and theater for disabled characters, played by disabled actors, are becoming more commonplace. Commercials with actors who are disabled are increasing. But as I mentioned, a lot more must be done. The pamphlet "Everything You Always Wanted to Know About Working with Performers with Disabilities But Were Afraid to Ask" was created by the three actors unions to be distributed to production companies, casting offices, agents, and others in the industry, to inform them of the facts about actors with disabilities. It can be accessed on the Internet through any of the acting unions.

I felt that the best way to deal with a chapter as important as disabilities was to have those people who are on the frontlines every day speak about the issue involved. I interviewed actors Kitty Lunn and Anita Hollander and the late actor-director Joseph Chaikin. I believe that you'll find their interviews to be informative and insightful.

Interview with Kitty Lunn

More than a twenty years ago, while preparing for her first Broadway show, Kitty Lunn had an accident that rendered her paraplegic. Through contact with the theatrical unions, she was introduced to the Performers with Disabilities Committee, which is dedicated to increasing employment opportunities for professional actors who are disabled and ready to seek employment. A year after joining the PWD Committee, she was asked to run for the Council of Actors' Equity (the first wheelchair-mobile person to ever hold a council seat). She was then elected to chair the Performers

Photograph by Eric Stephen Jacobs.
Pictured: Kitty Lunn

with Disabilities Committee for Actors' Equity.

Ms. Lunn is listed in the eighteenth edition of *Who's Who in American Women*. Recently, she founded *Infinity Dance Theater*, a nontraditional dance company for dancers with disabilities and nondisabled dancers beyond the age traditionally associated with performing.

Ms. Lunn serves on the National Board of the American Federation of Television and Radio Artists and continues to work as both an actress and dancer in theater, film, television, and concerts. Some of her TV, film, and theater credits include *Awakenings, Eyes of a Stranger, As the World Turns, Agnes of God,* and *Loving.*

Prior to your accident, how was your acting career going? What kind of work were you doing?

KL: It was going great, and I was preparing to do my first Broadway show. I was moving towards fewer musicals and less singing and dancing and more towards the dramatic. I made a very healthy living at that time, which included doing television commercials.

How has your career been affected by your accident?

KL: Disability diminishes opportunity. There's no way around that. That's the real truth about disability and the performing arts.

Writers and directors have found characters with disabilities fascinating for years. If you look over many of the Academy Award performances for the last decade, you'll notice a lot of those awards were given to actors who portrayed those characters with disabilities. The actors playing those roles, however, didn't have disabilities. There is a history of this kind of thing. For instance, many years ago, when they were shooting the movie *Showboat*, Lena Horne was rehearsing in the role for three months, but finally, it went to Ava Gardner because the producers just didn't feel comfortable about it. They didn't feel that most of America would accept a real African-American woman in the role, even though the character was African American. That kind of thing doesn't happen anymore because we have wonderful actors who are African-American and who can do those roles. Times have changed, although there is always room for improvement. But when it comes to disability, it still is perceived as an "acting" challenge, rather than something that the actor brings in his or her portfolio of abilities. It's considered a great challenge to teach an actor "how" to use a wheelchair or "how" to use sign language, rather than bring the disabled actor who already has those abilities to the roles.

Getting back to my career. Do I work as much as I worked before? Of course not. My commercial career stopped dead. In the fourteen years since I've been disabled, I believe I've done two commercials. I worked on and off on the daytime serial, *As the World Turns* when it was on the air. This was a role that was written specifically for me. Also, I've changed, too, as a woman getting older. So it probably would have happened naturally that my commercial career would have dwindled.

Specifically, what adjustments do you now need to make when working as an actor?

KL: The biggest hurdle that any actor with a disability has to overcome is stereotypical perceptions. The biggest barriers that I have, besides those stereotypical notions, is physical access to audition sites, to soundstages, and to theaters. This is particularly true in New York City. Today, many of the newer buildings being built demand physical access. This was not always true. In theaters, there have been many improvements for the audience members to have better access, but not always for the talent. I have also encountered some access difficulties at different locations when going to do a movie job.

I have worked diligently in the last twelve years to see that these things are dealt with, but in some cases, the producer is not always in control of the set, particularly if it's being done at a location.

What would you like those who are employing you as an actor and those you are working with (actors, directors, designers, etc.) to know when working with you or any other actor with disabilities?

KL: One example: many people, when seeing me roll down the street, make assumptions about me and my disability. One assumption is about my IQ. They assume that because I use a wheelchair that I have mental disability and that I'm hard of hard of hearing. These assumptions are made all of the time. For women particularly, they make assumptions about your sexuality, that you don't have any. Fear plays a huge part. People are afraid of anything that is different. For actors with disabilities, one thing you must do is put the people that you come in contact with at ease about your disability.

One thing you must include in the book is information about the ADA, the Americans for Disabilities Act, which was signed into law in 1990. It's a very wide and encompassing civil rights act that deals with employment and access to public places. But like most laws, the ADA had a lot of holes in it. The one thing that I want readers of your book to know, and that includes aspiring actors with disabilities who are thinking of coming to New York, is that the ADA was not intended to guarantee more than equal access. It is not an affirmative action legislation. It does not guarantee employment. It is not an entitlement legislation. The ADA says that an employer does not have the right to ask you about your disability at the audition. They can, however, ask the actor with the disability to demonstrate how he or she could perform the essential tasks of the job (i.e., the role), with or without a reasonable accommodation. The words "reasonable accommodation" are very important. The law puts the burden on the prospective employee, the actor, to state up front what "reasonable accommodation" would be for the actor to perform the role. The employer can't ask me why I use a wheelchair or anything about my medical condition, but they can ask me how I would perform my role.

In your article, "Breaking the Code," you say that "we must stop segregating people into 'special populations,' no matter how well meaning it may appear to be." In what ways do you feel that this can this be attained?

KL: I think one of the biggest deterrents to that is special education. We have to really look at how we educate our children. We have to change how we educate and give opportunities to children with disabilities. Most of the time in New York public schools, children with disabilities are segregated into special education, and not part of the education mainstream. Many of the teachers who work in special ed, although they are trying to help and be of service, do not believe that the children in their special ed classes will go on to higher education and the world of work. I'm talking here about public education.

As the chairperson of the Performers with Disabilities Committee of Actors' Equity, what things did you discover about how the unions dealt with disabled actors? Have things changed much?

KL: Things have changed dramatically, for the better. Back in 1990, when I was elected, none of Equity's contracts spoke of equal opportunities. Back then, there were a lot of misconceptions about disability. The Committee for Racial Equality did not want to include disability under the umbrella of nontraditional casting. That took the first two or three years to get all of that changed. It was really André De

Shields and the late Danny Straithorn who embraced the idea that disability belonged under the umbrella of nontraditional casting.

Actors' Equity took the lead on this and set the standard for the other unions to follow. I've worked very hard on the National Board of AFTRA to make sure that these principles were carried through in their contracts. It's been a little harder with SAG.

Actors with disabilities must become more active within the unions.

How do you suggest casting directors, producers, and directors offer people with disabilities the same opportunities as any other actor?

KL: The burden is not just on the employer; the burden is also on the actor. The actor with disability has to be the best trained in his craft, and that isn't easy. One of the recurring problems we have is that there aren't that many actors who are ready and qualified to handle the responsibility. Disability doesn't diminish talent; it does diminish opportunity. Disability doesn't give you talent that you don't already have, and there comes the entitlement mentality. We cannot expect a producer, a director, or a casting director to hire someone just because they have a disability. As well-trained actors with disabilities are given more opportunities, there will be a need for more facilities that are accessible. If an Actors' Equity audition is being held and a performer with disability wants to audition, but it isn't accessible, all that actor needs to do is tell the producer that he wants to audition, and it will be arranged. A mutual agreement as to where the actor can audition will be arrived at. In the Equity, SAG, and AFTRA contracts, if a blind performer has been called in to read, if they wish, with forty-eight hours notice, they can have the sides written in Braille. The producer is also responsible for hiring sign language interpreters for deaf performers. A deaf performer has the right to decline the interpreter. But contractually, the producer is obligated to provide the interpreter. Most individuals in America have gotten their perceptions about people with disabilities from telethons that are designed to tug at your heartstrings so you give them money.

What changes have you noticed in the entertainment industry towards people with disabilities in the last few years?

KL: People today are much more enlightened about people with disabilities. Many people with disabilities need specific and costly medical care. To pay those bills, they have to go on Medicare. To qualify to be on Medicare, you cannot be working. Therefore, there is a disincentive towards employment. There is stuff afoot that hasn't been passed yet, but which is a step forward. There is a law called the Work Incentive Act that deals with an individual with disability.

Here, they will be able to work, and they won't lose their Medicare and Medicaid coverage. It's going to take a generation or two to get many of the ideals now started into the mainstream.

What positive things do you see now occurring? What still needs to be done?
KL: Buses are now accessible, where ten, twelve years ago, they were not. As more people with disabilities pervade and invade the mainstream, it'll become more of the norm.

What advice do you have for actors with disabilities who are thinking of coming to New York to pursue an acting career?
KL: Number one, before they even get a bus ticket or drive here, the new actor coming to New York must ask him/herself, "How well trained and prepared am I?"

Second, and most important, especially for people in wheelchairs, accessible housing in New York City is extremely difficult to find. Start that networking process for finding housing, well, well, well in advance of actually coming here. For example, the West Side YMCA has only one wheelchair-accessible room—only one.

Also, get your day job lined up before you get here. New York is a very expensive place to live.

The burden for employment in this business is shared equally between the actor and the employer. You must be the best prepared that you can be as an actor.

Also—and this is just my feeling—your responsibility is to put the prospective employer at ease about you and your disability. One way to do this is to become comfortable with your own disability. So, all of your anger and angst about how unfair life is just wastes everyone's time, including your own. You should try to have a sense of humor about your life and disability.

The worst thing a person with disability can do at an audition is to try to give the impression that they don't need any accommodations, that they can leap tall buildings with a single bound, that they don't need any assistance of any kind, and then, after they get the job, make all these demands for accommodations. You must be up front as to what accommodations you will need to perform.

It's my opinion that if an actor has a physical disability, and I'm including blindness and deafness in that, I think that they should include it on their résumé. I include the universal symbol for a wheelchair on my résumé. It says I use a manual or power wheelchair. I think that this is really important. If an actor has an invisible or hidden disability, or one that can be handled with medication, then, I don't feel that it has to be mentioned on their résumé.

Photograph by Maurice J. Moran, Jr. Pictured: Anita Hollander

Interview with Anita Hollander

When she was in her twenties, Anita Hollander lost a leg to cancer. That certainly didn't stop her drive to sing and act. She has performed throughout Europe and America. Ms. Hollander has premiered works of composers and lyricists at Carnegie Hall, the Village Gate, Playwrights Horizons, and the O'Neill Center. Her original one-woman show, *Still Standing*, has been produced Off-Broadway, as well as nationally, at the White House, the Alabama Shakespeare Festival, Cleveland Playhouse, the Kennedy Center, and many other venues. She's played a tap-dancing nun in *Nunsense* and a three-legged Grizabella in *Cats* plus many other classic roles. She received a prestigious Helen Hayes Award nomination for Outstanding Lead Actress in a Musical. On television, she was a promo announcer for the NBC *Today* show and has appeared on *Law & Order, Oz, The Sopranos, All My Children*, to name a few. (www.anitahollander.com)

Prior to getting cancer, how was your acting career going? What kind of work were you doing?

AH: I began acting when I was eight, so I already had a résumé. At the point that I got cancer, I was doing my formal training at Carnegie Mellon. I was in my junior year (1977). (laughing) It certainly threw me off. I felt like this was one of my acting challenges. In my acting training, there were things like, "Here's my objective" and "Here's the obstacle" and "This is my motivation." It applied perfectly to what I was going through at the time. My whole mental state was that this was just an obstacle, a test to see if I was strong enough to have an acting career the way I wanted to have one. I know it seems kind of funny. I mean, here I was twenty-one years old, and this was just an acting exercise. It certainly was a shock to my system. I lost my voice from the whole experience, and I had to start all over again, with breathing and vocal training and all that. The surgery and the treatment at that hospital were very traumatic. My treatment was so bad that it was like they turned me from a twenty-one-year-old into a twelve-year-old. So I went back to my real life extremely timid and extremely small. I went back to school six weeks after the operation. I wanted to finish the year with my colleagues.

How has your life and career been affected since you lost your leg?

AH: The leg loss was five years later. Two weeks after the amputation, I was back in a show in Boston that I was in and directed. I went back to work on one leg. I went on stage with a bucket and a pole. They hadn't enough time to make a leg for me yet, since I wasn't healed enough. I was so determined, and there was no way I was stopping my life for this.

I had to adapt to having one leg and to deal with other people's reactions and perceptions to my having one leg, especially when walking into auditions with people that didn't know me. The difficult thing was walking into those auditions, and people were judging me on how I walked, not on my talent. I once walked into an audition and was told that I was not allowed to audition. Without knowing who I was, without looking at my résumé, the director said, "This isn't the right show for you." That wasn't true. It was a comedy, and I was doing comedy four or five nights a week at the Improv. The next day, the director spoke to her musical director, who wasn't at the audition. She said, "This woman showed up at the audition with one leg." The guy knew me; he had played for my act. He said, "Didn't you think she was fabulous?" The director said, "Well, I didn't let her sing." To which he replied, "Why didn't you let her sing? She's fabulous." She said, "I didn't want her to 'embarrass' herself."

The reason I even mention this story is that it's a real good example of people judging you before they know your work. This was in about 1983, my first year in New York. This was not the first time this kind of thing had happened.

In most respects, my life has been affected positively since the loss of my leg. Whether it's my own show or someone else's, people watching me seem to learn something positive and invaluable about performers with disabilities. It seems like writers love me, but sometimes producers and some casting directors are afraid of me.

What adjustments do you now need to make when working?

AH: Many of the producers and casting directors seem afraid to hire a disabled person. For me, with my leg, it's a snap-on-snap-off situation. I snap the leg on, I snap the leg off. After twenty-eight years of having one leg, it's not an issue for me. I prefer not to have to do stairs. But I do stairs when I have to.

Generally, how do you feel people respond to you in productions you're involved with?

I'd like to give you two examples of everything right and everything wrong. The first example was a daytime serial, the other was a very hot TV show that's now on the air. On the daytime, they brought me in to do a disabled role. They conferred with me on the script, went all out to treat me well. They realized it would be better if they sent a car for me. It would be better if I didn't have to walk the stairs. It would be better if the hair and makeup were on the same floor, rather than on separate ones. And in that building, the hair and makeup were four flights apart. If I politely asked about a correction about the disability, they were thrilled to make it, because they knew they had someone who knew what they were talking about.

A week later, there was another show, a TV show. I was asked to come out to a "casting call" for a role that was a one-legged character. When I got there, I found out it was not a casting call, but a production meeting to consult with me to be a photo double for a two-legged woman playing the one-legged character. They made me climb stairs to get to this production meeting, when in reality, there was an elevator that I could have taken, which was right behind the room where the meeting was. So rather than this being an audition, which I thought it was, they asked me to show them how the leg worked, how it went on and off. I was not being paid for this. They were telling me right to my face that I really didn't look anything like the actress I was supposed to photo double for. I asked them if they had had auditions for this role of a one-legged character, because the SAG contract says that they must. They said she had to have a Russian accent. So I said, "So, what's the problem? There are one-legged actors who can do a Russian accent." They said they hadn't seen any one-legged actors for the role and that they didn't care about the contract. I told them that they needed a consultant for disability, someone who can explain to them what they wanted to know. I said, "If you need a technical consultant, then we would need to negotiate that."

It was a very tense meeting. But for once in my life, I was not timid. I felt that this was a time for me to educate them about things. Usually, I'll say all the right things and try to get the job, but here was a situation where that just didn't feel appropriate. I felt that they were in the wrong, and I said, "I think this meeting is over." The upshot of all this is that they paid me for the meeting. They agreed to the price I asked for as a consultant, and they used me as the double.

You've said, "There is a difference between parading physically challenged people in front of an audience to perform and having talented artists who just happen to be disabled perform." Can you elaborate on this according to your experience?

AH: I think that sometimes people go out of their way to cast a disabled person to play a role that that person isn't ready to play. I feel that they are doing a disservice. Just because you want to have a disabled person on the stage, it might be a mistake. Because that disabled person might not be the best person for the role. However, people use that a lot to not even use a disabled actor. The truth is, in most cases when I've been involved with a disabled role, even though this might sound egotistical, I was right for the role. When a person is right for the role, and the person has a disability, it is a perfect marriage. I understand that acting is being things that you aren't. However, to disqualify a disabled actor for a disabled role because you think it might just be too easy for them, because they are already, I think is just out-and-out wrong.

Your show, Still Standing, came out on CD and is on the Internet (www. iTunes.com). What was the message you were trying to get across?

AH: It's a musical survival guide to life's catastrophes. It's fifteen songs to help not just disabled people deal with catastrophes, but everyone. What tools you need for survival, like a sense of humor, a perspective, a great imagination, a supportive family, love, and other things.

In your experience, how have things changed in the last few years as far as opportunities for actors with disabilities? What still needs to be done?

AH: I certainly continue to get work. And I'm excited about the promo work that I did on the *Today* show, because it's a job where my being disabled isn't of any concern. They didn't know that I was disabled when they hired me. Because I can go to this job without my leg on, I'm comfortable. I think Kitty Lunn had a lot to do with the positive changes that have occurred. But at the same time, I think that Hollywood is behind. Out there, in movies and TV, there's still a feeling that if you're disabled, you're not as good. I think the next hot or hip thing on television should be disability. Just as you've seen with blacks, gays, and Asians, you've discovered that these people were glamorous, sexy, and adorable, so, the same is true with people with disabilities. As far as those actors who won Oscars for playing disabled people, not one of them got the life behind the moves. Not one of them understood what was going on inside. The three actors unions (SAG, AFTRA & AEA) have joined to create the I.AM.PWD campaign: Inclusion in the Arts and Media of People With Disabilities (www.iampwd.org). It's a national civil rights campaign to transform people with disabilities into people with *visibility*, and give a face and a voice to the disabled community in the media. I am national co-chair of the campaign along with Robert David Hall of the TV show *CSI*.

What advice do you have for actors with disabilities who are thinking of coming to New York to pursue and acting career?

AH: Get training! If you want it badly enough, get training any way you can. I know that it's not always easy just to get training, but it'll be very important to you once you come to New York and try to get work. Read plays. Meet writers. If you like a particular writer's work, try to get to know him/her. Write them letters. Writers can be your best friend. If you do a reading for a writer and he likes how you read, he's going to take you with him as the play moves along. My whole career has been based on good writers. Representing good writers has been my foot in the door (laughs). Taking the positive route is the best way to go, but never be afraid to speak up when the situation calls for it. Not necessarily angrily, but speak up when you feel there has been an injustice. You can do it politely, even in a friendly, humorous way.

Interview with Joseph Chaikin

The late Joseph Chaikin was a world famous actor and director. In his memory, I'd like to publish this interview, one of his last. It's as pertinent now as it was when I interviewed him in 2001 for the first edition of this book. Mr. Chaikin directed one of the most influential experimental theater groups in the United States, the New York City–based Open Theater,

Photograph Copyright by Christopher Little. Pictured: Joseph Chaikin

which he founded in 1963 after working as an actor with the Living Theatre. Chaikin's work was honored with the Vernon Rice Award for "outstanding contribution to the theater." Chaikin was a six-time Obie Award recipient, including the very first Lifetime Achievement Obie awarded by the *Village Voice* in 1977. He was awarded two Guggenheim Fellowships, the National Endowment for the Art's first Annual Distinguished Service to American Theater Award, the Edwin Booth Award, and honorary Ph.D.s from Drake University and Kent State University. His book, *The Presence of the Actor*, was rereleased by TCG Publications in 1991. Chaikin was the first American director to be included in the Cambridge University Press's Directors in Perspective series on the world's most influential theater directors.

In 1984, Chaikin underwent open-heart surgery and experienced a stroke, which resulted in aphasia. His recovery process has been the source of inspiration for several theatrical pieces, including *The War in Heaven* (a collaboration with Sam Shepard), *The Traveler* (by Jean-Claude van Itallie), *Struck Dumb* (a collaboration with Jean-Claude van Itallie), and *Night Sky* (developed with Susan Yankowitz). Chaikin continued to direct productions in New York for the New York Shakespeare Festival, Manhattan Theatre Club, the Mark Taper Forum in Los Angeles, Atlanta's Seven Stages Theater, and San Francisco's Magic Theater, among others. An accomplished teacher, Chaikin conducted workshops and seminars throughout the United States, Europe, the Middle East, and South Africa.

In 1992, Chaikin directed Bill Irwin in an Obie-award winning production of *Texts for Nothing* by Samuel Beckett at the Joseph Papp Public Theater. From 1994 to 1996, Chaikin worked with author Susan Yankowitz on a new version of *Terminal,* a piece originally created by the Open Theater in 1970. Chaikin's 1996 collaboration with Sam Shepard, *When the World Was Green*, premiered at the Cultural Olympiad of the 1996 Summer Olympic Games in Atlanta and then played at New York's Public Theater, Cambridge's American Repertory Theatre, and most recently at the Singapore Arts Festival and the Chekhov Festival at the Moscow Arts Theatre.

How did you get started as an actor?

JC: I grew up in New York. As a child, I loved theater and films. I was not well as a child. When I was five years old, I had rheumatic fever and was very sick for two years. When I was ten years old, I was sick once again, but this time for a long time. My father taught Hebrew at the time. It was years later, when I went to Drake University, where I really discovered theater. I went there when I was sixteen years old, stayed for two years, and then came back to New York. When I came back to New York I started to study at HB Studio. At that time, I became familiar with Shakespeare. One of the people that impressed me quite a lot was Stella Adler, who I met during that time. I never studied with her though. It was during that time that I worked as a waiter. I met Sam Shepherd at the restaurant where I worked. He was a waiter, too. We became good friends back then and have been very close ever since. We talked all the time about theater, all the time. I was about eighteen years old.

My favorite acting teacher was a woman named Nola Chilton. She taught a style of acting similar to what Lee Strasberg was teaching, but much better than his technique. I thought she was terrific. Peter Brook was another mentor. I was directing a play by John Claude van Itallie, and Peter Brook invited me to go to London.

How important do you think acting training is for an actor?

JC: It's important, because to do Shakespeare, or my favorite, Beckett, you must understand the words, how to say them. Acting helps you learn the different physical life needed for characters and the music of the language. You must really want to do this acting thing. I believe actors should be discouraged. Jerzy Growtowski taught me to discourage actors, because then, only the best will stay and work and train.

What kind of training is the best training?

JC: The best kind of training is where you learn how to use words, language. I discourage acting for films; that's just not for me.

What do you focus on in your master class for actors and directors?

JC: I focus on using your voice and understanding language. The most important thing is to understand the music of the language. Shakespeare is very important to study. Acting should be surprising. I'm very critical in my class, and sometimes, my students feel bad. I don't work with beginning actors, only advanced actors.

In addition to language and speech, I focus on body work. I have problems with my body, but Wayne, the man I teach with, does some of the body work that I can't do. We teach together. I very much enjoy seeing good actors grow. It's very exciting. I had a directing student, and she was a very good student. I saw something she directed recently, and it was very good. That makes me very happy. As I've said before, the music and rhythm of language is very important. Beckett loved the music of language also. That's one of the reasons I'm so fond of his work.

Do you think acting and directing are skills that can be learned?

JC: Yes, yes, I do. But most important is talent. For instance, I'm going to begin auditions for Sam Shephard's new play at the Signature

Theatre. I was talking to my boss, Jim Houghton (artistic director of Signature), about the auditions. We'll see people once, maybe twice. If there's talent, we'll know. It'll be yes or no. (Note: The play was a major success).

Do you still act?

JC: Not much anymore; I prefer directing. When I was acting, I did Beckett, Brecht, and Shakespeare.

How did you go from acting to directing?

JC: I was acting with the Living Theatre years ago. It was very interesting, the Living Theatre. My friend, Gordon Rogoff, suggested that we start another theater together. So, we did start a theater that eventually became the Open Theater. It was there that I got into directing. I had learned things about acting and directing at the Living Theatre, but it was in the Open Theater that I really began to direct. I had also been trained to direct by Peter Brook in London.

Any early directing jobs that you really enjoyed?

JC: I loved directing Tennessee Williams. The characters are so beautiful. And I really enjoy Ionesco. I like the absurdity. And Albee's *Counting the Ways*.

Who are your favorite actors?

JC: Marlon Brando, who I met years ago, is a wonderful actor. He studied with Stella Adler. Brave, bold actor. I also love Maggie Smith.

How do you know when it's time to give up?

JC: I sometimes discourage actors, but you never know, an actor might bloom later on. It's hard to always know.

How has living with a disability (aphasia) affected you personally?

JC: After I had my stroke, my speech was much worse than it is now. Lots of training. JoAnne Akilitis was very helpful to me. She's a very kind and supportive woman. She encouraged me a great deal at a very tough time in my life. With her support, I began a project on disabilities at the Public Theater.

When I was younger, I was very pessimistic. After the stroke, I became much more optimistic. Right after the stroke, the right side of my body was in a lot of pain. Now, it's much better, but still not perfect. I could hardly walk back then. Part of my optimism is that I'm getting older, and I appreciate life much more.

How has disability affected your work?

JC: Mainly, the aphasia has affected me. Also, with my right arm, I've had to work on that. Before I had the stroke, I was working on Sam Shepherd's *War and Heaven*. I had to stop working on it. Sam was very kind. We continued work on the play later on. I work very hard on the aphasia. I'm missing words very often. My ideas and thoughts are the same, I just can't always find the words. But I notice that each year, I seem to be getting a little better. Years ago, Gordon Davidson invited me to Los Angeles to do a project on disabilities. I brought in Jean-Claude van Itallie, and we worked on this disabilities project together. It was called *The Traveler*. It was very good. I also worked with Susan Yankowitz on a play called *Night Sky*. It was very successful. The ideas of the play were mine, but Susan actually wrote the play.

Why focus on disabilities?

JC: Disabilities are very important. People assume that if a person has just one leg that their mind is also not working. This is wrong. People with disabilities are just as capable as anyone else to do many things that other people can do. There can be humor in being handicapped. It's not all so sad. I'm working with John Belluso, and he is a wonderful handicapped playwright who has found the humor in disabilities. People must understand that there is more to disabilities than just sadness. I very much admire John's work. He went to NYU. John is fast thinking, has fresh thoughts—wonderful writer. He is in a wheelchair.

THE NONTRADITIONAL CASTING PROJECT

The Nontraditional Casting Project (NTCP) is a not-for-profit advocacy organization that was established in 1986 to deal with problems of racism and exclusion in film, TV, and theater. This organization was specifically created to make certain that all minorities would be fairly represented in the workplace.

The following was reprinted with the kind permission of the Nontraditional Casting Project. I could have paraphrased the information here, but felt that it was important for my readers to read the language of the document as written.

The Nontraditional Casting Project (NTCP) is a not-for-profit advocacy organization established in 1986 to address and seek solutions to the problems of racism and exclusion in theatre, film, and television. The only organization of its kind in the country, NTCP's principal concerns are that artists who are African-American, Asian-Pacific-American, Caribbean Black, South Asian, Latino, Native American, deaf and hard-of-hearing, blind and low-vision, artists who have ambulatory disabilities or developmental disabilities are denied equitable professional opportunities; and that this exclusion is not only patently discriminatory, but a serious loss to the cultural life of the nation. Furthermore, this exclusion has resulted in a theatre, film, and television industry that does not accurately reflect the diversity of our society.

NTCP works to promote inclusive hiring practices and standards, diversity in leadership, and balanced portrayals of persons of color and persons with disabilities. NTCP considers diversity a comprehensive issue, which extends to the participation of those who make up the artistic team—actors, directors, designers, writers, stunt performers, choreographers—as well as the production team and administrative staff, board of directors, and the audience.

NTCP advocates the full participation of artists of color and artists with disabilities through the strengthening of culturally specific and disability-specific institutions, as well as through expanding opportunities at institutions that primarily produce or present work based in a European tradition.

Since its inception, NTCP has been a leading voice in the movement toward inclusion. As efforts to achieve broader diversity accelerate throughout the theatre, film, and television industry, NTCP is increasingly being called upon to assist casting directors, production companies, theatre organizations, film studios, and television networks with a range of needs, from consulting to casting.

NTCP's aim is to achieve a theatre, film, and television industry that accurately reflects our populace; where each artist is considered as an individual; where ethnic, cultural, and physical difference is understood and appreciated as part of one's individuality; where the stories being told reflect our communities; and where our individual humanity and forms of expression can be celebrated.

NTCP's work involves

- advocacy toward more inclusive standards and practices;
- consciousness raising and education;
- specific programs through which producers, directors, and casting directors can implement inclusion.

NTCP's Artist Files are a national resource of approximately 2,500 actors' résumés and photographs, as well as the résumés of writers, directors, choreographers, designers, and stage managers.

The Artist Files/Artist Files Online are made available to producers, directors, and casting directors in two formats: Pictures and résumés are maintained in binders at NTCP's New York office, available to the profession Monday through Friday by appointment, and the Files are available on the NTCP Web site. The binders are organized by cultural identification or physical accommodation, and beyond this, by gender, general age range, and alphabetically.

Access to Artist Files Online on their Web site is given to producers, directors, and casting directors who provide NTCP their professional credentials. If you are an artist—an actor, director, writer, designer, choreographer, stage manager—and you would like to be included in the Files, please send NTCP one black and white photograph and résumé. To ensure inclusion in the Files, actors of color are asked to enclose a covering note indicating his/her cultural identification and, for an actor with a disability, any accommodation used. Please indicate your union affiliation(s). Send to

Actor Files Online
Nontraditional Casting Project
165 West 46th Street
New York, NY 10036
(212)869-8530

Interview with André De Shields

In a career spanning forty years, **André De Shields** has distinguished himself as an actor, director, and educator. He is the recipient of the 2009 National Black Theatre Festival's Living Legend Award, the 2007 *Village Voice* Obie Award for Sustained Excellence of Performance and the 2009 AUDELCO Award for Outstanding Performance in a Musical/Male. He has acted in Broadway shows like *Impressionism* with Jeremy Irons and Joan Allen, Mark Medoff's *Prymate* (Drama Desk Nomination), *The Full Monty* (Tony Nomination), *Play On!* (Tony Nomination), *Ain't Misbehavin'* (Emmy Award) and *The Wiz* (Title Role), as well as films like *Extreme Measures* with Hugh Grant, *Prison* with Viggo Mortensen, and *The American Snitch*, and television shows including *Rescue Me*, *Life On Mars*, *Lipstick Jungle*, *Sex and the City*, *Cosby*, *Law & Order*, *As the World Turns* and *Another World*. Regionally, he has been seen in David Mamet's *A Life in the Theatre*, *Inherit the Wind*, *Death of a Salesman*, *Our Town*, *The Man Who Came to Dinner*, and Ibsen's *Ghosts* with Jane Alexander. He is an alumnus of both the University of Wisconsin-Madison and New York University (Gallatin School). A triple Capricorn, André is the ninth of eleven children, born and raised in Baltimore, Maryland. Visit *www.andre-deshields.com*.

ANDRÉ DE SHIELDS

Photograph by Lia Chang. Pictured: André de Shields

Why and when did you decide to move to New York to become an actor?

ADS: My move to New York came with the Organic Theater Company. I was working in Chicago. We had created the world's first science fiction, episodic, adventure play, called *Warp*. They brought it from Chicago to New York. The play opened at the Ambassador Theater on February 14, 1973, and closed four days later. So, there I was in New York, the center of the universe, where I knew I wanted to be. The Organic Theater Company returned to Chicago, but I decided to stay in New York. I didn't have a pot to piss in or a window to throw it out of, but there I was, where I wanted to be.

Did you have a strategy, a game plan before moving here?

ADS: The only strategy I had was that our show (*Warp*) was going to bring New York to its knees, take Broadway by storm, and we were going to be big stars. At least, that was the dream. I had no real strategy or game plan. I did have a friend who was living and working here in *Jesus Christ Superstar*. Her name was Charlotte Crossley. She invited me to sleep on her couch while I was getting on my feet.

What did you imagine it would be like?

ADS: Bright lights, big city, fast pace, tall buildings, everything. I thought I was going to make a million dollars and drive fast cars and meet beautiful people, be wined and dined. I thought I was going to be the next Sidney Poitier (my role model).

What was your first year in New York like? What were the adjustments you had to make?

ADS: The show closed, and I cried. After I cried, I partied. After I partied. I went to work at LaMaMa's for $25 a week. I was my friend's live-in maid. This friend I lived with went on to become one of Bette Midler's Harlettes. And I went on to choreograph the Harlettes.

If you had a chance to redo any part of that first year in New York (especially career-wise), what would it be?

ADS: I wouldn't redo it. I understand that my life and my career have unfolded perfectly. If I had been in the position of power to influence or change it, I would not then be on this path of destiny, which is absolutely correct for me right now.

Did you take classes when you first got here, and if so, with whom?

ADS: No, I didn't. All of the honing of my art in New York was done at LaMaMa. It was done at the Organic Theater Company in Chicago.

I've never trained formally. Ellen Stewart (LaMaMa) and Stuart Gordon (the Organic Theater Company) were my mentors.

What kind of survival jobs did you have? How did you get by?
ADS: I didn't have any survival jobs. I earned the little I did in the experimental theater world at LaMaMa and the small group of friends who loved me and took care of me.

How did you get an agent? How did you get to meet casting directors?
ADS: In the summer of '73, I was hired, after several auditions, by Peter Link of the Public Theater to do a concert at the Delacorte Theater in Central Park, entitled *Please Don't Let It Rain* (which, of course, it did). It was at that concert that I was noticed by Dulcina Eisen, a young associate at the Gage Group Agency. She asked me to come in for an interview. I did, and she liked me, and she asked me if I wanted to freelance with her. She started to send me out, which got me more and better auditions. That's how I got to know the casting directors in New York.

What were your first auditions/acting jobs like?
ADS: We immediately hit pay dirt with an audition for the American premiere of *Joseph and the Amazing Technicolor Dreamcoat* at the Playhouse in the Park Theater in Philadelphia. I was cast as Pharaoh in that production. After that, Dulcy got me an audition for this production of *The Wiz*. I auditioned for the Scarecrow and didn't make the cut. She sent me back for the role of the Tin Man, and I didn't get it. She sent me back, I auditioned for the Lion, and I didn't get it. She sends me back, and I auditioned for the Wiz, and I made it, I got the part. The reason she kept sending me back is because we both knew, Dulcy and I, that I was perfect for the Wiz. The producers didn't know that I was right for the Wiz, but each time I auditioned, I once again knocked at the door to let them know. I was persistent. They let me keep coming back, because they saw something in me, but they hadn't decided. I went back for that audition of the Wizard with all my ammunition: my five-inch silver platforms, my hot pants, my hair pulled back in a Jimi Hendrix, silver hoops in my ears, glitter, the whole thing. When I walked in, there was an audible gasp. When I sang for them, the composer said, "That's my Wiz!" He saw that I could do it, and I wasn't afraid to be outrageous. This story is a huge lesson that I tell to all my students when I teach. One of the lessons that you don't learn in acting schools is that you *can* change the minds of the creative team of a show. Sometimes, these casting breakdowns are lies, or they don't know what they want.

In experimental theater, which is where I was trained, you don't subscribe to this notion that you can be bored by a show, but smile all the way to the back. When you become bored in experimental theater, you must leave the show because you are no longer contributing to it. It is destroying the source of your talent to stay. I applied this to *The Wiz*. I was in the show for two years, one year on Broadway and one on the road. I woke up one morning: "Gee, I don't feel like going to work. But I will, I'll get through the show on automatic pilot." Now, that's the red flag for experimental theater artists. I gave two weeks' notice. They thought I was out of my mind. I left the show in August of '77. In September of '77, Bette Midler called and told me she was about to go on tour again, and she needed my services as choreographer. In November of '77, we opened at the Copacabana in New York. In December of '77, Richard Maltby asked me if I would be interested in working with him on this idea of a tribute to Fats Waller at the Manhattan Theater Club on East 73rd Street. So, all of this is really to show the beauty and the reward of that experimental discipline. If you feel that you are doing a show on automatic pilot, you leave, you take the jump, and your safety net will appear.

What do you feel are the main differences between living/working in New York versus Los Angeles? Do you have a preference for one over the other?

ADS: I prefer working in New York. The main difference is, when the work stops in New York, you can literally hustle your next job on the corner. In LA, there are no corners. I've spent some time in LA on national tours of shows that I was in. During those times that I was out there, I'd do the audition routine, which was totally different than the routine here in New York. First of all, the audition begins with trying to get into an agent's office. Here in New York, you don't have to start dressing up until you get the audition. In LA, you have to dress up to meet the agent. You have to go to the right party, air kiss the right people out there. I'm not dissing it; that's just the way it's done out there. New York people say, "Don't take it personally," and maybe there is some truth to that. In LA, I think it's one hundred percent personal. I like to live in New York. There certainly are pluses for living in LA or any other place for that matter. But when I think about the drug that New York is, I come back to stay. I must, I need, I prefer, I want to live in Manhattan. I guess the drug is the work, and New York is the pusher or the source. When I'm in another place and I can't go to the corner and make that buy, that score, that connection, then I know I have to go back to New York.

What advice (or warnings) do you have for actors who are thinking of moving to New York to start their careers?

ADS: I use this often with the young people that I work with. The first thing that my students ask when they are about to graduate is, "How do I get an agent?" And I say, "That's the last thing that you want. What you want to know is how to deal with the only two things that this industry guarantees. One is rejection, the other is insecurity. When you are lonely and can make a friend of insecurity, and when you're hungry and can eat rejection, you are then ready to come to New York."

What major changes have you noticed taking place in nontraditional casting from when you first began acting to the present?

ADS: My first professional show was *Hair* with the late Tom O'Horgan, in Chicago. *Hair* is the American tribal, love-rock musical, which had every color, every creed, every religion, every sexual persuasion that you could possibly imagine. However, there were no doctrines of nontraditional casting being articulated. That's just the way the world was. Thirty years later in New York, we have to legislate, as much as we have to legislate in the industry, nontraditional casting, multicultural, ethnic diversity, under that umbrella called "inclusion." And I'm all for that. What I'm learning is that everything old is new again. It's just packaged differently. The last bastion of exclusivity to fall is "The Great White Way," pun intended. In experimental theater, you have to go against the tradition. And the tradition in the world, the universe, is the domain of white men. To be nontraditional means you have to distribute the wealth.

What issues do you feel still need to be addressed in nontraditional casting?

ADS: The largest issue that needs to be addressed is the playwright. It is the playwright who is responsible for the reflection that is then revivified on the stage. If the playwright puts this on the page, then the creative team is obligated to present what the playwright wrote. It is a basic tenet of the theater to reflect society. When your society is multicultural, then, the playwright cannot use the excuse that "I can only write about what I know." You must write about what you see.

If there is a message you'd like to put out to producers, directors, and casting directors regarding nontraditional casting, what would it be?

ADS: Profit and truth in the living theater are not mutually exclusive. Chew on it.

Is there anything that you feel actors of color should be aware of before coming to New York?

ADS: This is the question that you must ask yourself: "Who, male or female, in the pantheon of actors of color has made a living on the New York stage?" The reason that I say ask yourself that question is, then, you can see what you are up against. Even the best of us, and I consider James Earl Jones and Cicely Tyson two of the best of us, no longer make a living on the New York stage. When I talk to my peers, they consider me an exception, because of *The Wiz, Play On, Ain't Misbehavin'*, and now, *The Full Monty*.

What are your plans for the future?

ADS: I have a story to tell, and part of the story, you've asked questions about. And I want to tell it in prose and poetry, not a play. I feel there is a book in me. There is a compendium of information in me that I will tell like a griot. A griot is an African term. In African tribal culture, the griot is responsible for keeping the oral history of his village, tribe, or nation. We African Americans here in America have borrowed that term. Although the oral tradition still exists here in the United States, I want to be a scribe, a griot, in book form, so that the history does not get sullied, or tainted, or conveniently changed. But I want to tell the story of the desert or monastery, if you will, that you must enter, the vow that you must take, if you want to become an actor in New York. Very specifically, as a theater actor in New York, without distracting oneself to television, movies, or Hollywood. If one is going to make a living as an actor in New York, it is tantamount to entering a monastery.

AN ACTOR'S ACTIONS

Many actors come to New York to pursue their dreams, but are stymied when opportunities present themselves, because they are unsure of how they are supposed to behave, "to be" in different situations. Even though they believe in their talent, they're not always sure of what is "personally" expected of them at auditions and in casting directors' and agents' offices. It's the not knowing that can be unsettling and can zap an actor's confidence. What follows are some ideas that may be of some use. These are based on my own perceptions and feelings, as well as those of many actors, casting directors, and agents that I interviewed. These are only suggestions. How you go choose to go about your career is, of course, always totally up to you.

Appropriate Behavior Between Actors and Casting Director and Agents

As has been said time and again throughout this book, always be respectful, professional, polite, and friendly at interviews and auditions As a very successful actor recently told me, "I've always behaved (at auditions and in interviews) as if I'm with a revered aunt. Sure, I want to be warm and open with her, but I don't tell her too much. I like to charm her, yeah, but not embarrass her or myself in any way."

Another suggestion came from an actor who said that for years, he always tried "too hard" at interviews and auditions. He thought by "blowing them away, making a big splash," he'd really impress them. One day, a helpful casting director, who believed in the actor's talent, told him that he should "try not to take all the air out of the room." The casting director told him to "share the space" with the person who was interviewing him: "Try not to make everything always about you. Try to find something of interest in the person who is interviewing you." I realize that interviews and auditions are very stressful, but they are part of the job, and you must come to terms with them. You must learn to not only accept them, but to embrace them, even make them enjoyable, if possible. It's a way to get to know another person. And yes, that casting director or talent agent is a human being. Try to relate to him as you would to any human being. Actors sometimes develop fantasies about people in power.

Appropriate Behavior in Rehearsal and Performance

After being cast in a show, many actors seem to become "instant family" with the others in the cast. The rehearsal period can become a wonderful time of bonding with others. Perhaps it's the tension of the rehearsal process or an individual's insecurities, but some actors have a tendency to cling onto others for support. This can sometimes make for an unpleasant situation. An actor's neediness can be draining on others in the cast. If another actor starts clinging to you in rehearsal, try to be supportive, but let her know that you have your own work to do and that she should try to find her way through her fears and insecurities. Try to be sensitive to the actor, but also make sure to take care of yourself and your needs. Neither abandon her, nor allow her to monopolize all your time. Try to find a supportive balance.

You may encounter actors who "act out" in any of a hundred ways during the rehearsal period. Some actors are egotistical or seem insensitive, or are control freaks or constantly apologizing, or blabbermouths, etc. The bottom line is to always try to find the balance of doing what you need to do for yourself first, so that you can get the most out of the rehearsal period. Try to maintain a friendly, but professional relationship with everyone in the company. Remember, many of these people can become a strong part of your future networking group. Alienating anyone for whatever reason can never be helpful. Try to be diplomatic and fair, truthful to yourself as well as others.

Knowing how intimate you should get with other members of a company during rehearsal, or even in production, is purely a personal thing, but most professionals agree that it's always risky to become "involved" with someone from a company while in rehearsal or production. Things can go wrong in personal relationships between members of a company that may affect the production as a whole in some way.

Social Behavior with Industry People

Once again, "professionalism" is the operative word here. Next comes "friendly and positive." Some actors mistakenly believe that as they get to know agents or casting directors better, they can be "totally open" with them, use them as parents or shrinks. I'm all for an actor being friendly—but to a degree. You must always be clear that what you're developing with them is a business relationship, not a buddy-buddy friendship. It is inappropriate for you to reveal too much about your personal life. I know that some actors develop very close relationships with their agents or with some casting directors. For some, this closeness is not a problem, but for others, there may be complications down the line that they'll regret. How much you decide to open up is totally up to you.

Actors should not allow themselves to become too involved with a talent agent's or casting director's personal life. There have been many stories where actors, while just trying to be supportive of an agent going through a divorce or breakup, become their confidant or best friend. In some cases, what happens is that they inadvertently become part of the problem rather than the solution. This adversely affects the business aspect of their relationship, and in some cases can be detrimental. How familiar you want to be with your agent or with a casting director is up to you, but once again, please try to maintain the business aspect at all costs.

Quite often, agents or casting directors will ask you to join them to see a play or movie that one of their clients is in. There is certainly no harm in doing this. It can be an excellent opportunity for you to deepen your business relationship. On your "date," you should be friendly and open, but once again, to a degree. If you become too informal, too relaxed, too cozy, you may be sending out signals that you don't mean to.

Then there are the situations where a friendly business date with a casting director or agent becomes "something more." I think that it's obvious that you shouldn't drink too much alcohol during the evening. You don't want to say or do things that you will regret the next morning. There are thousands of casting-couch stories floating around New York and Los Angeles; don't add yours story to the heap. Never put yourself in a place where an uncomfortable situation can occur. Always meet professional people in a public place, such as a restaurant or at the theater, and certainly never at their hotel room (the lobby is fine, thank you) or at their apartment.

And one last thing: Even if you have sincere feelings for your agent, perhaps you'd like to date them, may I suggest that you find a new agent first. Then, if you wish, dating your former agent is fine.

I know that to some, much of this might seem somewhat puritanical. Perhaps it is, but it's also the best way I can advise to not complicate business relationships in a business where, so often, the lines between social and business can become very blurry.

Being "Gracious"

For a long time, I've wanted to mention to actors the importance of being gracious in this business. Not only do I feel that it's important in networking, but it's also important in all interactions. *Webster's* defines gracious as "marked by kindness and courtesy" and "characterized by charm and good taste." In a business where large egos and insecurities are everywhere, it is quite important to try to be as pleasant as you can be with everyone that you come in contact with. There can be a tremendous amount of rejection in this business. Being able to lift yourself up, pull yourself together, and move on is always difficult. Taking the high road in all interactions is something you should always attempt to do. So many actors in this business, from years of rejection, unfortunately become bitter and resentful. Everyone responds better to the actor who is kind and considerate. As Mary Harden of Harden Curtis Associates says (see her interview in chapter 15), "Always remember that the people that you're dealing with in this business are human beings." We sometimes think of those in power as people whom we can use in some way, and therefore, we don't treat them with the same humanity and dignity that we'd treat anyone else in our lives.

If agents or casting directors do something nice for you, give you a tip about a job, come to see you in a show that you're performing in, let them know how appreciative you are. Send them a note, give them a call. If a casting director calls you directly for an audition or work, send her a note letting her know how appreciative you are. If someone compliments you on a performance that she saw you in, let her know how (sincerely) appreciative you are that she took the time to mention it to you.

You may not book a job just because you're pleasant, but how people in the industry think of you, your reputation, is quite important. It may be just as important as your picture and résumé, and it will follow you wherever you go in this business. There are some actors who have reputations of "being difficult." Yes, people who are difficult, not courteous, may work in the business, but people dread being in their company. In the long run, these actors may not work as much as they could. There are other actors, however, who are known for their humanity, their kindness to others. Everyone wants to work with them. They make the workplace a better place to be. And yes, in the end, the kinder, more gracious actor probably does get more work than the actor who gives people a hard time. But it's not just about working in this business, it's about how you choose to work, the way you interact with others, the quality of how you choose to live your life. Please take what I'm saying to heart.

PART VI

A Life in Show Business

PATHS TO SUCCESS

Arriving in New York can be overwhelming. You have your dream, and now you need to strive to fulfill it. The secret to starting out is to have a daily itinerary for the first month or so. There is so much to see, do, plan, and accomplish. In the actor interview section coming up, Lisa Emery discusses how she was overwhelmed for almost the entire first year or so after she arrived in New York. Other actors have also told me of how overwhelming New York can be. As I suggest in the beginning of the book, one of the ways to deal with this is to make several shorter trips to the city *prior* to actually moving here.

The First Week in New York

When all the preliminary work has been done and you've packed and moved to the city, you should already have a well-planned itinerary. The more you work out *prior* to arriving, the less overwhelming those first few weeks will be. One thing about itineraries: you should always be flexible and prepared to make any necessary adjustments. Being calm but focused those first few weeks will be a great help in settling into your new life in the city. One priority at the beginning will be where you'll live, your home base. Once you have a temporary or permanent place to work out of, here are some things you'll need to do during that first week or two:

- You will want to make certain domestic arrangements, so that you are hooked up and comfortable in your new space. These include getting phone and cable hookups arranged, adding any necessary or decorative touches to your surroundings, and finding the most convenient grocery stores.
- If you know any people in the city, this is a good time to give them a call and let them know you're here, perhaps get together for coffee. Keep yourself busy and focused. The first few weeks may bring on loneliness and homesickness.
- Find a job that will work compatibly with auditions and classes.
- Interview and audit any teachers and classes that you're thinking of taking.
- Start looking into photographers for your headshots.

- Once you're into a groove with your career, keep the momentum going. You should do something for your career every day.
- Networking leads to interviews. Interviews lead to auditions. Auditions lead to work. Work begets work.

Ten Things That It Takes to Make It as an Actor In New York

1. Talent
2. Perseverance
3. Professionalism
4. Confidence
5. Good networking skills
6. Perseverance
7. A good working strategy
8. Ability to deal with rejection
9. Luck
10. Perseverance

Yes, perseverance is listed several times. It is the one thing that will carry you from one goal to another in a business that can be extremely difficult. Why some actors click early in their careers and others take twenty years, no one can really say. Quite often, it's luck, being in the right place at the right time. Sometimes, it's knowing the right people who can help you along. Sometimes, it's type. If you're a young character actor, you may not work a great deal until you've "aged" into your type. Sometimes, it's talent. Some actors' talents don't bloom right away; sometimes their talent "opens up" as they work more and develop inner confidence. There are so many reasons why a career does and doesn't take off. You have to believe in yourself and your talent, and yes, you have to persevere, no matter what.

When Is Enough Enough?

The answer to this question is totally subjective and totally personal. The truth is, each actor has his own answer. I've known actors that gave up after only six months of trying. I know of others whose careers took thirty years to take off. But for each one of them, there is the story of the actor who arrives in New York and, within a year, gets a contract on a daytime serial. Or the actor who books five national commercials in the first six months that she's here. So much of this business is luck and timing. How long you hold out depends on you. Certainly, finances are a consideration. You've got to earn a living. But it all really comes down to how strong your dream and determination are. If you'll recall, at the beginning of the book, I mentioned that actors come to New York because they have a dream about an acting career. How much you want it is everything. How many years of your life you're willing to dedicate to this dream is up to you. When is enough enough? Only when you, and you alone, say it is. You are the only one who has the power (and yes, the perseverance) to latch on to your dream.

NEW YORK ACTOR STORIES

I decided to have a section of actor interviews, because I felt that reading about other actors' struggles and solutions might serve as a source of information and inspiration. As you'll notice, some of these actors had a very rough time trying to make it in the business. But for others, it was just a walk in the park. Their stories are true reflections of the way that this business can work.

Henry Winkler
Photograph copyright by Carol Rosegg. Pictured: Henry Winkler

When Henry Winkler created "The Fonz" (Golden Globe for Best Actor in a Comedy Series) for *Happy Days*, television history was created. The black leather jacket he wore in the show now hangs in the Smithsonian. The character made him an international star. Most recently, he received an Emmy nomination for Outstanding Actor for his appearance on *The Practice*. He presently can be seen on the TV series, *Royal Pains,* and in the films, *The*

Hillers and *Running Mates*. His many films include *The Lords of Flatbush, Crazy Joe, Nightshift* (Golden Globe nomination), *Down to You (*with Freddie Prinze, Jr.), *Little Nicky,* and *The Waterboy* (with Adam Sandler, for which he earned a Blockbuster Award nomination for Favorite Supporting Actor), *Scream,* and *Ground Control* (with Kiefer Sutherland and Kelly McGillis).

Mr. Winkler has appeared on many television shows and made-for-TV movies, including *The Mary Tyler Moore Show, Rhoda, The Bob Newhart Show,*

A Child Is Missing, Battery Park, and *Dead Man's Gun.* In association with partner John Rich, he sold two television series to ABC-TV, *Mr. Sunshine, Arrested Development* and *MacGyver. MacGyver* ran for seven seasons.

Mr. Winkler's personal commitment to helping others is well known. Much of his work has been with children's organizations, which include United Friends of Children, Children's Action Network, Toys for Tots, National Committee for Arts for the Handicapped, and the Special Olympics, among many others.

Why and when did you decide to move to New York to become an actor?

I was born and raised here. I went to the McBurney School, then to Emerson College, and then to graduate school (Yale). I thought I'd never leave New York. I thought my entire career would be here in New York. I was trained for the theater. The time that I went to California, a lot of the "New York" actors all were shocked. Of course, they all eventually came out there and asked if I could set them up. I left for California on September 18, 1973, I landed at two forty-five in the afternoon, and I never came home.

I was in the repertory theater at Yale for a year and a half. After that, I got a job at the repertory theater in Washington, the Arena. I was fired after three weeks of rehearsal. I then put my snow tires back on my car and drove to New York. I cried the entire way. I thought, no one is going to hire an actor who's been fired. When I arrived, I started doing plays for free at the Manhattan Theatre Club. I did Lynne Meadow's first play in New York City. I worked at theaters like the Cubiculo and the St. Clement's church space.

Did you have a strategy, a game plan before moving here?

I had no strategy at all. My plan was that I was just going to get an acting job, and that was it. I was driven, and that's all there was to it. I set my mind to it, and I was going to get it!

What did you imagine it would be like?

I never even thought about any of it. I just had blinders on. I was determined that I was going to get an agent, get work. I was tenacious. I got an agent for commercials. Someone sent me to meet Tina Jacobson. She was with another agency, but was going to start her own agency, and asked me to come with her. I said, "Sure." We were incredibly successful. I sometimes booked two or three jobs a week. So, my first year in New York was successful enough that I could do free plays at night. I earned enough money in that year for me to go to California, supposedly for one month.

What was your first year in New York like?

I was in New York for about a year to a year and a half. I auditioned for a movie called *The Lords of Flatbush* and got it. Then I got the film, *Crazy*

Joe, with Peter Boyle. Also during that time, I got a Broadway play. Saying that the play didn't do to too well is an understatement. I say that I was on Broadway from eight to eleven. One month after I went to California, I got the Fonz (*Happy Days*). There was an angel on my shoulder.

If you had a chance to redo any part of that first year, what would it be?

Well, for one thing, I would have worked on my fear. I would have worked on how difficult it was for me to get out of my own way in auditions. For commercials, I allowed my instinct to take over. I did anything that came into my mind. But when it came to theater, I made it so important that I psychically stumbled. One thing that came out of that was eventually learning how important it is to truly trust your instincts.

Did you take classes when you first got here?

I didn't take any classes, but what I did was, I worked with a group called Off the Wall. It was an improv group.

What did you do for a survival job? How did you find a place to live?

I worked in a travel agency, Europa Car, whose selling point was that you when you fly with them to Europe, you'd get a car to drive there.

Lewis J. Stadlen had an apartment that I rented on West 72nd Street. I was born and raised on West 78th Street. It was a one-bedroom apartment that I paid $174 a month for.

How did you get agents and casting directors to become aware of your work?

People came to see my work at the Cubiculo and places like that. My agent, Joan Scott (at that time), I got through a young lady that I was dating at school. She introduced me. The way that I met a lot of the casting directors was through my agent submitting me to them. I met them at the auditions.

What do you think the main differences are between living and working in New York versus LA?

I think that starting in New York, working in theater, studying here, gives you a foundation for everything else. Because acting is acting is acting. The level of intensity of filling the space and all that is different when you do movies as opposed to theater. But the very basis of your training as an actor will work for you whether you do a radio play or a television show or a movie or a stage play.

New York is a very exciting city. You can walk from neighborhood to neighborhood. It's alive, visceral. In LA you have to drive everywhere; there are no seasons. In my heart, I've never left New York. But I have a wonderful life in LA For me, being bicoastal is not feasible.

What advice (or warnings) do you have for actors who are thinking of moving to New York to start their careers?

You have to think of yourself as that toy that looks like a clown, with sand on the bottom, that when you punch it, it comes right back up. I think you must remember, it's really a very difficult occupation.

Number two, you cannot allow yourself to be defined by rejection. The casting director and directors are not defining you as a person. On that particular audition, you weren't right for this job. We, as actors, are so willing to personalize that rejection.

It's really important that you keep your eye on the prize. My lawyer once said to me, "If you sit at the table long enough, the chips will come to you."

You must train yourself, be prepared. Listen to your instincts. I cannot say that enough. Every time that you have an initial visceral reaction to something and you try to second-guess it, it will not work out well. Every time I've ever made a professional decision where I've gone against that initial reaction, where I knew in my gut not to do it, and I did, fate came up and hit me in the head with a hammer. Your instincts will always let you know what you need to do. Whenever you go to an audition, make one instant choice about the material. It doesn't matter if you're right or wrong, because there is no right or wrong. By making one choice, you will separate yourself out from thousands of other actors. There is no "safe."

Debra Monk
Photograph by John Hart. Pictured: Debra Monk

Debra Monk has won the Tony Award (*Redwood Curtain*), the Emmy Award (for Katie Sipowicz on *NYPD Blue*), the Obie Award (*The Time of the Cuckoo*), the Drama Desk Award (*Oil City Symphony*), and the Helen Hayes Award (*The Three Hotels*). Other Broadway plays include: *Steel Pier* (Tony nomination), *Company,* *Nick and Nora, Pump Boys and Dinettes,* and *Picnic* (Tony nomination), among others. Some of Ms. Monks films include: *Devil's Advocate, First Wives Club, Reckless, Quiz Show, The Bridges of Madison County, Fearless,* and *In and Out*. Recently, she appeared in *Curtains* on Broadway and *Love, Loss, and What I Wore*, Off-Broadway. Most recently she appeared on the TV series *Damages, Grey's Anatomy, Ghost Whisperer, and Brothers and Sisters*.

Why did you decide to move to New York?

I moved here in 1974. I moved to New York, because it was the only place to go. I had been in graduate school in Texas. I had an MFA in acting from Southern Methodist University.

Did you have a strategy, a game plan before moving here?

No, I was really stupid. I thought because I had my M.F.A., things were going to happen fast. I thought I was going to come here and do Ibsen and Shakespeare, but I couldn't even get a commercial. My first year in New York was very humbling.

I thought I was going to get work right away. I thought they'd all love me, and I'd get work right away. I didn't have an Equity card, so I couldn't go to Equity auditions. And even the non-Equity auditions were difficult. I didn't have an agent.

What was your first year in New York like?

I was going to auditions when I could get them. I started studying at HB Studios, but I didn't study long, because I had just come out of a very intense program at SMU. I was *so* trained that I didn't want to take any more classes; I just wanted to work. I worked as a temporary secretary. I was living with the man I was going to marry. The one thing I didn't have to worry about was an apartment; he had one. I moved in with him.

If you had a chance to redo that first year in New York, what would you do differently?

I thought about that question a lot. For me, I think I needed the humbling experience of that first year. I came out of graduate school kind of cocky; I think a lot of kids do. I really can't think of anything I could have done differently, given the situation. I sent out all the pictures, the postcards, made rounds—but nothing. There was hardly any response to me. I had my monologues all ready, but I couldn't get a chance to do them. I couldn't get anything.

What were your first auditions in New York like?

The only auditions I got were non-Equity.

What were your first acting jobs in New York? Do you remember how you got them?

The first job I got was playing Hortense the maid in a non-Equity production of *The Boyfriend* at a dinner theater in Raleigh, North Carolina. My first job in New York was at the Colonnades Theater Lab. The man I was living with and I both auditioned for the Colonnades, but he got into the company and I didn't. So for a year, I worked on my audition pieces. I would go to productions at the Colonnades and hung out there and got to know the people there. A year later, I auditioned, and this time I got in. But when I got in, there was nothing for me to do. They had already cast the next year's play from their company.

So I ended up sitting at home doing nothing—I wrote a very funny letter to the artistic director of the company. I said that I knew I was just out of school, and I knew that I had lots to learn, but if there's not a part in the show for me, let me do something, let me be your assistant, let me understudy for free, let me be part of the company—something. I wrote some other very funny things in the letter that I can't really say here. Anyway, I got in. He called me after he got the letter, laughing hysterically, saying, "You're absolutely right, you should be in some of our productions." I became his assistant. What eventually happened was, there were no understudies there, and this woman in the company became ill. Long story short, I got to do her role. She had to leave the company, and I continued in the role.

I worked with that company until it closed. And even though the company was high profile in New York, I still couldn't get an agent. After that company closed, I got a job as a waitress. I was fascinated with being a waitress. I took notes even. I was auditioning as much as I could, but nothing. Finally, I got together with some friends from graduate school and decided to write a piece. None of us had an agent, we weren't working, and we started writing *Pump Boys and Dinettes*. That was around 1978. We opened late night at Heebie Jeebies, got producers to see the show, and then opened Off-Broadway. That gave the break to make money, to be able to live. But I still couldn't get an agent, even after the show moved to Broadway. Most people believed that I was the character in the show, a country-western performer.

How did you get agents and casting directors to become aware of your work?
After the show closed, I did a production of it in a mall in St. Louis. I needed the job, but I was afraid I was only always going to be doing this one show. There was a girl in the show who did have an agent, and she was constantly flying back and forth to New York to do auditions. One of the other places she was going to audition was at the Actors Theater of Louisville. I had always wanted to work there, but I couldn't get an agent. So on my day off, I flew to the Actors Theater of Louisville on my own, knocked on the door, and said "I want to audition for you." They said, "You can't do that." I said, "Look, I have to fly back today. Is there anybody here I can talk to?" So I talked to Jon Jory's assistant, and she said, "Look, we just don't do this. Besides, Jon isn't even here, he's in New York. You can't just come here and audition." I said, "Can you at least hear my piece?" She said "Okay." So I auditioned for her. After the audition, I said to her, "If there is anything that you think I'm right for, I'll fly here to audition for you." So I left, finished my gig in the mall, moved back to New York. I still couldn't get an agent.

Then one day, I get a call from Jon Jory's assistant. She says Jon is coming to New York to audition actresses, and Jon wants to see you. What had happened was, this actress in one of their productions was tragically killed in a car accident. William Mastrosimone had written this play for her, and she had died on the way to Louisville. So, Jon came to New York to replace this actress. And as he was leaving to go to New York, his assistant said to him, "By the way, while you were away, this woman auditioned here. Perhaps you should see her when you're in New York." I got the audition. The play was *The Undoing*. And I got the part. And I went to Louisville. It was very difficult, because they were all in mourning for this wonderful actress who had died. Jon was wonderful to me. I did the play, and it went very well, and Jon and I started working together. We became great collaborators. I worked there for three years, 1983, '84, and '85. I worked there for six months out of each year. Everyone goes to Louisville, and finally, I got an agent. So when I came back to New York, people knew who I was.

When I got back, my friend Mark Hardwick said, "We've been playing with some funny ideas for a musical with, like, Laurence Welk kind of music. We thought it might be funny if you played the drums in it." I did play the drums. So, long story short, we created *Oil City Symphony*, and it was a big hit, got great reviews. My career really took off after that. Don Scardino saw me in that show, and I got *Women and Wallace* at Playwrights Horizons, a part of the Young Playwrights Festival. I got involved with that group of people and worked there for a few years. From there, I auditioned for The Lab at Circle Rep. It was there that someone said to me, "You shouldn't be auditioning for them, they should be asking you." And I said, "Well, they're not. What should I do, sit around and wait?"

So that's one thing I want to say to young actors: Don't think, "I shouldn't have to do that." Because you know what? Maybe you *do* have to do that. Sometimes, you have to swallow your pride if you want something bad enough. At the Lab, you did readings of plays. And I did a reading of a Craig Lucas play, *Prelude to a Kiss*. Long story short, the play took off and went to Off-Broadway and then Broadway. That was my first Broadway play. And I met Lanford Wilson while I was involved with Circle Rep. And he wrote a part for me in his new play, *Redwood Curtain*. I ended up doing that play on Broadway (and winning a Tony). That play really changed my career. And once I was on Broadway, I started getting movie auditions.

Do you have a preference between New York and Los Angeles?

LA is just not for me. I don't like having to always be in a car. Out there, you feel very isolated. I don't like the living conditions out there. And for me, emotionally, soulfully, there is nothing like live theater. I think of TV and film as a source of money, so that I can do theater.

Any advice for young actors who are thinking about moving to New York to start their careers?

Many of the things that happened in my career never would have happened if I didn't do things for myself. I had to do all the footwork Things like flying out to Louisville from that mall. Nobody has ever handed me anything until I got in there and showed myself.

If you don't want this more than anything, don't come here. Unless you have a great passion for this, you won't be able to sustain the rejection.

Dylan Baker

Photograph by Andrew Brucker. Pictured: Dylan Baker

TV audiences will recognize Mr. Baker from the series *Kings, Drive* and *The Book of Daniel*, and from regular appearances on *Law & Order, The Good Wife, Monk* and *The West Wing*. He has acted on Broadway in *God of Carnage, November, Mauritius, La Bete* (Tony and Drama Desk nominations) and *Eastern Standard* (Theater World Award) and Off-Broadway in *Homebody Kabul, The Common Pursuit,* and *Not About Heroes* (Obie Award). His film credits include *Revolutionary Road, Spiderman II and III, The Road to Perdition, Thirteen Days, Happiness, The Long Walk Home,* and *Planes, Trains, and Automobiles.* As a director, Mr. Baker has brought over a dozen plays to the stage, the last being *The Torch-Bearers* at the Williamstown Theater Festival.

Why and when did you decide to move to New York to become an actor?

It's difficult for me, because I always felt New York was where I was headed ever since I was a kid. I grew up in a midsize town in Virginia. When I got out of college, I worked at the Folger Shakespeare Theatre in Washington. But I was always headed towards New York. I always felt that I needed to go there if I was going to pursue theater. I never even thought about LA. I felt that the stage was what acting was about. I thought I'd just go to New York and start pounding the pavement. After the Folger, two things happened. I had a friend who took over the Boston Shakespeare Company, and he asked me to do some parts there. I was excited about that, but what also happened was, I got accepted into the Yale School of Drama. I was actually planning to go to Boston, but my friend, Kent Thompson, made me realize that in the three years at Yale, I'd probably meet people that work in the theater more than if I walked the streets of New York for ten years. After Yale, I immediately found a place to live in New York, but then went to Williamstown for the summer and did my first professional Equity job. Two plays that I did at Williamstown, *To Whom It May Concern* and *Not About Heroes,* both moved Off-Broadway. *Not About Heroes* was a two-hander that opened at the Lucille Lortel Theatre And so, I got to do my first Off-Broadway job, and I got an Obie Award.

Did you have a game plan when you moved here?

I really didn't have a strategy, so to speak. My game plan was always, do as much summer Shakespeare as possible. That way, when I went in, I'd have something behind me. I didn't know what to expect in New York. I didn't know anything about agents, workshops, or anything.

Did you take classes when you first got here and, if so, with whom?

I joined up at the Actors Studio, because my wife was a member there. But as soon as I got in, I got a job and didn't go. I never really followed up on the Actors Studio. I took some lessons with Peter Flood. I'd call him up every now and then when I had an audition. He helped me with *La Bete.*

Where did you live when you first got here?

I lived in four different places my first year in New York. Lots of problems with sublets and such.

What were your first acting jobs in New York like?

My first job was at the Lucille Lortel Theater. It was like a dream come true. It was a gorgeous theater. I was playing opposite Edward Hermann and Dianne Wiest. Ed and I actually had to go up to the Sherry Netherland and do the play for Ms. Lortel herself. And she decided she wanted to do it.

How did you get agents and casting directors to become aware of your work?

The agents came up to Yale and to Williamstown. So I had an agent before I got to New York.

Which do you prefer, Los Angeles or New York?

I'm much more into living in New York, because I like people. The way LA is set up, it's antisocial. I hate to say it, but bars are an important part of my life. That's where you meet people and talk. Like going to the West Bank Café to meet some friends. In LA, you have to worry about driving home if you've had a few drinks. In LA, it's higher profile out there. Doing a film in LA is different than doing a film in Paduca. I did one play, and that's the last one I'll do. I worked for the Pasadena Playhouse. We reopened that space. The businesspeople out there don't go to plays. To them, plays are a sign of weakness and are a distraction. The feeling is, actors are doing a play because they can't get a film.

What advice do you have for actors who are thinking about moving to New York to start their careers?

Do your work beforehand. Have a résumé of experience; don't come here fresh off the boat. Try to work outside of New York before you get here. Keep the phone number of every single person you've ever known, or your sister or brother have ever known, who have moved to New York. Just call them up for connections for a place to live or whatever you ever need. I feel that generally, people in New York are fairly helpful.

Lisa Emery

Photograph by Blanche Mackey. Pictured: Lisa Emery

Ms. Emery's Broadway credits include *The Smell of the Kill, The Women (revival) Present Laughter, Jackie: An American Life, Burn This, Rumors,* and *Passion.* Off-Broadway, she has appeared in *Dinner with Friends, Far East, What the Butler Saw, Curtains, Marvin's Room, The Matchmaker,* and *Talley and Son,* and regionally, she has worked for Williamstown Theatre Festival, Hartford Stage, Huntington Theatre, Walnut Street Theatre, and Portland Stage. She has appeared in the TV series *Fringe, Law & Order: Criminal Intent, Canterbury's Law,* and *Damages.*

Why and when did you decide to move to New York?

I moved here on Valentine's Day in 1978. The reason I came here, really, was because the guy that I was seeing at the time, well, actually living with, wanted to move here. So I just said "okay." I was acting in Philadelphia at the time. I had grown up in the Philadelphia area. I was non-Equity, but working all the time. Still, I wasn't able to support myself acting.

Did you have a strategy before moving here?

I had no strategy, no game plan. I just wanted to be with this guy. Well, of course, our relationship fell apart immediately after I moved here.

What was your first year actually like?

It was awful. I spent so much time sleeping that first year. I was constantly being bombarded with visual and auditory stimulus here. I was very unhappy with this guy, and he was leaving—not a great time. My mother was very ill with cancer, so I was going back and forth between New York and Philadelphia. It was probably the worst year of my life. So, I figured, since I didn't know anyone here in New York and I didn't know how to break in, I'd audition for Circle in the Square's two-year school. And I got in. So I went back to school.

If you had a chance to redo any part of that first year in New York, what would it be?

I don't think I'd redo any of it. The reason is, I'm so happy where I am now, and I really believe that everything you do leads to the next thing. I remember I got an audition for ABC. They weren't seeing people for a specific show, but for a young talent program. I auditioned for Irene Selznick, and then, all of a sudden, I was offered this holding contract with ABC, where they would pay me like $10,000 not to do anything, except be with them. And I said no. I said, no! I was working on this new play in the Lab at Circle Rep called *Diary of a Shadow Walker*, and I thought that ABC might make me do something like *Charlie's Angels* or something. Sometimes, I wonder what would have happened if I had signed that deal with ABC. I wonder what that might have led to. But I don't regret it at all. I had no rights by that contract; they had all the rights, and I didn't like that.

What kind of survival jobs did you have?

I waited tables, tended bar, things like that. One of my first jobs was, I walked around with a sandwich board up and down Fifth Avenue. And the sign said, "Welcome to the Whorehouse." It was advertising for *The Best Little Whorehouse in Texas*. This other girl and I were so humiliated that we used to duck into a bathroom and hide. I also worked at the Bronx Zoo and ushered at the Delacorte Theater and answered phones at a brothel. The brothel job was very convenient. It was open at night, and I had my days free.

How did you find a place to live when you first got here?

I came to New York on weekends with this guy I was seeing then, and we'd look for an apartment. It was nothing like it is now, trying to find a place to live. We found a great place on 13th Street.

What were your first acting jobs in New York like?

A guy that was waiting tables with me recommended me for a job. I remember it was at somebody's loft on 14th Street. The play was called *The Eternal Song of Walt Whitman*, and I got the job. I was the narrator. We did, like, five or six performances for a handful of people. And I remember this guy had snakes and dogs and cats. It was horrible and seedy.

I worked for a lot of those little New York theaters that first year. I started working with the Lab at Circle Rep, and I was auditioning a lot for those plays. That was about 1979. I started slowly, but surely working there in different Lab plays.

My first Equity job was through Circle Rep. Marshall Mason was directing a play called *In Connecticut*, by Roy London. It was done at the Geva Theater, upstate New York. They were hoping that it would come to New York City, but it never did. But I got my Equity card. Then, I did regional jobs. My first regional job was in Portland, Maine (Portland Stage Company). I did Lanford Wilson's *Talley and Son*, up at Saratoga, then in New York City.

How did you get agents and casting directors to become aware of your work?

I was pretty shy or lazy that way. I just kind of hoped that people would see me at Circle Rep, in those Lab plays, or in the different plays I was doing outside of the Lab. I remember Fifi Oscard and Michael Hartig's office sent people down to see actors in the plays I was involved in, and out of that, I met those agents.

The first agent who ever really believed in me was Bob Barry, who I just loved. It was a very small agency, just him. He sent me out on stuff. The whole meeting-casting-director thing was slow and steady. I'd meet them when I went out on auditions at their offices. When I did *Talley and Son* here in the city, I got to meet a lot of people through that. I feel really lucky to have gotten hooked up with Circle Rep and all the people that I met there. Circle Rep got me really working.

The way that I got my present agent was that I was understudying Joan Allen in *Burn This*, and I got to go on. At that time, I thought I had to parlay this into something. I invited a handful of agents that I thought were good agents. One of them was my agent. But I felt I was in a good position at that time. I was in a good play with a wonderful role. I felt confident about everything.

Do you have a preference between New York and Los Angeles?

I went to LA to do *Rumors*. I had done it on Broadway, and then went out to LA to do it. It was a fantastic summer. But generally, I don't go out there looking for work. I have gone out on spec only a couple of times. It's not for me. I've never felt comfortable knocking on someone's door and just saying,

"Here I am." I always felt that if someone saw my work and they liked it, then the right thing would happen. But to go out there where no one knows me and say, "Here's my résumé," it's not for me.

I enjoyed my three months in LA doing *Rumors*. It's fantastic when you're out there making money. I went out there a couple of times with my husband, and we stayed at the Oakwood, I think it's called, and we looked for work. I found it very depressing. I felt like I was a fish out of water. No one knew me, and I felt like I was starting all over. The stuff that I was auditioning for didn't interest me creatively at all.

Any advice for actors thinking of moving to New York?

Don't listen to the people who tell you how hard it is. Come here when you're young and are willing to live with, like, six roommates. Have a cold eye about what you're doing, but do it anyway. Work begets work. Have a strong network of people in the business; it can be very helpful. You can meet people easily if you try hard enough. One thing that has served me is, I don't read reviews until after the show is over. I know most people don't do this, but it's worked for me. You kind of know when things are good or not, just the way people are around you. But I found that it's not good for me, no matter what people say. It just interferes.

Becky Ann Baker

Becky Ann Baker, by Tom Bloom

Becky Ann Baker has done many Broadway shows, including *Best Little Whorehouse in Texas, Streetcar Named Desire, Titanic, Assassins, All My Sons,* and *The Good People,* as well as Off-Broadway and regional theater. On television, she is best known as the mom on *Freaks and Geeks,* and of her films, her favorite is *A Simple Plan.* She is also experienced in commercials, voice-overs, and books on tape. She is a member of the Actor's Studio, a Usual Suspect at the New York Theatre Workshop, and an Artistic Associate of the Williamstown Theatre Festival. She feels incredibly lucky to be in this business.

Why and when did you decide to move to New York?

I honestly don't ever remember *not* wanting to move to New York City, it must have been the old movies I watched! I thought I could leave West Springfield High School and move to New York to become a chorus girl, but my parents insisted on two years of college. Since I had never been to a large city, it was probably wise.

Did you have a strategy before moving here as to how you were going to find acting work?

I stayed four years at Western Kentucky University getting a B.A. in theater and a minor in dance. The head of the theater department, Dr. Bill Leonard, suggested an apprentice program at the Barn Theatre in Augusta, Michigan for the summer after I graduated. He had worked there and I apprenticed, over two summers, getting my Equity card with Tom Wopat, Dana Delaney, and Patricia Wettig. I worked there as an Equity member for many summers afterwards.

What was your first year in New York actually like?

I lived with four other women in a three-bedroom walkup on Bank Street. It was fantastic. We each paid $105. A month! Every time one of us got a job we celebrated. It was just like my favorite movies that brought me to New York. My first paying theater job was a non-Equity tour of Lil' Abner (Moonbeam Mc Swine)! I was in heaven! Then I went back to the Barn to get my Equity card.

If you had a chance to redo any part of that first year in New York what would it be?

Not a single thing. I'm still so close to the women that I lived with then, all apprentices at the Barn.

What kind of survival jobs did you have?

My second day in New York I passed a bar that was looking for bartenders and waitresses. Two of my roommates and I were given jobs. I was a bartender and they were waitresses. It turned out to be a Mob-run topless dancer bar! We were in leotards, not topless, but we only lasted a few weeks before we were fired; they thought we were undercover police. It was too bad, we were making so much money!

How did you find a place to live when you first got here?

We found our brownstone fifth-floor walk-up in an ad in some local paper. We were sure that it was illegal. We had to pay in cash on the first of the month.

What were your first acting jobs like?

After I got my Equity card my second summer at the Barn, I came back to New York City and went to every Open Equity call for dancers and singers. "Cattle calls," they were called. My first chorus job was to go to Knoxville, Tennessee to the Clarence Brown Theatre and work on a show that turned out to be *Sugar Babies*. By the time *Sugar Babies* came to New York, I was already in the original cast of *The Best Little Whorehouse in Texas,* so I stayed there. The show ran for four years. It was like going to grad school, I learned so much.

How did you get agents and casting directors to become aware of your work?

I invited agents to see me in *Whorehouse* after I took over principal roles. I worked freelance with some but it never clicked until I met the Gage Group. I have been with them ever since.

Do you have a preference between New York and Los Angeles?

LA is terrific for making money, and we have spent many different seasons there, but my heart is in New York, because you can work in the theater much more. Working on new plays with the playwright is my favorite thing to do in this business.

Any advice for actors thinking of moving to New York?

These days grad school is a good idea for meeting agents and casting directors. I think it's a lot harder to get started these days and any way to get connected is helpful. The internships and apprentice programs are still a great way to start out. Best of luck!

APPENDIX A

Talent Agents, New York. This is an abridged list from Sue Henderson's Labels. I've included the most well-known and active agents in the New York City area.

Abrams Artists • NATR, A, E, S, ATA, D, W
275 7th Avenue, 26th floor • New York, NY 10001
(646)486-4600 • david.marmanillo@abramsartny.com • www.abramsartists.com

Access Talent, Inc • A, S
171 Madison Ave.. Ste. 910 • New York, NY 10016
212-684-7795 • chascowing@accesstalent.com • www.accesstalent.com

Bret Adams • A, E, ATA, NATR, W
448 W. 44 St. • New York, NY 10036
212-765-5630 • bretadamsltd@bretadamsltd.net

Agents for the Arts, Inc. • E, S
203 W. 23 St. 3 fl. • New York, NY 10011
212-229-2562

Andreadis Talent Agency • NATR, A, E, S
119 W. 57 St. Ste. 711 • New York, NY 10019
212-315-0303 • andreadis@verizon.net

Arcieri & Associates • S, A
305 Madison Ave. Ste. 2315 • New York, NY 10165
212-286-1700 • talent@arcieritalent.com • www.arcieritalent.com

Artists Agency, Inc. • A, W, P, D, PKG
230 W. 55 St. Ste. 29D • New York, NY 10019
212-245-6960

Artists Entertainment Agency • A, NATR
165 W. 46 St. Ste. 1114 • New York, NY 10036
212-869-7093

Artists Group East • S, A, E, D
1650 Broadway Ste. 610 • New York, NY 10019
212-586-1452

Atlas Talent • A, S, NATR, ATA
15 E. 32 St. 6 fl. • New York, NY 10036
212-730-4500 • www.atlastalent.com

Avalon Artists Group NY • A, E
143 W. 29 St. Suite 1103 • New York, NY 10001
212-868-3200 • erica@avalonartists.com • www.avalonartists.com

Bauman, Redanty & Shaul • NATR, ATA, A, E
1650 Broadway Ste. 1410 • New York, NY 10019
212-757-0098

The Bethel Agency • E, A, S
P. O. Box 21043 Park West Sta. • New York, NY 10025
212-864-4510

Bloc NY • S, E
137 Varick St. 6 fl. • New York, NY 10013
212-924-6200 • info@blocnyc.com • www.blocnyc.com

Judy Boals, Inc. • E, W, S, NATR
307 W. 38 St. Ste. 812 • New York, NY 10018
212-500-1424 • info@judyboals.com • www.judyboals.com

Don Buchwald & Associates • A, E, W, D, S
10 E. 44 St. 5 fl. • New York, NY 10017
212-867-1070

Carson Adler Agency, Inc. • NATR, A, E
250 W. 57 St. Ste. 2030 • New York, NY 10107
212-307-1882 • www.carsonadler.com

Carson Organization, Ltd • A, E, NATR
419 Park Ave. South Ste. 606-607 • New York, NY 10016
212-221-1517

Clear Talent Group • E, A, NATR, ATA
325 W. 38 St. #1203 • New York, NY 10018
212-840-4100 • www.cleartalentgroup.com

CornerStone Talent Agency • A, E
37 W. 20 St. Ste. 1108 • New York, NY 10011
212-807-8344

Creative Artists Agency • A, E
162 5th Ave. 6 fl. • New York, NY 10010
212-277-9000

Cunningham, Escott, Slevin & Doherty • NATR,A, E, S
257 Park Ave. South Ste. 900 • New York, NY 10010
212-477-1666 • info@cesdtalent.com • www.cesdtalent.com

Ginger Dicce Talent Agency • S, A, E
56 W. 45 St. Ste. 1100 • New York, NY 10036
212-869-9650

Douglas, Gorman, Rothacker & Wilhelm, Inc. (DGRW) • NATR, A, E, V
1501 Broadway Ste. 703 • New York, NY 10036
212-382-2000 • info@dgrwinc.com

Dulcina Eisen Associates • S, A, E
154 E. 61 St. • New York, NY 10065
212-355-6617

Endeavor Talent Agency • ATA, E, A, W, D, S
152 W. 57 St. 25 fl. • New York, NY 10019
212-625-2500

Jim Flynn Agency • E, A, S
307 W. 38 St. Ste. 801 • New York, NY 10018
212-868-1068

Frontier Booking International • A, E
1560 Broadway Ste. 1110 • New York, NY 10036
212-221-0220 • www.frontierbooking.com

The Gage Group • A, E, NATR, ATA
450 7th Ave. Ste. 1809 • New York, NY 10123
212-541-5250

Garber Talent Agency • S, A, E
2 Pennsylvania Plaza Ste. 1910 • New York, NY 10121
212-292-4910

Generation TV • S, A, E
20 W. 20 St. Ste. 1008 • New York, NY 10011
646-230-9491 • info@generationmm.com • www.generationmm.com

Gersh Agency New York, Inc. • A, E, D, S, W
41 Madison Ave. 33 fl. • New York, NY 10010
212-997-1818 • www.gershagency.com

Peggy Hadley Enterprises, Ltd. • A, E, S, V
119 W. 57 St. PH North • New York, NY 10019
212-246-2166 • phadleyent@aol.com

Harden-Curtis Associates • ATA, A, E
850 7th Ave. Ste. 903 • New York, NY 10019
212-977-8502 • www.hardencurtis.com

Hartig-Hilepo Agency, Ltd. • A, E, S
54 W. 21 St. Ste. 610 • New York, NY 10010
212-929-1772 • info@hartighilepo.com

Eileen Haves Talent Representative • NATR, A, E
P. O. Box 677 • New York, NY 10028
212-249-0033

Henderson/Hogan Agency • A, E
850 7th Ave. Ste. 1003 • New York, NY 10019
212-765-5190 • abutler@hendersonhogan.com

Barbara Hogenson Agency • W, P, D
165 West End Ave. Ste. 19C • New York, NY 10023
212-874-8084

Independent Artists Agency • S, A, E
330 W 38 St. # 1204 • New York, NY 10018
646-486-3332

Ingber & Associates • A, E, NATR
1140 Broadway Ste. 907 • New York, NY 10001
212-889-9450

Innovative Artists • A, E, ATA, S
235 Park Ave. South 10 fl. • New York, NY 10003
212-253-6900 • www.innovativeartists.com

International Creative Management • A, E, W, D, V, ATA
825 8th Ave. 26 fl. • New York, NY 10019
212-556-5600 • www.icmtalent.com

Jordan, Gill & Dornbaum Talent Agency, Inc. • A, E, S
1133 Broadway Ste. 623 • New York, NY 10010
212-463-8455

Stanley Kaplan Talent Agency • NATR, A, E
139 Fulton St. Ste. 503 • New York, NY 10038
212-385-4400

Kazarian, Spencer, Ruskin & Associates • A, E, ATA
311 W. 43 St. Ste. 1107 • New York, NY 10036
212-582-7572

Kerin-Goldberg & Associates • A, E, S
155 E. 55 St. Ste. 5D • New York, NY 10022
212-838-7373

Archer King • S, A, E, W, D
1650 Broadway Ste. 407 • New York, NY 10019
212-765-3103 • akingltd@yahoo.com • www.archerkingltd.com

Kolstein Talent Agency (KTA) • A, E, NATR
247 W. 38 St. #1001 • New York, NY 10018
212-937-8967 • info@kolsteintalent.com • www.kolsteintalent.com

The Krasny Office, Inc. • S, A, E
1501 Broadway Ste. 1303 • New York, NY 10036
212-730-8160

Lally Talent Agency • NATR, A, E, S
630 9th Ave. Ste. 800 • New York, NY 10036
212-974-8718

Bernard Liebhaber Agency • A, E, NATR, S
352 7th Ave. • New York, NY 10001
212-631-7561

The Luedtke Agency • A, E, W, V, ATA, S
1674 Broadway Ste. 7A • New York, NY 10019
212-765-9564

William Morris / Endeavor Agency LLC • A, E, W, D, ATA, S
1325 Avenue of the Americas 15 fl. • New York, NY 10019
212-586-5100 • www.wma.com

Nicolosi & Co. Inc. • NATR, A, E
150 W. 25 St. Ste. 1200 • New York, NY 10001
212-633-1010 • jnicolosi@nicolosi-co.com • www.nicolosi-co.com

Fifi Oscard Agency, Inc. • A, E, W, D
110 W. 40 St. Ste. 704 • New York, NY 10018
212-764-1100 • agency@fifioscard.com • www.fifioscard.com

The Meg Pantera Agency • A, E, S, V
138 W. 15 St. 1 fl. • New York, NY 10011
212-219-9330

Paradigm Agency • A, E, ATA, S, D, W
360 Park Ave. So. 16 fl. • New York, NY 10010
212-897-6400 • www.paradigmagency.com

Phoenix Artists Inc. • A, E, NATR, ATA
321 W. 44 St. Ste. 401 • New York, NY 10036
212-586-9110 • phoenixartistsinc@yahoo.com

Professional Artists • S, A, E, W
321 W. 44 St. Ste. 605 • New York, NY 10036
212-247-8770

RadioActive Talent Inc. • A, S
243 5th Ave. #505 • New York, NY 10016
Doesn't want phone listed. • www.radiotv.com • www.myspace.com/radiofreeny

Schuller Talent (New York Kids) • S, A,
276 5th Ave. Ste. 204 • New York, NY 10001
212-532-6005 • margaret@schullertalent.com • www.schullertalent.com

Sheplin-Winik Artists • E
676-A 9th Ave. Box 164 • New York, NY 10036
646-246-8853

Anthony Soglio Agency • E
423 Madison Ave. • New York, NY 10017
212-751-1850

Ann Steele Agency • NATR, A, E
330 W. 42 St. 18 fl. • New York, NY 10036
212-629-9112

Stewart Talent New York • A, E, S
318 W 53 St. Ste. 201 • New York, NY 10019
212-315-5505 • www.stewarttalent.com

Peter Strain & Associates, Inc. • ATA, A, E
321 W. 44 St. Ste. 805 • New York, NY 10036
212-391-0380

The Talent House • E
325 W. 38 St. Ste. 605 • New York, NY 10018
212-957-5220 • assistant@talenthousenyc.com

Talent Representatives, Inc. • A, E, W, NATR
1040 1st Ave. #307 • New York, NY 10022
212-752-1835

TalentWorks, Inc. • A, E, ATA, S
220 E. 23 St. Ste. 303 • New York, NY 10010
212-889-0800

The Mine • E, ATA, NATR
347 W. 36 St. #203 • New York, NY 10018
212-612-3200 • talent@the-mine.com • http://www.the-mine.com

Hanns Wolters International, Inc. • S, E
211 E. 43 St. Ste. 505 • New York, NY 10017
212-714-0100 • hannsw@aol.com

Ann Wright Representatives • S, A, E, W
165 W. 46 St. • New York, NY 10036
212-764-6770

Babs Zimmerman Productions, Inc. • E
305 E. 86 St. Ste. 17FW • New York, NY 10128
212-348-7203

APPENDIX B

New York Personal Managers (This is an abridged list from Hendersons Labels. These are the most active managers in the New York City area)

Amy Ambrosino
A.M. Ambrosino Mgmt.
POB 307
New York, NY 10044

Herb Rothman
American Talent Mgmt.INC.
928 Broadway #506
New York, NY 10010

Sandy Gunar
Avanti Talent Mgmt.
332 Bleecker St. #E13
New York, NY 10013

Emily Gerson Saines
Brookside Talent Mgmt.
250 W. 57 St. #2303
New York, NY 10107

Howard Rapp
Charles Rapp Enterprises
55 Broad St. 26 Fl.
New York, NY 10004

Dick Woefle
Choice Talent & Model Mgmt.
505 8th Ave. #802
New York, NY 10018

Breanna Benjamin
Creative Talent Co.
165 W. 46 St. #1210
New York, NY 10036

Liz Gallagher
DGS Talent Mgmt.
43 W. 68 St. Ste. 5A
New York, NY 10023

Laura Kossoff
Dreamweavers Mgmt.

532 LaGuardia Pl. #310
New York, NY 10012

Dick Fox
Fox Entertainment Co.
1650 Broadway #303
New York, NY 10019

Sid Gold
Goldstar Talent Mgmt.
240 Central Park South #8B
New York, NY 10019

Seth Greenky
Green Key Mgmt.
251 W. 89 St. #4A
New York, NY 10024

Ingrid French
Ingrid French Mgmt.
928 Broadway #302
New York, NY 10010

Jeff Mitchell
J. Mitchell Mgmt.
70 W. 36 St. #1006
New York, NY 10018

Jaime Baker
Jaime Baker Mgmt.
311 W. 43 St. #1106
New York, NY 10036

J. Herman/Emily Gipson
Josselyne Herman Mgmt.
345 E. 56 St. #3B
New York, NY 10022

Joyce Chase
Joyce Chase Mgmt.
2 5th Ave.
New York, NY 10011

Karen Riposo
KPA Mgmt.
355 8th Ave. 7-C
New York, NY 10001

T. Lehrman/L. Bush
Landslide Mgmt.
155 E. 76 St. #12A
New York, NY 10021

Lloyd Kolmer
Lloyd Kolmer Co.
65 W. 55 St.
New York, NY 10019

Marilyn Zitner
Marilyn Zitner Mgmt.
16 Penn Plaza #722
New York, NY 10001

Christopher Silveri
Prestige Entertainment
143 W. 29 St. #1103
New York, NY 10001

Henry Ravelo
Ravelo Artists Mgmt.
484 W. 43 St. #10C
New York, NY 10036

Richard Rosenwald
Richard Rosenwald Assoc.
300 W. 55 St. #5Y
New York, NY 10019

Rita Powers
Rita Powers Mgmt.
295 Greenwich St. #513
New York, NY 10007

Rochelle Shulman
RKS Mgmt. Ltd.
975 Park Ave. #10C
New York, NY 10028

Philip Rose
Rosalee Productions

137 W. 78 St. #1 Garden
New York, NY 10024

Rosella Olsen
Rosella Olson Mgmt.
319 W. 105 St. #1F
New York, NY 10025

Roxy Horen Mgmt.
300 W. 17 St.
New York, NY 10011

Donna DeStefano
Sirensong Enterprises Inc.
853 Broadway #1406
New York, NY 10003

J. Steinberg/E. Steinberg
Steinberg Talent Mgmt.
1560 Broadway #405
New York, NY 10036

Suzanne Schachter
Suzelle Enterprises
853 7th Ave. #8D
New York, NY 10019

Michael Farkas(Young Adults)
Talented Managers
65 W. 90 St. #7D
New York, NY 10024

M. Leone/ T. Leone
Terrific Talent Assoc. Inc.
419 Park Ave. So. #1009
New York, NY 10016

Tina Thor
TMT Entertainment
648 Broadway #1002
New York, NY 10012

Katherine Atkinson
Washington Square Arts
310 Bowery 2 Fl.
New York, NY 10012

APPENDIX C

New York, Primetime, Series, And Extra Work Casting (And The One Remaing New York Soap Opera) Source: Henderson's Labels)

Julie Madison
ABC / One Life To Live
157 Columbus Ave. 2 Fl.
New York, Ny 10023
212-456-3580   Principals
Assistant
Sheryl Baker-Fisher

Victoria Visgilio
ABC / One Life To Live
157 Columbus Ave. 2 Fl.
New York, Ny 10023
212-456-3580
Principals & U/5's

John Ort
ABC / TV Studio
157 Columbus Ave. 2 Fl.
New York, Ny 10023
212-456-7777 X 4313
Primetime Casting

Marci Phillips
ABC / TV Studio
157 Columbus Ave. 2 Fl.
New York, Ny 10023
212-456-7777 X 3306
Primetime Casting

Janet Murphy
ABC / TV Studio
157 Columbus Ave. 2 Fl.
New York, Ny 10023
212-456-7777 X 4703
Primetime Casting
    Associate
    Matthew Maisto

Amy Herzig (V. P.)
CBS-TV
51 W. 52 St. 5 Fl.

New York, Ny 10019
212-975-3851
Primetime Casting

Michal Zecher
CBS-TV
51 W. 52 St. 5 Fl.
New York, Ny 10019
212-975-3851
Primetime Casting
    Talent Coordinator

Katharina Eggmann
CBS-TV
51 W. 52 St. 5 Fl.
New York, Ny 10019
212-975-3851
212-975-4321
Primetime Casting

Nevitt Greene
Americas Most Wanted
2 Bethesda Metro Ctr. #800
Bethesda, Md 20814
202-204-2600
TV   Principals

Meredith Marciano
Amerifilm Casting Inc.
151 1st Ave. #225
New York, Ny 10003
646-498-6252
917-715-4291 (Hotline)
All Areas Background
Www.Amerifilmcasting.Com
Info@Amerifilmcasting.Com

Beth Bowling / Kim Miscia
Bowling/Miscia Casting
609 Greenwich St. 6 Fl.

New York, Ny 10014
212-609-0556
Film & TV   Principals
  Gossip Girl

Heather Comer
Deanna Gallucio
C&G Casting
440 9th Ave. 8 Fl. #24
New York, Ny 10001
212-404-3188
Film, TV & Commercials
Background
  Candgcasting@Gmail.Com

Ali Merhi / Todd Feldman
Central Casting Ny
875 6th Ave. 24 Fl.
New York, Ny 10001
646-205-8244
646-964-6512 (Hotline)
917-484-9840 (Sag/Aftra)
917-484-9850 (Non-Union)
All Areas
Www.Centralcasting.Org
Passwordrequest@Centralcasting.Org
Backgroundsubmissions@Gmail.Com
Background
  Other Casting Directors
  Lucy Pho
  Tiffany Moon
  Jeni Thornell
  Sara Conte
  Stephanie Hunter
  Joy Shean
  David Waldron

Billy Hopkins
Chrystie Street Casting
55 Chrystie St. #501
New York, Ny 10002
212-966-6000
Film & TV   Principals
  Other Casting Director

Suzanne Crowley
Associate
Jessica Kelly
  Info.Chrystiestreetcasting@
  Gmail.Com

Amy Christopher
Fox-TV / Casting
1211 6th Ave. 20 Fl.
New York, Ny 10036
212-556-2480
TV   Primetime
Associate
  Clint Alexander

Gayle Keller
Gayle Keller Casting
609 Greenwich St. #4a
New York, Ny 10014
646-278-7516
TV & Film   Principals

Lynn Kressel / Suzanne Ryan
Lynn Kressel Casting
W. 23 St. Pier 62 #304
(Hudson River)
New York, Ny 10011
212-414-2941
Film & TV   Principals
Associate
  Claire Traeger

Lynn Kressel
Jonathan Strauss
Lynn Kressel Casting
W. 23 St. Pier 62 #304
(Hudson River)
New York, Ny 10011
212-414-0575
Film & TV   Principals
Associate
  Philip Huffman
  Jonathan@Jonathanstrauss-
  casting.Com

Kimberly Hope
Lynn Kressel Casting
W. 23 St. Pier 62 #308
(Hudson River)
New York, Ny 10011
212-336-6374
TV   Principals
    Associate
    Faryn Einhorn

Talent Manager / Casting
Mtv: Music Television
Mtv2 / Mtvtr3s / Mtvu
1515 Broadway 23 Fl.
New York, Ny 10036
212-846-7072
TV
    Www.Mtv.Com

Jennifer Mcnamara Shroff
(V. P. Casting)
NBC-TV
30 Rockefeller Plaza #1623e
New York, Ny 10112
212-664-5517
Film & TV   Principals
    Other Casting Director
    Marcia Debonis
    Associates
    Trey Lawson
    Jessica Daniels
    Katja Blichfeld

Katie Hockmeyer
NBC / Jimmy Fallon Show
30 Rockefeller Plaza 7 Fl.
New York, Ny 10112
212-413-6520
TV   Primetime
    Background & Skits

Ayala Cohen / Marci Klein
NBC / Saturday Night Live
30 Rockefeller Plaza

New York, Ny 10112
212-664-4511
TV   Principals
    Primetime

Matt Mchugh
NBC / Saturday Night Live
30 Rockefeller Plaza
New York, Ny 10112
212-664-4511
TV   Primetime
    Background & Skits

Brian Siedlecki (Talent Exe.)
NBC / Saturday Night Live
30 Rockefeller Plaza
New York, Ny 10112
212-664-4511
TV   Primetime
    Background & Skits

Kerry Barden / Paul Schnee
Barden / Schnee Casting
150 W 28 St. #402
New York, Ny 10001
212-727-7600
All Areas   Principals
    Associate
    Allison Estrin
    Bardenschnee1@Mac.Com

Jill Greenberg-Sands
Nickelodeon / N Network
1515 Broadway 38 Fl.
New York, Ny 10036
212-846-4976
212-258-7500 (Other Cd's)
TV Other Casting Directors
Leslie Zaslower
David Doan
    Associate
    Danielle Pretsfelder

Barbara Mcnamara
Barbara Mcnamara Casting

249 W. 34 St. #500
New York, Ny 10001
212-645-6051
212-479-7880 (Call Times)
All Areas Except Theatre
Background
    Associate
    Sean Marks
    Talent@Barbmcasting.Com

Julie Tucker / Ross Meyerson
Tucker / Meyerson Casting
568 Broadway Ste. 301
New York, Ny 10012
212-334-1167
Film & TV
Principals
    Associates
    Cj Molidor
    Jtcasting@Yahoo.Com

Geoffrey Soffer Casting
Silver Cup Studios East
34-02 Starr Ave. 2 Fl.
Long Island City, Ny 11101
718-906-3225
TV   Principals
    Associate
    Candice Alustiza
    Assist@Soffercasting.Com

Lee Genick
Sylvia Fay/ Lee Genick
And Associates
71 Park Ave.
New York, Ny 10016
212-889-2626
212-479-8569 (Hotline)
All Areas
    Background
    Other Casting Director
    Fleet Emerson
    Associate
    Ronen Glevint

Sag Members
Must Attend Open Call
To Register
Non-Sag
Submit By Mail Only
Contact@Sylviafaycasting.Com

Sheila Jaffe / Susan Paley Abramson
Jaffe Abramson Casting
%HBO
1100 6th Ave. 13 Fl. #49
New York, Ny 10036
212-512-1000
Film & TV   Principals

Cindy Tolan
Cindy Tolan Casting
609 Greenwich St. 6 Fl.
New York, Ny 10014
212-219-5094
Film, TV & Theatre   Principals

Mark Saks / Scott Free / Rsa Films
Mark Saks Casting
270 Lafayette St. #203
New York, Ny 10012
212-343-2020
Film & TV   Principals
    Associate
    Chrissy Fiorilli

Meredith Tucker
Meredith Tucker Casting
% Actors Alliance
330 W 38 St. #710
New York, Ny 10018
212-279-3330
Film & TV   Principals
    Boardwalk Empire
    Enlightened
    Associate
    Julie Schubert

Grant Wilfley
Grant Wilfley Casting

123 W. 18 St. 8 Fl
New York, Ny 10011
212-685-3537
646-747-1579
212-685-3168 (Hotline)
Union Registration 1-4 Pm Weds.
All Areas   Background
    Casting Associates
    Sabel
    Melissa Braun
    Allison Hall
    Richard Burridge
    Mihal
    Www.Gwcnyc.Com
    Info@Gwcnyc.Com

Dan Duckworth
Aaa Voice Casting
123 W. 18 St. 7 Fl.
New York, Ny 10011
917-363-9877
Voice Work Only   Associates
    Carole Duckworth
    Jen Duckworth
    Www.Voiceoverunlimited.Com
    Aaavoicecasting@Aol.Com

Doug Aibel
Doug Aibel Casting
Vineyard Theatre
108 E. 15 St.
New York, Ny 10003
212-353-3366 X 220
Theatre, Film & TV   Principals
    Associate
    Henry R. Bergstein

Alaine Alldaffer
Alaine Alldaffer Casting
% Playwrights Horizons
416 W. 42 St.
New York, Ny 10036
212-564-1235
Film, TV & Theatre   Principals

Associate
Lisa Donadio
Www.Playwrightshorizons.Org

Tom Wojtunik
Astoria Performing Arts Ctr.
Pob 195
34-23 Steinway St.
Astoria, Ny 11101
718-393-7505
Theatre Only Accepts Actors, Directors
And Tech Résumés
    Www.Apacny.Org

Jennifer Feraday
Background/Foreground Inc.
601 W. 26 St. M224
New York, Ny 10001
212-609-1103
All Areas Except Theatre Principals &
Background
Union & Non-Union
Www.Bgroundinc.Com
Www.Fgroundinc.Com

Barbara Barna
Barbara Barna Casting
249 Smith St. Pmb 122
Brooklyn, Ny 11231
718-855-9522
Film, TV & Comedy Principals
(Real People Types)
Www.Barbarabarnacasting.Com
Subs@Barbarabarnacasting.Com

Bradley Baron
Bradley Baron Casting
Pob 1023
Fort Lee, Nj 07024
201-313-1107
All Areas Background
Do Not Send 8x10s
Send Post Cards Only
    Associate
    Pamela Kramer

Harriet Bass
Harriet Bass Casting
648 Broadway #912
New York, Ny 10012
212-598-9032
Film, TV & Theatre   Principals
Union Only
    Associate
    Eileen Mccabe

Eve Battaglia
Eve Battaglia Casting
% Oval Concierge
276 1st Ave.
New York, Ny 10009
212-777-1449
Film & TV   Principals

Jerry Beaver
Jerry Beaver & Associates
484 W. 43 St. #19n
New York, Ny 10036
212-244-3600
All Areas Principals
No Visits

Jay Binder
Jay Binder Casting
321 W. 44st. #606
New York, Ny 10036
212-586-6777
Film, TV & Theatre
Www.Bindercasting.Com
Principals
Associates
Jack Bowdan
Mark Brandon
Sara Schatz
Nikole Vallins
Info@Bindercasting.Com

Judy Bowman
Judy Bowman Casting Inc.
140 Cabrini Blvd. #10
New York, Ny 10033

212-501-3520
All Areas Except Print Principals

Stacy Seidel / Lisa Fischoff
Broadcasters
420 Lexington Ave. Ste. 1934
New York, Ny 10170
212-986-5257
All Areas Primarily Principals
A Division Of Hsr/Ny
Stacybc@Hsrny.Com
Lisabc@Hsrny.Com

Ellen Chenoweth
Ellen Chenoweth Casting
% Post Factory
161 6th Ave. 11 Fl.
New York, Ny 10013
212-627-1662
Film   Principals
        Associate
        Amelia Rasche Mccarthy

Howard Cherpakov
Howard Cherpakov Casting
150 W. 28 St. #701
New York, Ny 10001
212-643-2602
Film, TV & Theatre   Principals

Kathleen Chopin
Kathleen Chopin Casting
12 W 32 St. #12n
New York, Ny 10001
212-358-9346
Film & TV   Principals
        Associates
        Rori Bergman
        Anne Davison

Deborah Brown
Deborah Brown Casting
160 West End Ave.
New York, Ny 10023
212-724-3447

AN ACTOR'S GUIDE—MAKING IT IN NEW YORK CITY

Film, TV & Theatre   Principals
Do Not Send 8x10

Kristine Bulakowski
K. Bulakowski Casting
Pob 670 Prince St. Sta.
New York, Ny 10012
212-769-8550
212-769-8550 (Hot Line)
All Areas Background
Associate
Driss Tijani
Kbcasting@Cs.Com

James Calleri
Calleri Casting
70-A Greenwich Ave. #162
New York, Ny 10011
212-488-2190 (P)
Film, TV & Theatre   Principals
Associates
Erica Jensen
Paul Davis
Geoff Josselson
Www.Callericasting.Com

Betsy Capes
Capes Casting
826 Broadway 4 Fl.
New York, Ny 10003
212-777-2240
All Areas Principals
Contact By Mail Only
Www.Capesco.Com

Robin Carus
Robin Carus Casting
Pob 1586
New York, Ny 10028
212-861-6359
Film, Theatre & Industrials   Contact
By Mail Only

Don Case
Donald Case Casting, Inc.

386 Park Ave. South #809
New York, Ny 10016
212-889-6555
All Areas Primarily Principals
Other Casting Directors
Rachel Silver
Donna Cassell
Tisha Ioli
Dcasecasting@Hotmail.Com

Liz Ortiz Mackes
Casting Solutions
P. O. Box 20164
New York, Ny 10011
212-875-7573
All Areas Primarily Principals
Union & Non-Union
Associate
Cahill Connolly
Www.Castingsolutions.TV
Castsolutions@Aol.Com

Michael Cassara
Michael Cassara Casting
333 W 39 St. #601-A
New York, Ny 10018
212-564-6700
Film, TV & Theatre   Principals
Submissions@Michaelcassara.Net
Www.Michaelcassara.Net

Sharon Chantiles
Jeffrey Vigneault
**Chantiles/Vigneault
Casting**
39 W. 19 St. 12 Fl.
New York, Ny 10011
212-924-2278
All Areas   Principals
Submit By Mail Only

David Clemmons
David Clemmons Casting
265 W. 30 St. 2 Fl.
New York, Ny 10001

212-594-7434
Primarily Theatre Principals
Associate
Joy Dewing
Info@Clemmonscasting.Com
Www.Clemmonscasting.Com

Bob Cline
Bob Cline Casting
676-A 9th Ave. #160
New York, Ny 10036
212-726-3329
Primarily Theatre Principals
Associate
Tina Marie Libby
Contact By Mail Only

Rich Cole
Rich Cole Casting
648 Broadway #912
New York, Ny 10012
212-614-7130
Theatre Only Principals

Jackie Kelly
Complete Casting
457 W. Walnut St.
Long Beach, Ny 11561
516-431-2620
All Areas Except Theatre Principals &
Background
Other Casting Director
Margaret Dwyer

Byron Crystal
Byron Crystal Casting
Pob 191
New York, Ny 10276
212-229-0684
Commercials, Film, TV   Background
Contact By Mail Only

Sue Crystal
Sue Crystal Casting
251 W. 87 St. #26

New York, Ny 10024
212-877-0737
All Areas Principals & Background
Suecrystal@Earthlink.Net

Merry Delmonte
Merry Delmonte Casting
575 Madison Ave. 10 Fl.
New York, Ny 10022
212-757-9838
All Areas Except Theatre
Principals & Background

Donna Deseta
Donna Deseta Casting
584 Broadway #1001
New York, Ny 10012
212-274-9696
All Areas   Principals
Other Casting Directors
Becky Moore
David Cady
Www.Donnadesetacasting.Com

Lucy Baker / Kyle T. Coker
Donna Deseta Casting
584 Broadway #1001
New York, Ny 10012
212-274-9696
All Areas   Background
    Indicate Sag Membership
    & Background Work On Photo
    Www.Donnadesetacasting.Com

L. Digiaimo / L. Digiaimo Jr.
Lou Digiaimo Casting
37 Lehigh Way
Oakland, Nj 07436
732-277-0984
Film Only   Principals

Casting Dept.
Disney Theatrical Prod.
% New Amsterdam Theatre
214 W. 42 St.

New York, Ny 10036
212-827-5400
Theatre   Principals
   Union Only
   Www.Disneyonbroadway.Com

Stephanie Dalle-Molle
Pennie Dupont
Pennie Dupont Casting
36 Perry St.
New York, Ny 10014
212-255-2708
Film   Principals
   Pd@Verizon.Net

Elisbeth Jameson
Ej Casting
151 1st Ave. #131
New York, Ny 10009
212-995-2428
Film, TV & Commercials
Background

Daryl Eisenberg
Daryl Eisenberg Casting
180 West End Ave. #17g
New York, Ny 10023
646-678-4000
   All Areas   Principals
   Www.Decasting.Com
   Info@Decasting.Com

Sean Powers
Rita Powers
Extras Casting
295 Greenwich St. #513
New York, Ny 10007
212-965-1683
All Areas Except Theatre   Background
   Booked77@Aol.Com

Alison Watters
Extra Extra Casting
1202 Lexington Ave. #282
New York, Ny 10028

212-560-6567
   Film & Commercials
   Background
   Www.Extraextracastings.Com
   Extraextracastimg@Yahoo.Com

Destiny Lilly
Extra Talent Agency
1133 Broadway #1201
New York, Ny 10010
212-807-8172
Film, TV & Commercials
Background
Actorinquiry@Extratalentagency.Com

Alan Filderman
Alan Filderman Casting
333 W. 39 St. Ste. 601a
New York, Ny 10018
212-695-6200
Film, TV & Theatre   Principals

Alexa Fogel
Alexa Fogel Casting
% Actors Alliance
330 W 38 St. Ste. 505
New York, Ny 10018
212-594-8095
Film & TV   Principals
   Associates
   Christine Kromer
   Nadia Lubbe

Janet Foster
Janet Foster Casting
3212 Cambridge Ave.
Bronx, Ny 10463
718-549-6066
Film, TV & Theatre   Principals
Jfostercasting@Optonline.Net

Kelly Foster
Kelly Foster Casting
% Overland Entertainment
257 W. 52 St. 5 Fl.

New York, Ny 10019
212-262-1270
Corporate Films & TV   Principals

Casting Department
Godlove & Co. Casting
151 W. 25 St. 11 Fl.
New York, Ny 10001
212-627-7300
All Areas Except Theatre   Principals
    Casting Directors
    Linda Godlove
    John Doyle
    Www.Godlovecasting.Com

Brette Alysse Goldstein
Brette Goldstein Casting
630 9th Ave. Ste. 1410
New York, Ny 10036
646-431-5244
Film, TV & Theatre   Principals

Amy Gossels
Amy Gossels Casting
1471 3rd Ave.
New York, Ny 10028
212-717-4277
All Areas Except Theatre Principals &
Background
    Associate
    Eliza Khan

Donna Grossman
Donna Grossman Casting
% Aqua Studios
12 W. 27 St. 10 Fl. N.
New York, Ny 10001
212-598-2344
All Areas   Principals & Background
    Associate
    Lisa Feiner
    Www.Donnagrossmancasting.
    Com

Jen Halpern
Jen Halpern Casting

Pob 1061
New York, Ny 10028
917-438-9120
All Areas Except Theatre Principals &
Background

Carol Hanzel
Carol Hanzel Casting
48 W. 21 St. 7 Fl.
New York, Ny 10010
212-242-6113
All Areas Principals & Background
    Associate
    Colleen Piquette

Judy Henderson & Assoc.
330 W. 89 St.
New York, Ny 10024
212-877-0225
All Areas Principals
    Associates
    Kimberly Graham
    Doug Henderson

Linda Lipson
Herman/Lipson Casting, Inc.
630 9th Ave. Ste. 1410
New York, Ny 10036
212-807-7706
All Areas Principals & Background
Contact By Mail Only
Other Casting Director
Barry Shapiro
Myhighprofile@Gmail.Com

Neil Myer / Brooke Thomas
House Productions
450 W. 15 St. #202
New York, Ny 10011
212-929-0200
All Areas Except Theatre Principals
    Other Casting Directors
    Mary Egan Callahan
    Rebecca Yarsin
    Cristina Schulman

Www.Houseprod.Com
Brookc@Houseprod.Com

Stuart Howard
Stuart Howard Assoc., Ltd.
151 W. 26 St. 7 Fl.
New York, Ny 10001
212-414-1544
All Areas Principals & Background
Other Casting Director
Amy Schecter
  Associate
  Paul Hardt

Craig Lechner
Impossible Casting
122 W. 26 St. 6 Fl.
New York, Ny 10001
212-255-3029
All Areas Principals & Background
  Associate
  Matthew Wulf
  Info@Impossiblecasting.Com

Avy Kaufman
Avy Kaufman Casting
180 Varick St. 16 Fl.
New York, Ny 10014
212-620-4256
Film, TV & Commercials   Principals
  Associates
  Leeba Zakharov
  Sabrina Hyman

Karen Etcoff
Kee Casting
Pob 3175
Guttenberg, Nj 07093
201-854-6396
212-465-7206 (Hot Line)
212-502-0308 (Call Times)
All Areas   Background
  Associate
  Bill Tripician
  Www.Keecasting.Biz

Judy Keller
Judy Keller Casting
247 W. 38 St. 7 Fl.
New York, Ny 10018
212-463-7676
All Areas Principals & Background
  Associate
  Natalie Delange
  Www.Judykellercasting.Com

Kevin Kennison
K2 Casting At ABC Film Video
303 5th Ave. #1002
New York, Ny 10016
212-686-3490
All Areas Principals & Background
Union / Non-Union
Kevin@Abcfilmvideo.Com

Jodi Kipperman
Kipperman Casting, Inc.
12 W. 37 St. 3 Fl.
New York, Ny 10018
212-736-3663
All Areas Principals & Background
  Associates
  Anthony Pichette
  Allynn Simons
  Casting@Kipperman.Com
  Www.Kipperman.Com

Stephanie Klapper
Stephanie Klapper Casting
39 W. 19 St. 12 Fl.
New York, Ny 10011
646-486-1337
All Areas Principals
Contact By Mail Only

Ellen Lewis
Ellen Lewis Casting
% Post Factory
161 6th Ave. 11 Fl.
New York, Ny 10013
212-627-1662 X206

Film & TV   Principals
   Associate
     Meghan Rafferty

Liz Lewis
Liz Lewis Casting
151 W. 19 St. 3 Fl.
New York, Ny 10011
212-645-1500
All Areas Principals & Background
   Other Casting Directors
     Angela Mickey
     Lynn Taylor
     Nikki Vitale
     Lisa Rubenstein
     Jennifer Ajemian
   Www.Lizlewis.Com

Vince Liebhart
Vince Liebhart Casting
70 A Greenwich Ave. #102
New York, Ny 10011
Unlisted
Film, TV & Theatre   Principals

Wendy Litwack
% Aqua Studio
12 W. 27 St.
New York, Ny 10001
212-686-0014
Commercials & Webisodes Principals
& Background
Needs Non-Union

Joan Lynn
Joan Lynn Casting
1461 1st Ave. Ste. 355
New York, Ny 10065
212-535-5305
All Areas Principals & Background

Amanda Mackey
Mackey/Sandrich Casting
75 Leonard St. #5sw
New York, Ny 10013

212-343-3660
Film Principals
   Associate
     Jandiz Estrada

Nancy Piccione
Manhattan Theatre Club
311 W. 43. St. 8 Fl.
New York, Ny 10036
212-399-3000
   Theatre Principals
   Other Casting Director
   Kelly Gillespie

Jamibeth Margolis
Jamibeth Margolis Casting
676a 9th Ave. Box 126
New York, Ny 10036
212-330-8608
Film, TV & Theatre   Principals

Martine Dorfman
Martine Casting
163 3rd Ave. #176
New York, Ny 10003
212-217-0369
Commercials Principals & Background
Primarily Non-Union

Pat Mccorkle
Mccorkle Casting Ltd.
575 8th Ave. 18 Fl.
New York, Ny 10018
212-244-3899
Film, TV & Theatre   Principals
   Associate
   Joe Lopick

Mele Nagler
Melcap Casting
260 W. 44 St. 3 Fl.
New York, Ny 10036
212-575-1987
Film, TV & Theatre   Principals
   Other Casting Director

David Caparelliotis
Associate
Stephanie Yankwitt

Beth Melsky
Beth Melsky Casting
928 Broadway #300
New York, Ny 10010
212-505-5000
All Areas Principals & Background
Contact By Mail Only
Other Casting Directors
Nancy Frigand
Richard Reed
Shadd Sutton
Laura Richard
David Bellatoni

Matthew Messinger
Matthew Messinger Casting
244 W. 72 St.
New York, Ny 10023
212-877-2598
All Areas & Voice Work Principals
Www.Matthewmessingercasting.Com
Mattcast1@Nyc.Rr.Com

Norman Meranus
Norman Meranus Casting
201 W. 85 St. #16d
New York, Ny 10024
212-799-0352
Film & Theatre   Principals
Contact By Mail Only

Jeff Mitchell / Jennifer Rudolph
Mitchell Rudolph Casting
70 W. 36 St. #1006
New York, Ny 10018
212-679-3550
Film, TV & Theatre   Principals
Www.Mrcast.Com

Barry Moss/Bob Kale
Mka Casting, Ltd.

484 W.43 St. #28r
New York, Ny 10036
212-307-6690
Film, TV & Theatre   Principals
No Drop Off's
Other Casting Director
John Anastasi

Arnold J. Mungioli
Mungioli Theatricals, Inc.
151 W. 26 St. 7 Fl.
New York, Ny 10001
212-337-8832
Film, TV & Theatre
Principals
Contact By Mail Only
Www.Mungiolitheatricals.Com

Elissa Myers / Paul Fouquet
Elissa Myers Casting
333 W. 52 St. #1008
New York, Ny 10019
212-315-4777
Film, TV & Voice Work   Principals
Associate
Sarah Tillson
Www.Elissamyers.Com

Jack Doulin (Cd)
Ny Theatre Workshop
83 E. 4 St.
New York, Ny 10003
212-780-9037
Theatre Principals
Jackd@Nytw.Org
Www.Nytw.Org

Cody Beke / Lang Fisher
Onion Network Inc.
536 Broadway 10 Fl.
New York, Ny 10012
212-431-0538
212-627-1972
TV Principals & Background
Electronic Submissons Ok

Www.Theonion.Com
Casting@Theonion.Com

Ellyn Long Marshall
Orpheus Group Inc.
1180 6th Ave. #1920
New York, Ny 10036
212-957-8760
All Areas Principals
Contact By Mail Only
Other Casting Director
Marie Nelson
Orpheusgroupny@Yahoo.Com

Kristen Paladino
Paladino Casting
159 W. 25 St. 2 Fl.
New York, Ny 10001
212-741-2224
All Areas Except Theatre Principals
    Other Casting Director
    Lori Malkin
    Associate
    Emily Derr
    Www.Paladinocasting.Com
    Talent@Paladinocasting.Com

Erica Palgon
Erica Palgon Casting & Beyond
217 E 86 St
Pmb 133
New York, Ny 10028
212-580-6151
All Areas

Vinnie Potestivo
Vinnie Potestivo Casting
135 W 26 St. 12 Fl.
New York, Ny 10001
646-808-1351
Film, TV & Hosting Other Casting
Director
Cristine Cowan
Www.Vinniep.Com

Laura Richin
Laura Richin Casting
33 Douglass St. #1
Brooklyn, Ny 11231
718-802-9608
Film, TV & Theatre   Principals
Richincasting@Aol.Com

Judy Rosensteel
Judy Rosensteel Casting
43 W. 68 St. 4 Fl.
New York, Ny 10023
212-595-1607
Commercials & Voice Work Principals

Laura Rosenthal / Maribeth Fox
Laura Rosenthal Casting
401 Broadway #711
New York, Ny 10013
212-431-2611
Film & TV   Principals
    Other Casting Directors
    Ali Farrell
    Geoffrey Miclat
    Associate
    Jodi Angstreich

Jim Carnahan
Roundabout Theatre Co.
231 W. 39 St. 12 Fl.
New York, Ny 10018
212-719-9393
Theatre Principals
    Associates
    Carrie Gardner
    Steve Kopel
    Kate Boka

Tara Rubin
Tara Jayne Rubin Casting
570 7th Ave. #401
New York, Ny 10018
212-302-3011
Film, TV & Theatre   Principals

Associates
Eric Woodall
Laura Schutzel
Merri Sugarman

Jennifer Rudin
Jennifer Rudin Casting
16 W 23 St. 4 Fl.
New York, Ny 10010
212-827-5400
Film & Theatre   Principals

Cindi Rush
Cindi Rush Casting
20 W. 20 St. #300
New York, Ny 10011
212-414-2838
Film, TV & Theatre   Principals
    Associate
    Michele Weiss

Casting Dept.
Howard Schwartz Recording
420 Lexington Ave. Ste. 1934
New York, Ny 10170
212-687-4180
Voice Work Principals

Carol Nadell
Selective Casting
Pob 1538
Radio City Station
New York, Ny 10101
212-757-1510
Industrial Films Principals
Seeks Foreign Speaking Talent
    Associate
    Lena Kaminsky
    Www.Selectivecasting.Com

Sherie L. Seff
Sherie L. Seff Casting
400 W. 43 St. #9b
New York, Ny 10036
212-947-7408

Theatre Principals
Slscasting@Aol.Com

Susan Shopmaker
Susan Shopmaker Casting
545 8th Ave. 23 Fl
New York, Ny 10018
212-686-5502
All Areas Principals & Background
    Associate
    Randi Glass
    Info@Susanshopmakercasting.
    Com

Mark Simon
Mark Simon Casting
240 W. 44 St.
New York, Ny 10036
212-302-9540
Musical Theatre Principals
    Associate
    Jeff Davolt

Caroline Sinclair
Caroline Sinclair Casting
131 Varick St. #930
New York, Ny 10013
212-929-1002
All Areas Principals
    Associate
    Bettina Bilger

Carrie Faverty / Tony Mennuto
Sound Lounge Casting
149 5th Ave. 12 Fl.
New York, Ny 10010
212-388-1212
Voice Work

Laura Stanczyk
Laura Stanczyk Casting
1674 Broadway 7 Fl.
New York, Ny 10019
212-757-9456
Film, TV & Theatre   Principals

Ilene Starger
Ilene Starger Casting
Pob 246 Fdr Sta.
New York, Ny 10150
212-563-7990
Film & TV   Principals

Elsie Stark
Elsie Stark Casting
Stark Naked Productions
39 W 19 St. 12 Fl.
New York, Ny 10011
212-366-1903
All Areas Principals & Background
    Associates
    Elizabeth Gans
    Joyce Batson
    (Background)
    C. B. Maltese
    They Have A Spanish Dept.
    Info@Starknakedproductions.
    Com

Adrienne Stern
Adrienne Stern Casting
32 Court St. #1501
Brooklyn, Ny 11201
718-522-0208
Film, TV, Theatre & Commercials
Principals & Background
Sternprojects@Yahoo.Com

Irene Stockton
Irene Stockton Casting
261 Broadway #2b
New York, Ny 10007
212-964-9445
Film & Theatre
Principals
Stocktoncasting@Aol.Com

Jill Strickman
Strickman-Ripps, Inc.
66 W. Broadway #602
New York, Ny 10007

212-966-3211
    Commercials Principals &
    Background
    Other Casting Directors
    Jennifer Kitchin
    Mary Anne Driscoll
    Kristin Danas
    Nadette Stasa
    Kathy Foronjy
    Associate
    Paige Barr

Dani Super
Dani Super Casting
34 W. 27 St. 11 Fl.
New York, Ny 10001
Unlisted
All Areas Except Print
    Danisupercasting@Gmail.Com

Daniel Swee
Daniel Swee Casting
Lincoln Center Theater
150 W. 65 St.
New York, Ny 10023
212-501-3230
Theatre & Film Principals
    Associate
    Camille Hickman

Tuffy Questell
Tec Casting
Pob 523
Bronx, Ny 10462
212-712-7467
All Areas Background
Submit By E-Mail
    Associates
    Serena Rosario
    Rara Taylor
    Teccasting@Gmail.Com

Bernard Telsey
Telsey + Company
311 W. 43 St. 10 Fl.

New York, Ny 10036
212-868-1260
    All Areas Principals
    Other Casting Directors
    David Vaccari
    Will Cantler
    Bethany Berg
    Tiffany Little Canfield
    Craig Burns
    Rachel Hoffman
    Associates
    Justin Huff
    Bess Fifer
    Carrie Rosson
    Abbie Brady

Jordan Thaler
The Public Theatre
425 Lafayette St.
New York, Ny 10003
212-539-8550
Theatre Principals
Other Casting Director
Heidi Griffiths

Todd Thaler
Todd Thaler Casting
130 W. 57 St. #10a
New York, Ny 10019
212-246-7116
Film & TV   Principals

Molly K. Meado
Theatreworks / Usa
151 W. 26 St. 7 Fl.
New York, Ny 10001
212-647-1100
Theatre Principals
    Associate
    Taryn Anderson
    Www.Theatreworksusa.Org
    Casting@Twusa.Org

Lisa Todd
Lisa Todd Casting

164 W 25 St. #14f
New York, Ny 10001
Unlisted
Film

Jim Kozloff
Vh1 Casting & Talent Relations
345 Hudson St. 2 Fl.
New York, Ny 10014
212-258-7800
TV Principals

Laura Verbeke
Laura Verbeke Casting
132 E. 43 St. #737
New York, Ny 10017
917-747-3038
Film, TV & Theatre Background
Electronic Submission Ok
Laura.Verbeke@Yahoo.Com

Steve Garrin
Videoactive Productions
1560 Broadway Ste. 610
New York, Ny 10036
212-541-8106 (No Calls /
No Visits)
Voice Work Principals
    Associates
    Louise Moore
    Emily Degrass
    Www.Videoactiveprod.Com
    Vworks@Aol.Com

Meg Simon
Warner Brothers TV
1325 6th Ave. 32 Fl.
New York, Ny 10019
212-636-5145
TV Principals
Casting Associate
Findley Davidson

Kathy Wickline
Wickline Casting
1080 N. Delaware Ave. #700

Philadelphia, Pa 19125
215-739-9952
All Areas Principals & Background
   Associate
   Molly Mendte
   Info@Wicklinecasting.Com

Scott Wojcik / Gayle Seay
Wojcik/Seay Casting
247 W. 38 St. 7 Fl.
New York, Ny 10018

212-929-2339
All Areas Principals & Background
Www.Wscastingonline.Com
Info@Wscastingonline.Com

Liz Woodman
Liz Woodman Casting
245 W. 107 St. #8f
New York, Ny 10025
212-787-3782
Theatre Principals

APPENDIX D
Suggested Reading

Adler, Stella. *The Technique of Acting.* New York: Bantam Books, 1998.

Alterman, Glenn. *Promoting Your Acting Career.* New York: Allworth Press, 1998.

———. *Creating Your Own Monologue.* New York: Allworth Press, 1999.

———. The Perfect Audition Monologue, Lyme, New Hampshire, Smith and Kraus, 2003.

———. *Two Minutes and Under.* Lyme, New Hampshire: Smith and Kraus, 1993.

Caine, Michael. *What's It All About?* New York: Random House, 1992.

Callan, K. *The New York Agent Book.* Studio City: Sweden Press, 1989.

Chekhov, Michael. *To The Actor.* New York: Harper and Brothers, 1953.

Hagen, Uta. *A Challenge for the Actor.* New York: Scribner's, 1991.

———. *Respect for Acting.* New York: Macmillan, 1973.

Henderson, Sue. *Henderson's Personal Managers Directory.* New York: Hei Publications, 2000.

Henry, Mari Lyn, and Lynne Rogers. *How To Be A Working Actor*, 5th ed. New York: Back Stage Books, 2007.

Kozlowski, Rob. *The Actors Guide to the Internet.* Portsmouth, New Hampshire: Heinemann, 2000.

Lewis, Robert. *Advice to the Players.* New York: Stein and Day, 1980.

Meisner, Sanford, and Dennis Longwell. *On Acting.* New York: Random House, 1984.

Shurtleff, Michael. *Audition.* New York: Bantam, 1980.

APPENDIX E
Suggested Periodicals, Publications, and Guides

American Theater Magazine, published ten times a year by Theater Communications Group, 355 Lexington Avenue, New York, New York 10017.

Back Stage, published weekly by BPI Communications, Inc., 1515 Broadway, New York, New York 10036.

Directory of Professional Theatre Training Programs (Jill Charles), published yearly by Dorset Theater Festival and Colony House, Box 591, Dorset, Vermont 05251.

The Regional Theater Directory, published yearly by Theater Directories, P.O. Box 519, Dorset, Vermont 05251.

Summer Theater Guide (John Allen), published yearly by Theatre Guide Update, Box 2129, New York, New York 10185.

Theatrical Index, published weekly by Price Berkley, 888 Eighth Avenue, New York, New York 10019.

GLENN ALTERMAN

Glenn Alterman is a multiaward-winning playwright and the author of nineteen best-selling theater-related books (including eight books of original monologues). Nearly all of his books have gone on to multiple printings. He is also a screenwriter, an actor, a successful New York City commercial print model, and a highly respected monologue/audition acting coach.

His books include *The Perfect Audition Monologue, Glenn Alterman's Secrets To Successful Cold*

Photograph by Robert Kim

Readings, Sixty Seconds To Shine—101 *One Minute Original Monologues, Creating Your Own Monologue, Promoting Your Acting Career, Two Minutes and Under (Original Monologues for Actors, Volumes 1, 2, and 3), Street Talk (Original Character Monologues for Actors), Uptown (More Original Monologues For Actors), The Job Book: One Hundred Acting Jobs for Actors, The Job Book 2: One Hundred Day Jobs for Actors, What to Give Your Agent for Christmas, Monologues of the Stars,*, and *Two Minute Monologues. Two Minutes and Under, Street Talk,* and *Uptown* were the number one best-selling books of original monologues in 1992, 1993, and 1995, and along with *Creating Your Own Monologue, Promoting Your Acting Career, The Job Book, The Job Book 2,* and *Two Minutes and Under,* were all "Featured Selections" in the Doubleday Book Club (Fireside Theater and Stage and Screen Division). Most of his published works have gone on to multiple printings.

As a playwright, Mr. Alterman is the recipient of the first Julio T. Nunez Artist's Grant, the Arts and Letters Award in Drama, and scores of playwriting awards. His play *The Pain in the Poetry* was published in 2009 *The Best Ten Minute Plays For 2 or More Actor (Smith and Kraus) and The Best Short Plays- Volume 8 (licensed by Playscripts). After* is in 2011 *The Best Ten Minute Plays For 2 or More Actors (Smith and Kraus).* Several of his plays have been finalists at the Actors Theater of Louisville's Humana Festival.

Mr. Alterman's plays, *Like Family* and *The Pecking Order,* were optioned by Red Eye Films (with Alterman writing the screenplay). His play, *Solace,* was produced Off-Broadway by the Circle East Theater Company (formerly Circle Rep Theater Company). *Nobody's Flood* won the Bloomington National Playwriting Competition, as well as being a finalist in the

Key West Playwriting Competition. *Coulda-Woulda-Shoulda* won the Three Genres Playwriting Competition twice, two years in a row. The prize included publication of the play in the Prentice Hall textbook, used in college theater departments all over the country. There have been dozens of productions in the U.S. and Europe.

Mr. Alterman wrote the book for *Heartstrings: The National Tour* (commissioned by DIFFA, the Design Industries Foundation for Aids), a thirty-five city tour that starred Michelle Pfeiffer, Jennifer Holliday, Kelsey Grammer, Susan Sarandon, Marlo Thomas, and Sandy Duncan. Other plays include *Kiss Me When It's Over* (commissioned by E. Weissman Productions), starring and directed by André De Shields; *Tourists of the Mindfield* (finalist in the L. Arnold Weissberger Playwriting Competition at New Dramatists); and *Street Talk/Uptown* (based on his monologue books), produced at the West Coast Ensemble.

Spilt Milk received its premiere at the Beverly Hills Rep/Theater 40 in Los Angeles. The *Danger of Strangers* won Honorable Mention in the Deep South Writers Conference Competition, was a finalist in the George R. Kernodle Contest, was selected to be in the Pittsburgh New Works Festival and has had over 35 productions, including at Circle Rep Lab and the West Bank Downstairs Theater Bar (starring James Gandolfini). There have been many productions of his original monologues play, *God In Bed*, both in the United States and in Europe.

Mr. Alterman's work has been performed at Primary Stages, Ensemble Studio Theater (EST), Circle in the Square Downtown, HERE, LaMaMa, Circle Rep, in the Turnip Festival, at the Duplex, Playwrights Horizons, at several theaters on Theater Row in New York, as well as at many theaters around the country.

Mr. Alterman has been a guest artist and given master classes and seminars on "The Perfect Audition Monologue" and "The Business of Acting" at such diverse places as the Governor's School for the Arts in Norfolk, Virginia, the Edward Albee Theater Conference (Valdez, Alaska), Southampton College, Western Connecticut State College, Broadway Artists Alliance, The American Federation of Television and Radio Artists (AFTRA), the Dramatists Guild, the Learning Annex, the Screen Actors Guild, the Seminar Center, and at many acting schools and colleges all over the country and in Europe.

In 1993, Mr. Alterman created the Glenn Alterman Studios, where actors receive monologue/audition coaching, as well as career preparation. He was named "Best Monologue/Audition Coach in the Tri-State Area" by Theater Resources Magazine and first runner up as "The Best Private Acting Coach In New York", by the readers of *Back Stage*. He presently lives in New York City, where he's working on several new plays, acts in TV commercials, and coaches actors.

On the Web, he can be reached at *www.glennalterman.com*.

INDEX

extra work
don'ts of, 216–217
dos of, 217
interview with actor doing, 217–220
interviews with extra casting directors,
213–217
on SAG project, 135

facts, about New York City, 8–21
Fay, Sylvia, 214
Fifth and Madison Avenues from 57th to
79th streets, 30
The Film Center Café, 33
Financial District/Lower Manhattan, 9
shopping, 28
theaters in, 10
Fitzgerald, Ella, 16
Flatiron District/Union Square, 13
rent costs, 23
shopping, 29
Flea Theater, 10
folk music, 31
food prices, 6
Frenkel, Nick, 147–152

Gallery Players, 18
Garcia, Risa Bramon, 59
geography, New York City, 8–9
Gillespie, Dizzy, 32
*Glenn Alterman's Secrets To Successful
Cold Readings* (Alterman), 91
Go Forth Productions, 19
Goff, Thom, 120–123
Goldblum, Tracy-Lynn, 207–209
Gotham Comedy Club, 32
Gracie Mansion, 16
graciousness, 267–268
Graham, Martha, 40
Gramercy Park, 13, 23
Grand Central Terminal, 14
the Great White Way. *See* theaters
Greenwich Village, 22, 29
grunge clubs, 31
Guggenheim Museum, 16
Gym Bar, 33

hair, 66
half-price theater ticket booth (TKTS), 6
Hamilton, Alexander, 10
Harden, Marcia Gay, 51

Harden, Mary, 141–144
Harlem, 16, 23
Harry Warren Theatre, 18
heading, résumés, 73
headshot photographers
actors interviewing with, 55
finding right, 55
interviews with, 63–69
listings of popular, 70–71
photo reproduction studio with, 69–70
headshots
advice and tips, 67–68
casting directors on, 59
commercial, 56–57
corporate, 57
cost of photo session and
reproductions, 54–55, 66–67
8" x 10", 60
finding right photographer, 55
interviewing with photographer, 55
legit, 57
makeup in, 58, 66, 68–69
in NYC and L.A., 63–64
photo shoot post production, 59–60
photo shoot preparation, 56–59
purpose of, 54
samples, 61–62
shopping, 55–56
types of, 56–57
Heights Players Theatre, 18
Hell's Kitchen, 22
Henderson, Sue, 104
Henrietta Hudson, 33
Herald Square, shopping in, 29
HERE Arts Center, 11
Hogs and Heifers, 33
Holiday, Billie, 16
Hollander, Anita, 248–252
housing. *See* rent costs
Howard, Michael, 38, 39–46
Huminska, Janice, 29

image consultants, 98–99
Impact Theatre Company, 18
improvisation classes, 49
industry people, social behavior with,
266–267
information sources
for nightlife, 31
voice-over work, 191

Books from Allworth Press

Allworth Press is an imprint of Skyhorse Publishing. Selected titles are listed below.